Medical Law in Slovenia

Medical Law in Slovenia

Second Edition

Viktorija Žnidaršič Skubic

This book was originally published as a monograph in the International Encyclopaedia of Laws/Medical Law.

Founding Editor: Roger Blanpain
General Editor: Frank Hendrickx
Volume Editor: Herman Nys

Wolters Kluwer

Published by:
Kluwer Law International B.V.
PO Box 316
2400 AH Alphen aan den Rijn
The Netherlands
E-mail: international-sales@wolterskluwer.com
Website: lrus.wolterskluwer.com

Sold and distributed by:
Wolters Kluwer Legal & Regulatory U.S.
7201 McKinney Circle
Frederick, MD 21704
United States of America
E-mail: customer.service@wolterskluwer.com

ISBN 978-94-035-3465-7

e-Book: ISBN 978-94-035-3470-1
web-PDF: ISBN 978-94-035-3471-8

The Author

Dr Viktorija Žnidaršič Skubic was born in Ljubljana, Slovenia, in 1972. She obtained her Bachelor's in Law from the University of Ljubljana, Faculty of Law, in 1996 with a thesis on the question of maternity and paternity for the children, conceived with the help of Biomedically-assisted Procreation (BMAP). For this work, she was awarded the University of Ljubljana Award: The Prešeren Prize. She continued her studies at University of Ljubljana with postgraduate programme in Civil and Commercial Law. She obtained her PhD in 2001 by defending a thesis *Property Relations between Spouses*. In 2006, she passed the State Exam of Public Administration. Since 1996, she has been employed at the Faculty of Law of the University of Ljubljana, first as a junior researcher, subsequently as an assistant, assistant professor, associate professor and from 2014 on as a full professor for Civil and Commercial Law. She teaches Civil Medical Law, Law of Inheritance, Personal Law and Civil Law – General Part. She also teaches a subject 'Law and Ethics in Health Care' at the College for Physiotherapy in Ljubljana. Since 2004, she has also been employed as a researcher at the Institute for Comparative Law at the Faculty of Law in Ljubljana. She has published several academic articles and has delivered papers at national and international conferences, her major interest being Medical law, Law of Inheritance, Personal Law and Family Law. She cooperated, as an associate and as a leader, in many national and international research projects. She was appointed as a member of a drafting commission for the Family Code and the Infertility Treatment and Procedures of Biomedically-assisted Procreation Act. She was a member of State Commission for BMAP, and she is a member of Ethical Commission for Transplantations. Besides Slovenian, the author speaks fluently English, French, Croatian and Serbian.

The Author

Table of Contents

Table of Contents

List of Abbreviations

BMAP	Biomedically-assisted Procreation (*Oploditev z biomedicinsko pomočjo*)
CAM	Complementary and Alternative Medicine (*Komplementarna in alternativna medicina*)
CIOMS	Council for International Organizations of Medical Sciences (*Svet mednarodnih organizacij medicinskih znanosti*)
DRG Model	Diagnosis Related Groups Model (*Model skupine primerljivih primerov*)
KZ-1	The Criminal Code (*Kazenski zakonik*)
NIPH	National Institute for Public Health (*Nacionalni inštitut za javno zdravje*)
NLHEF	National Laboratory for Health, Environment and Food (*Nacionalni laboratorij za zdravje, okolje in hrano*)
No.	Number (*Številka*)
OG	Official Gazette (*Uradni list*)
OG RS	Official Gazette of Republic of Slovenia (*Uradni list Republike Slovenije*)
OG RS – IT	Official Gazette of Republic of Slovenia – International Treaties (*Uradni list Republike Slovenije, Mednarodne pogodbe*)
OG SRS	Official Gazette of Socialist Republic of Slovenia (*Uradni list Socialistične Republike Slovenije*)
OJ EU	Official Journal of European Union (*Uradni list Evropske unije*)
AMPMD	Agency for Medicinal Products and Medical Devices of the Republic of Slovenia (*Javna agencija Republike Slovenije za zdravila in medicinske pripomočke*)
SFRY	Socialist Federal Republic of Yugoslavia (*Socialistična Federativna Republika Jugoslavija*)
sq. km	Square Kilometre (*Kvadratni kilometer*)

List of Abbreviations

UEMS	Union Européen des Médecins Spécialistes (*Evropsko združenje zdravnikov specialistov*)
UPB1	Official Consolidated Text Number One (*Uradno prečiščeno besedilo številka ena*)
UPB2	Official Consolidated Text Number Two (*Uradno prečiščeno besedilo številka dve*)
WHO	World Health Organization (*Svetovna zdravstvena organizacija*)
§	Paragraph (*Odstavek*)

General Introduction

§1. General Background of the Country

I. Geography and Climate

1. Slovenia (officially the Republic of Slovenia) is located on the southernmost part of Central Europe and the northernmost part of the Mediterranean. The country borders Italy to the west, Austria to the north, Hungary to the southeast and Croatia to the east and south. It is located on the crossroads of the Alpine, Mediterranean, Pannonian and Dinaric worlds. The country's surface area is 20,273 sq. km, and the average population density is 103.4 inhabitants per sq. km, placing it among the relatively densely populated countries of Central Europe. The capital of Slovenia is Ljubljana. It is at the same time the country's largest city with a total of 289,830 inhabitants.[1] The Slovenian coast on the Adriatic Sea is 46.6 km long. The highest peak in the country is Mount Triglav (2,863.65 m).[2]

2. Slovenia is the meeting point of four large geographical units: The Alps, the Pannonian Basin, the Dinaric Mountains and the Mediterranean. It is therefore geographically divided into the Alpine, Pannonian, Dinaric and Mediterranean regions. Slovenia has nine characteristic landscape types: Alpine mountains, foothills and plateaus, Pannonian hills, Dinaric plateaus, valleys and boxes, Mediterranean hills and plateaus.

3. The richness of Slovenia's nature is showcased by the country's immense geological and climate diversity. A mainly mountainous and hilly country, Slovenia's average height is 556.8 m above sea level. The highest areas are in the northwest part of the country, where the Alps are located. The altitude gradually decreases over the Karst and Alpine foothills towards the west with the lowest point at the coast and through sub-Pannonian regions to the east.

4. The described relief is in close connection to the country's climate. Southwest Slovenia thus has a strong Mediterranean climate influence – the sub-Mediterranean climate. This area has the warmest and mildest climate in the country, as the sea influence mitigates the winter cold and summer heat. This climate is characterized by mild winters and the biggest number of sunny days in the

1. *See* https://www.stat.si 7 Sep. 2020.
2. *See* https://old.delo.si, 5 Dec. 2021.

country. It is mainly distinguished from Mediterranean climate due to larger quantity of rainfall and somewhat lower temperatures. Moderate continental climate meanwhile covers most of Slovenia. The average temperature in the coldest month is below 0°C. The eastern edge of that climate already has a summer excess of rainfall, typical of continental European climate. The winters are quite cold and the summers quite hot. Alpine climate is characteristic for Alpine mountain ranges, their pertaining mountain valleys and some high Dinaric plateaus. This is the harshest climate in the country with colder temperatures than in other regions throughout the year. These are also the areas with the largest amount of rainfall, which mainly falls as snow during the cold part of the year.

5. Slovenia is rich in water sources. Ground water and various springs represent the main source of drinking water. The main watercourses are the rivers Mura, Drava, Soča, Sava, Savinja and Krka. Apart from Savinja and Krka, all the rivers flow through several countries and represent important water resources for Slovenia's neighbours as well. In the majority of cases, Slovenian rivers flow towards the Danube, but some also flow towards the Adriatic. Slovenia's hydrological situation is problematic in certain areas, which are prone to flooding and water-caused erosion. Torrential waters are quite common. Slovenia also boasts numerous discovered Karst caves, a large number of gorges and natural as well as man-made lakes in the mountains and on the plains. Slovenia also has a sea and flysch seacoast.

6. Slovenia can be described as a heavily forested country. A telling piece of information is that 58.2% of the country is covered with forests. Agricultural lands cover almost 40% of its area with the remaining 3% taken up by buildings. Slovenia is, among the European countries, the country with the lowest share of agricultural and cultivated land. Agricultural land is mainly utilized for meadows and pastures, followed by fields, gardens and vineyards, and orchards in the last spot. The overgrowth of farmland is the most common in the Dinaric and steep Alpine positions and sub-Alpine regions.

7. One of Slovenia's main assets is its biotic and regional diversity, often mentioned in literature. Slovenia is among the countries with the highest biotic diversity in the European Union (EU). Scientists assess that the number of species that can be found in the country is between 45,000 and 120,000 of which 26,000 animal and plant species have been researched. What is extraordinary is a large number of endemic species, i.e., species that mainly reside in Slovenia. There are nearly 800 such animal species and 66 plant species. [3] Almost 11% of Slovenian territory is

3. *See* https://www.arso.gov.si, 7 Sep. 2020.

currently under nature conservation protection. The largest area is taken by the Triglav National Park with 83,982 ha.[4] An increase in protected areas to 20% is gradually planned.[5]

8. Slovenia's natural resources mainly include forests, while the country is not particularly rich in ores. There are some brown coal, lignite, lead and mercury ores. The Alpine area is rich in hydropower resources.

II. Cultural Composition

9. The Republic of Slovenia is inhabited by Slovenians and the two autochthonous national minorities, the Italian (living in the ethnically mixed area of the Slovenian Istria) and the Hungarian (living in the ethnically mixed area of Prekmurje) as well as a separate Romany ethnic minority. All three communities enjoy constitutional protection (Articles 64 and 65 of the Constitution).[6]

10. The official language in the Republic of Slovenia is Slovenian, alongside Italian and Hungarian in the areas with the Italian or Hungarian minorities. Slovenian is the mother tongue for Slovenian minorities in neighbouring countries and some emigrants. All together some 2.4 million people are supposed to speak Slovenian.[7]

11. The ethnic composition in the Republic of Slovenia is as follows: Slovenians 83.06%, Serbians 1.98%, Croatians 1.81%, Muslims (including Bosniaks) 1.6%, Hungarians 0.3%, Italians 0.1%, others 2.2 and the rest are undetermined.[8]

12. There are forty-three religious communities registered in Slovenia. The majority of the population (57.8%) declare themselves as Roman Catholics, with members of the Islamic community at 2.4%, Orthodox at 2.3% and Protestants at 0.8%. About 10.1% of the population declare themselves to be atheists.[9]

III. Political System

13. Slovenia became an independent state on 25 June 1991 by adopting the Basic Constitutional Charter on the Independence and Sovereignty of the Republic

---

4. *See* https://www.tnp.si, 5 Jan. 2021.
5. *See* A. Pogačnik, P. Gabrijelčič & A. Zavodnik, *Mednarodna izhodišča in prostorski razvoj Slovenije* (*Slovenia's International Positions and Spatial Development*) (Fakulteta za gradbeništvo in geodezijo, Univerza v Ljubljani 2001), 11.
6. OG RS, Nos 33l/1991, 42/1997, 66/2000, 24/2003, 69/2004, 68/2006, 47/2013, 47/2013, 75/2016.
7. *See* https://www.dnevnik.si, 5 Jan. 2021.
8. *See* http://www.stat.si, 5 Jan. 2021.
9. *Ibid.*

of Slovenia.[10] With the Constitutional Charter, which forms the basis of the Slovenian constitutional system, Slovenia assumed absolute power on its territory and broke ties with the former Socialist Federative Republic of Yugoslavia.

14. On 23 December 1991, the National Assembly adopted the Constitution of the Republic of Slovenia, which pursuant to the Basic Constitutional Charter was in its capacity, as the supreme legal act of the new-founded state. With the new Constitution, the country established the foundations of national authority and also the status of individuals in the Republic of Slovenia. Slovenia became a full-fledged member of the EU on 1 May 2004.

15. The Constitution of the Republic of Slovenia guarantees a democratic political system based on parliamentary authority, the rule of law and a welfare state. The most important constitutional principles are that of power being vested in the people, the division of powers, the right to self-determination, the protection of human rights, special rights for the Italian and Hungarian national minorities, the division of state and church and the right to local self-government. The Constitution also deals with the protection of individual human rights, the system of government (particularly the three branches of powers: legislative, executive and judicial), economic and welfare rights, public finances, constitutionality, legality and the procedure for amending the Constitution.

16. Making amendments to the Constitution of the Republic of Slovenia is a challenging process, as each change requires an absolute two-thirds majority in the National Assembly. As an additional safeguard, at least thirty deputies can file a request to have the amendment put to a referendum. Amendments to the Constitution are confirmed in a referendum if the majority of the voters back them, but only if a majority of all eligible voters cast their ballots.

17. Slovenia is a territorially unified and indivisible state where local self-government is guaranteed. The state and religious communities are separated. Laws and other regulations must comply with generally accepted principles of international law and with treaties that are binding for Slovenia. Ratified and published treaties are applied directly.

18. Slovenia employs a (partial) bicameral parliamentary system, consisting of the National Assembly and the National Council. The first chamber (i.e., the National Assembly), which is made up of ninety deputies, performs the main legislative tasks. The deputies are elected in universal, equal, direct and secret voting. One deputy of the Italian and one deputy of the Hungarian national minorities are always elected to the National Assembly. The National Assembly is elected for four years.

10. OG RS, Nos 1/1991, 19/1991.

19. The National Council is the second chamber, performing a predominantly consultative function to the first chamber. It is a representative body for social, economic, professional and local interests and is composed of forty members, including representatives of employers, representatives of employees, representatives of farmers, crafts and trades and independent professions, representatives of non-commercial fields, and representatives of local interests. Members of the National Council are elected for a term of five years.

20. The National Council may propose to the National Assembly the passing of laws; it conveys to the National Assembly its opinion on all matters within the competence of the National Assembly; it can send a law back to the National Assembly for a revote prior to its promulgation; it can issue a call on a referendum as referred to in Article 90, paragraph 2 of the Constitution; it can also enquiry on matters of public importance as referred to in Article 93 of the Constitution.

21. The President of the Republic of Slovenia represents Slovenia and serves as the Commander-in-Chief of its defence forces. The President is elected in direct, general elections by secret ballot for a five-year term but for a maximum of two consecutive terms. The Constitution grants the President the following principal powers: to call elections to the National Assembly; to promulgate laws, to appoint state officials where provided by law, to appoint and recall ambassadors and accept accreditation letters from foreign diplomatic representatives, to issue instruments of ratification, to decide on granting clemency and to confer decorations and honorary titles.

22. The Government holds executive power in the Republic of Slovenia. It is composed of the Prime Minister and ministers. The ministers are independent and accountable to the National Assembly within the scope of their powers.

23. The President puts forward the Prime Minister – designate to the National Assembly after holding consultations with the leaders of deputy groups. The Prime Minister is elected by a majority of votes of all deputies in a secret ballot. The ministers are appointed and dismissed by the National Assembly at the Prime Minister's proposal.

24. Judges are independent in performing their judicial function. The office of a judge is permanent and is incompatible with posts held in other state bodies, local self-government bodies, bodies of political parties, etc. They are bound by the Constitution and laws. Judges are elected by the National Assembly on the proposal of the Judicial Council. Courts in Slovenia are organized in three instances: the first instance courts consist of local and district courts; the second instances are the higher courts; and the third instance is the Supreme Court in Ljubljana. The Supreme Court decides on ordinary and extraordinary legal remedies and performs other functions determined by law.

25. Slovenia's Constitutional Court is composed of nine justices, who are appointed by Parliament on the proposal of the President of the Republic. The Constitutional Justices are appointed for a nine-year term. The Constitutional Court *inter alia* decides on the conformity of laws with the Constitution and on constitutional complaints stemming from violations of human rights and fundamental freedoms by individual acts. The Constitutional Court in principle decides on a constitutional complaint only if legal remedies have been exhausted.

IV. Population and Vital Statistics

26. On 1 April 2020, Slovenia had 2,097,195 inhabitants, with 1,051,066 males and 1,044,795 females. On the same date, 1,940,844 citizens of the Republic of Slovenia and 156,351 foreigners lived in the country.[11]

27. The age structure in Slovenia is as follows: 15.1% of inhabitants are less than 15 years old, 64.7% are between 15 and 64 years old and 20.2% are older than 65 years. The average age is 43.5 years. The annual growth of the population is negative at -0.6 per 1,000 inhabitants. About 7.8 people per 1,000 immigrate to Slovenia annually. The average life expectancy in Slovenia is 78 years for men and 83.7 years for women.[12]

28. Data for Slovenia, similar to other developed countries in Western Europe, shows that it is demographically a so-called old country. We can see discernible shifts in the population pyramid during the time of both World Wars, when a distinct drop in the number of births can be detected. The reasons for that lie in uncertain conditions during the war and active participation of males in it (in a slightly larger percentage during World War I than in World War II).[13] Direct consequences of both conflicts are also evident in the distorted ratio between men and women with the former suffering a higher mortality rate during the fighting. After World War II, the Republic of Slovenia experienced a detectable baby boom. Between 1949 and 1953, there were more children born than at any time after the war in absolute terms, averaging at about 34,000 births a year. This growth is attributed by the experts to the appearance compensation, i.e., postponing births from the time during the war to after it and the changes and improvements in social and economic conditions. Apart from the so-called post-war baby boomers, another surge in births appeared in 2008 in the group of population aged between 26 and 32 years. These are the offspring of the first baby boom generation and the second generation of immigrants, i.e., children born to immigrants from the former Yugoslavia. From the year 2006

11. *See* https://www.stat.si, 7 Sep. 2020.
12. *Ibid.*
13. The reason being that Slovenians were then mainly fighting on fronts abroad, which kept a large part of the male population between 18 and 41 years of age far away from home for several years. For more details, *see* documents of Slovenian Statistical Office of the Republic of Slovenia, http://www.stat.si, 21 Dec. 2020.

Slovenia has again experienced a growing trend in the number of childbirths, a consequence of postponing pregnancies by women from the first baby boom generation. However, in 2018 and 2019, we saw a slight decline in births.[14]

29. In Slovenia the population consists of 51.2% of man and 49.8% of women. Up to the age of 59 years, the number of men exceeds the number of women in all age groups. This is the consequence of the ratio among newborns and the gender composition of immigrants. The share of women in the population begins to overtake men after the age of 60 years, as women generally live longer than men.

30. The inhabitants of Slovenia most often fall ill due to circulatory diseases (39.7% of all deaths), followed by various cancers (31.7% of all deaths), external reasons, respiratory diseases, gastrointestinal diseases and other causes.[15]

It has been estimated that the growth in the number of cases of cardiovascular diseases was caused by modern lifestyle, such as sedentary life with limited motion, industrial food diet with a lot of fats and cholesterol and smoking. The growth in such diseases was also influenced by the changes in family and social relations, including the increasing individualization and the appearance of smaller and dispersed families, which has resulted in less social support for an individual.[16]

Cancers affect men (53.9%) slightly more than women (46.1%) in Slovenia. The total relative share of survival is 57%. The most common type of cancer for men is prostate cancer and for women breast cancer.[17] According to research data, Slovenia also has a worryingly high percentage of deaths due to injuries and poisoning. The latter are designated as a public health issue, as the mortality from such causes, despite a dropping trend, is still among the highest in Europe. This is especially true for mortality as a result of excessive alcohol consumption. [18]

V. Social and Cultural Values

31. Values can be defined as guidelines for life or a thickened product of all that a society cherishes and what guides and motivates its norms. We could label values as a kind of abstract of the internal norms and goals of a society or culture. Values are generally quite stable and long lasting, and a change in their orientation also alters the culture and vice versa.[19]

Research, carried out by experts multiple times in the last twenty years, shows that the most important individual values for Slovenians are health, love, freedom,

---

14. *See* https://www.stat.si, 7 Sep. 2020.
15. *See* https://www.stat.si, 21 Dec. 2020.
16. *See* V. Zadnik & J. Šelb, *Osnovni vzroki smrti s kazalniki umrljivosti v Sloveniji v letu 2001* (*Main Causes of Death with Mortality Indicators*) 433 (2003).
17. *See* https://www.onko-i.si, 21 Dec. 2020.
18. *See* https://www.nijz.si, 21 Dec. 2020.
19. For more details, *see* J. Musek, *Raziskovanje vrednot v Sloveniji in vrednotni univerzum Slovencev* (*Research of Values in Slovenia and the General Values of Slovenians*) 1, http://www.prihodnost-slovenije.si, 21. Dec. 2020.

peace, family values, honesty, friendship and justice.[20] The differences between value orientations can be discerned according to gender, age, education, social and economic status, marital status, number of children and largely also in terms of an individual's religious and political orientation. The link between political and religious beliefs is especially marked in Slovenia, and it is the religious values (out of all categories of values) that can serve as the best pointer to an individual's political beliefs.[21] It is interesting to note that certain differences between values also appear in various Slovenian regions, but are not pronounced enough to be able to state an individual's regional origin with a sufficient amount of certainty on the basis of his or her value orientation. Speaking in terms of development, the so-called Dionysian values[22] have seen the largest growth in the transition period from socialism to capitalism. This is mainly attributed to the increase in individualism, private initiative and entrepreneurial mentality. Research in Slovenia has also shown that Slovenians not only value democratic values (tolerance, equality, autonomy, freedom) about as much as citizens of other developed and democratic nations and cultures, but that they also hold social and family values, health and safety to a relatively high esteem.[23]

32. As is true for the rest of the developed world, values are not present enough in contemporary education in Slovenia. Despite certain warnings and critiques by scientists, education is still strongly marked with permissive and postmodernist thinking. Research results show that values are a key component of the educational system and that shaping values is one of education's main if not the most important aim. However, the actual conditions in Slovenia point to the fact that they are very deficient in the education process.[24]

§2. General Description of the Health System

I. General Overview of the Healthcare System

A. *General*

33. The healthcare system is a complex organizational system, connecting numerous political, administrative, public and private manufacturing and service activities. Healthcare has been organized in the Republic of Slovenia with the aim to provide maximum efficiency in connecting and coordinating the interests of all

20. *Ibid.*, at 4.
21. This means that we will find but a few religious voters, who vote for the left and few non-believers voting for the right. The author sees the cause for that in the circumstances during the transition from socialism to capitalism, when the parties could not utilize their own tradition of political discourse, simply because such discourse has not existed before. *Ibid.*
22. Divided into hedonistic (sensual, health, security – such as happiness, fun, exciting life, pleasure, enjoyment) and power (status and patriotic – power, reputation, fame, money, political success, love for one's country). For more details, *see ibid.*, at 3.
23. *Ibid.*, at 9.
24. *Ibid.*, at 13.

stakeholders in the area. Slovenia employs a so-called tripartite system of management, which includes users of healthcare services, performers of healthcare services and the state. These three stakeholders are organizationally separated with the state holding a superior position. However, all three groups try to agree about their mutual interests regarding the management of the system through talks and negotiations.

34. The main interest of healthcare service users is to be and stay healthy and receive adequate medical care in case of illness. The porters of their interests in the healthcare system are the health insurance companies: these are public or private entities, which provide health insurance to their clients in exchange for payments.

All performers of healthcare services are employed in the healthcare sector, performing healthcare activities and, alongside material goods such as buildings and equipment, constituting the healthcare service. The performers provide preventive and curative treatment as well as non-health services and carry out educational and research activities in the area of health.

35. The state is represented by numerous institutions, with the main ones being the Ministry of Health and the Health Insurance Institute of Slovenia (Institute). The main function of the Institute is to carry out compulsory health insurance, i.e., provide for effective collection and distribution of public funds for good quality implementation of the rights.[25] The Constitution binds the state to provide for the existence and functioning of the healthcare system, which allows the performance of the state's public social tasks. The tripartite system is semi-autonomous in its functioning as the state retains key competencies and plays the main role in making key decisions. The remaining two stakeholders mainly take part in rationalizing the performance of healthcare activities and the functioning of the health insurance system.[26]

B. Regulation of the Healthcare System

1. Constitution of the Republic of Slovenia

36. The Constitution of the Republic of Slovenia guarantees the citizens the right to social security under conditions set down in the legislation. The state is obliged to provide compulsory health insurance. A special constitutional provision (Article 51) deals with the right to healthcare. It states everyone has the right to healthcare under the conditions set down in a separate act. The law determines the scope of rights of publicly funded healthcare.

---

25. The Institute operates ten regional units. It also operates an Information Centre and the Directorate. *See* http://www.zzzs.si, 21 Dec. 2020.
26. N. Vencelj, *Sistem zdravstvenega varstva v Republiki Sloveniji – analiza ukrepov za zmanjševanje izdatkov za zdravila* (*Healthcare System in the Republic of Slovenia – An Analysis of Measures to Reduce Costs for Medicinal Products*) 11–13 (Fakulteta za družbene vede, Univerza v Ljubljani 2004).

2. Legislation

37. The framework laws defining the health insurance system in Slovenia are the Health Care and Health Insurance Act[27] and the Health Services Act.[28] Several other acts (described in more details in the following chapters) also play a role, especially the Patients' Rights Act.[29]

3. Public Healthcare Service

38. The public healthcare system in the Republic of Slovenia is divided into primary, secondary and tertiary levels.

39. The primary level encompasses basic healthcare and pharmacies. Basic healthcare services are carried out within the network of healthcare institutions and posts, which have to be provided (in principle) by local communities. These enable rapid and direct link to the healthcare service, including emergency aid, community nursing and the like. Pharmacies are part of healthcare activities, providing medicinal products to individuals, healthcare institutions and other organizations. Medicinal product supply includes prescription drugs, non-prescription drugs and magistral creation of drugs. Pharmacies offer a service to the public and can be either public or private institutions (with a concession). Apart from their basic service, pharmacies can also carry out other activities, such as selling prosthetic appliances, body care and other health protection products, veterinary products etc.[30]

40. Secondary healthcare activity meanwhile encompasses specialists, who are tasked with continuing treatment of an individual, who was referred to them from the primary level. Secondary healthcare services take place in specialist outpatient clinics, general and specialized hospitals. Specialist outpatient services follow-up or supplement core healthcare activities and include in-depth diagnostics, disease treatment and outpatient rehabilitation. They can be carried out by hospitals, spas or private practitioners – specialists in individual fields. Physicians performing specialist outpatient activities as private practitioners, specialists in a community health centre or a spa contact appropriate hospitals in case of professional or organizational issues. Specialist outpatient institutions must include suitable laboratory and other diagnostic facilities for performing their services. Specialist hospital services include in-depth diagnostics, treatment and medical rehabilitation, healthcare, accommodation and food in general and specialist hospitals. A general hospital is a

27. OG RS, Nos 72/2006-UPB3, 114/2006-ZUTPG, 91/2007, 71/2008 Constitutional Court decisions: U-I-163/08-7, 76/2008, 118/2008 Constitutional Court decisions: U-I-163/08-12, 47/2010 Constitutional Court decision: U-I-312/08-31, 62/2010-ZUPJS, 87/2011, 40/2012-ZUJF, 21/2013, 91/2013, 99/2013, 111/2013, 95/2014, 47/2015, 61/2017, 64/2017, 23/2019.
28. OG RS, Nos 23/2005-UPB2, 15/2008-ZPacP, 23/2008, 58/2008-ZZdrS-E, 77/2008-ZDZdr, 40/2012-ZUJF, 14/2013, 88/2016, 64/2017, 1/2019, 73/2019, 82/2020, 152/2020.
29. OG RS, Nos 15/2008, 55/2017, 177/2020.
30. *See* Pharmacy Practice Act (ZLD – 1), OG RS, Nos 85/2016, 77/2017, 73/2019.

healthcare institution for treatment of several types of illnesses with a specialist outpatient service and accommodation at least for the areas of internal medicine, surgery, paediatrics, gynaecology and obstetrics. A specialist hospital is a healthcare institution for specialist outpatient and hospital treatment of a specific disease or a specific population group, which has to fulfil the same conditions as a hospital, but with accommodation, diagnostic and other capacities adjusted for its purpose.

41. Tertiary healthcare services encompass specialist outpatient and hospital activities of clinics and institutions. Their activities include performing the most demanding healthcare services (out or inpatient), which are not performed at lower levels due to their professional, personnel, technological and organizational complexity. Tertiary healthcare services also encompass scientific, research and educational activities. Healthcare services or programmes, performed on the tertiary level, are determined by the Ministry of Health.

Healthcare services on both, secondary and tertiary levels, include also activities of public health and those connected to public health in the area of health, environment and food.

a. Health Insurance

42. The health insurance system in force in Slovenia was implemented in 1992. It is based on the Austro-Hungarian system, which itself derives from the so-called Bismarck concept[31] (also termed the partner model) of national health insurance, which has proven to be quite successful in practice. This model is based on the principles of compulsory public insurance as prescribed by law. In order to make it work, all inhabitants with an income must pay their predetermined share of contributions to a specific institution, which manages health insurance and is by nature a non-profit institution. Individuals without income are, under the principle of solidarity, also entitled to basic health insurance. The state is tasked to adopt regulations which insurance companies must carry out, and it supervises the execution of such measures.

43. The principal law in the area of health insurance is the Health Care and Health Insurance Act.

The first part of the Act deals with health insurance, which encompasses everything regarding strengthening health, disease prevention, early detection, timely treatment, care and rehabilitation of the sick and injured. The Act states that everybody has the right to the best possible health and the obligation to take care of one's own health. Everybody is also entitled to healthcare and must contribute to its implementation according to his or her abilities. Healthcare also includes rights from health insurance, which ensures social security in case of illness, injury, birth or death.

---

31. Established in 1889 by the German Chancellor Otto von Bismarck. The nowadays Republic of Slovenia then belonged to the Austro-Hungarian Empire, which was the third country in the world to adopt Bismarck's model.

The second part of the Health Care and Health Insurance Act regulates compulsory and voluntary health insurance. Compulsory health insurance is of principle importance as it serves to exercise the right to social security in case of illness or injury, as stipulated by Article 50 of the Constitution of the Republic of Slovenia. This provision is upgraded by Article 51 of the Constitution, which sets down the constitutional right to healthcare.

i. Compulsory Health Insurance

44. The main institution in the area of health insurance in the Republic of Slovenia is the Institute. Voluntary health insurance is provided by individual insurance companies.

When dealing with health insurance, several other laws need to be mentioned apart from the Health Care and Health Insurance Act, as they also influence the execution or implementation of this Act. These are primarily the Health Services Act and Medical Services Act[32] and the Patients' Rights Act. The most important implementing regulation in this area is the Compulsory Health Insurance Rules.[33] The rules are, alongside some other implementing regulations, jointly adopted by the Institute as the operator of compulsory health insurance and the Minister of Health. The Compulsory Health Insurance Rules include more detailed provisions on insured persons, the contents of individual rights and the procedure of their implementation.

45. Compulsory health insurance is obligatory: a certain group of people is included in it automatically upon fulfilling the prescriptions set by law. For example, when an individual concludes an employment contract or independently carries out commercial or professional activity in the Republic of Slovenia as his or her main occupation,[34] he or she is automatically included in compulsory health insurance. Insured persons cannot select their insurance company, cannot determine the amount of insurance and do not have to conclude an insurance contract. The circle of insured persons also includes his or her family members, but only the insured persons are obliged to pay health insurance contributions.

46. Persons insured under compulsory health insurance can be divided into four groups:[35]

(1) active insured persons (employees, self-employed, farmers and members of their households, etc.);
(2) recipients of various social grants (also recipients of permanent financial aid);
(3) other individuals with income; and

32. OG RS, Nos 72/2006-UPB3, 15/2008-ZPacP, 58/2008, 49/2010 Constitutional Court decision: U-I-270/08-10, 107/2010-ZPPKZ, 40/2012, 40/2017, 64/2017, 49/2018, 66/2019.
33. OG RS, Nos 30/2003 (35/2003 amended), 78/2003, 84/2004, 44/2005, 30/2011, 49/2012, 106/2012, 99/2013, 25/2014, 85/2014, 10/2017, 64/2018, 4/2020.
34. *See* Art. 15 of the Health Care and Health Insurance Act.
35. A. Bubnov Škoberne & G. Strban, *Pravo socialne varnosti* (*Social Security Law*) 278 (GV Založba 2010).

(4) citizens of the Republic of Slovenia with permanent residence in the Republic of Slovenia (these are entered into compulsory health insurance by the municipality of their permanent residence if they do not have an income or of the income that does not reach a set quota).

The Health Care and Health Insurance Act requires that family members of an insured person can be insured as such if they have a permanent residence in the Republic of Slovenia (unless otherwise provided for immediate family members by an international treaty) and if they also meet other legal requirements.

47. The Act differentiates between immediate and wider family members. Immediate family includes spouses (dependent on the insured person, but not insured themselves), divorced spouses (if the insured person is obliged to pay alimony), cohabiting partners (if he or she has cohabited with the insured person for at least two years) and the insured person's children. The children are counted as immediate family until they reach the age of 15 years (the age when they can first seek employment) or the age of 18 years (when they become of legal age). After turning 18 years, they can only be counted as immediate family if they continue with their education, but only until they reach 26 years. An exception to that are children, who are incapable of work and are insured throughout the entire period of disability. Until the acceptance of the Civil Union Act in 2016 (ZPZ),[36] which came into use on 24 February 2017, homosexual partners in civil unions (formal and informal) were not considered as members of the immediate family. They became treated equally only after passing of the mentioned act. Now they are equalized with spouses and cohabiting partners in their rights and duties on all of the legal areas (except on the two, explicitly mentioned in law).[37] This means that if they entered formally in their civil union, they have the same legal status as spouses. If they live in an informal civil union, they are equalized with cohabitation: in that case their partnership should last at least two years before they receive the right to be insured by their informal civil union partner.

48. Pursuant to the Act, wider family members include stepsons or stepdaughters (if they are provided for by the insured person), grandchildren, the insured person's brothers and sisters, other children who do not have parents or for whom parents are unable to provide and the insured person's parents (father, mother, spouse or cohabiting partner of one of the parents or adoptive parents) if they live in the same household with the insured person, lack the means for independent sustenance and are permanently and completely incapable of working.

49. Classical cases of compulsory health insurance include insurance in case of illness, injury (both private and professional cases), motherhood or death. These are

36. OG RS, No. 33/2016.
37. Partners in homosexual civil unions (formal or informal) are not allowed to use BMAP procedures and to joint adoption of a child. *See* Art. 2 para. 3 of the Civil Union Act.

the so-called health cases.[38] They can also result in a need for medical care, with concurrently (or independently) appearing loss of income. In the first case, the insured persons have the right to health services and accessories and in the second, mainly, the right to monetary compensation.

50. The rights, stemming from compulsory health insurance in the Republic of Slovenia, are:[39]

- right to preventive healthcare services;[40]
- right to outpatient medical and dental care;
- right to hospital treatment;
- right to medical care in social security centres;
- right to treatment and care at home;
- right to medicinal products;[41]
- right to bandage materials;
- right to technological medical devices;[42]
- right to medical rehabilitation; and
- right to treatment abroad.

51. The Health Care and Health Insurance Act ranks individual rights to healthcare services according to the share insured persons have to pay by themselves. The first category includes those rights, which do not require additional payments, as they are fully paid for by the Institute.[43] Those are the following rights:

(1) regarding certain charges (e.g., all preventive services);
(2) regarding a specific group of individuals (children, pupils, students and women with regard to birth control, pregnancy and childbirth);
(3) regarding specific illnesses (injury at the workplace, occupational illnesses, HIV, contagious diseases, malign, muscular and several other severe illnesses); and
(4) regarding certain services (e.g., emergency medical aid, emergency ambulance transports).

38. For more details, *see* A. Bubnov Škoberne & G. Strban, *Pravo socialne varnosti* 280 (*Social Security Law*) (GV Založba, 2010).
39. These are the rights derived from the Health Care and Health Insurance Act and the Rules on Compulsory Health Insurance.
40. More detailed provisions on preventive healthcare services can be found in the Rules on carrying out preventive healthcare at the primary level, OG RS, Nos 19/1998, 47/1998, 26/2000, 67/2001, 33/2002, 37/2003, 117/2004, 31/2005, 83/2007, 22/2009, 17/2015, 47/2018, 57/2018 in 57/2018). The compulsory vaccination programme is determined in the annual Immunoprophylaxis and Chemoprophylaxis programme, published on the basis of the Communicable Diseases Act (ZNB), OG RS, Nos 33/2006-UPB1, 49/2020, 142/2020.
41. For more details, *see* the Medicinal Products Act (ZZdr-2), OG RS, Nos 17/2014 and 66/2019.
42. For more details, *see* Medical Devices Act, OG RS, No. 98/2009-ZMedPri.
43. *See* Art. 23 of the Health Care and Health Insurance Act.

For all other charges or services, the Act sets the lowest or highest percentages of the value of services and items that are being paid for by the Institute. The remaining costs must be covered by the individual himself or herself or by the voluntary insurance, concluded by the individual.[44] To illustrate how this works in practice, we will take a look at services linked to treating subfertility and BMAP, sterilization and artificial pregnancy termination, where up to 80% of the costs are paid for by the Institute. Dental prosthetics for adults or devices to improve vision of adults are meanwhile only covered to the amount of 50%.

52. Theoreticians have been criticizing this system of top-up payments as being discriminatory, as it does not allow for implementing the constitutional principle of a social state, equality, social security and healthcare. Especially vulnerable are people with lower income or those in a less favourable financial situation. To solve this problem, which has become quite pressing in practice, theoreticians proposed a system of top-up payments, where payments by individuals would be calculated as a percentage of their or household income.[45] This is also the path considered by the state *de lege ferenda* (more details in a dedicated chapter).

53. As was already mentioned, compulsory health insurance also allows the insured persons to receive monetary payments. The first among these is the right to monetary compensation during temporary absence from work, which replaces the lost income. The duty to provide for such salary compensation is divided between the employer and the Institute's purse.[46] The employer is obliged to pay out the compensation for the first thirty working days of absence. This period is relative as it is reset for every individual absence, regardless of the cause of the illness or injury. However, illness or injury contracted outside of work falls under absolute time limitations, with the employer having to pay compensation for up to 120 working days in a year. This limitation does not apply for occupational disease or injury at work. However, special rules do apply regarding recurrence (resurgence of illness after apparent recovery). If the time period between absences lasts for less than ten days, the monetary compensation must be paid for by the Institute from the recurrence onwards. The amount of the compensation in case of occupational disease or injury at work is 100% of the employee's average monthly wage over the past three months. Compensation in case of injuries and diseases, contracted outside of work, meanwhile amounts to 80% of the employee's salary in the past month. The Fiscal Balance Act[47] brought a considerable decrease in the amount of compensation for the first ninety days of absence from work, reducing it from 90%

---

44. Top-up payments range from 5% to 90% of the price of a healthcare service or accessory. In case of social necessity the state can pay the missing part (amount) to the full value of a certain kind of health service. This can be done only if the prescribed declaratory procedure has shown that a person has this right according to s. 3 Art. 24 of Health Care and Health Insurance Act.
45. A. Bubnov Škoberne & G. Strban, *Pravo socialne varnosti* (*Social Security Law*) 291 (GV Založba 2010).
46. For more details, *see* Arts 28–35 of the Health Care and Health Insurance Act.
47. OG RS, Nos 40/2012, 96/2012, 104/2012, 105/2012, 25/2013, 46/2013, 56/213, 63/2013, 99/2013, 101/2013, 107/2013, 85/2014, 95/2014, 24/2015, 90/2015, 102/2015, 63/2016, 77/2017, 33/2019, 72/2019, 174/2020.

of the average monthly salary of the beneficiary to 80% in case of disease.[48] The Institute as a rule pays out monetary compensation from the thirty-first day of the employee's absence onwards.[49] The compensation sum depends on the cause of inability to work: it is higher in case of occupational diseases and injuries at work, lower in case of illness contracted outside the workplace and slightly lower still in case of injury outside of the workplace. The highest and lowest compensation amounts are also set: compensation must not be lower than the guaranteed minimum wage and not higher than the salary the employee would receive for his or her work.

54. Monetary charges also include travel expenses (the right to reimbursement of transport, food and accommodation expenses during travel and stay in a different town).The right to funeral and death grant was – until November 2013, when the Social Assistance Payments Act[50] was changed and amended – a universal right, paid to family members of the deceased upon death. This was a traditional obligation of compulsory health insurance, even if death was not caused by disease or injury. Theoreticians have been calling for the elimination of funeral and death grants in their universal form for a long time.[51] Now the two rights became social rights, in the shape of so-called exceptional financial social assistance. They are allocated only to the socially weaker persons, based on the fulfilment of legally regulated conditions. Basically it means that family of the deceased has to be poor and it does not reach certain income limits or other prescribed censuses.[52] Due to the special rule of Social Assistance Payments Act [53] the two specific forms of financial social assistance are not to be paid back to the state on the event of death of the receiver from his or her legacy. It is namely the case for many other forms of financial social assistance received by beneficiary.[54]

Under certain circumstances insured persons have the right to treatment abroad. Slovenian insured persons can exercise planned treatment abroad and receive payment for it in line with three basic conditions.

48. For more details, *see* Art. 6 of the Fiscal Balance Act.
49. Because of the COVID-19 pandemic Slovenia accepted many intervention measures, among them also the Act Determining the Intervention Measures to Contain the COVID-19 Epidemic and Mitigate its Consequences for Citizens and the Economy (OG RS, Nos 49/2020, 61/2020, 152/2020, 175/2020). One of the changed regulations, in order to help economy in the difficult times, is also the rule of obligation to pay for the salary compensation for workers on sick leave. It is now, for the limited period of pandemic, the Institute who pays the amount from the first day of an employee's absence on.
50. OG RS, Nos 61/2010, 40/2011, 14/2013, 99/2013, 90/2015, 88/2016, 31/2018, 73/2018.
51. For more details, *see* A. Bubnov Škoberne & G. Strban, *Pravo socialne varnosti* (*Social Security Law*) 298–299 (GV Založba 2010).
52. For more details, *see* Art. 34a and 34b of Social Assistance Payments Act.
53. *See* s. 4 of Art. 39 of Act on Amendments and Supplements of Financial Social Assistance Act, OG RS, No. 99/13.
54. *See* V. Žnidaršič, *Dedovanje po prejemniku denarne socialne pomoči* (*Inheritance after the Recipient of Financial Social Assistance*), No. 2/3 *Delavci in delodajalci*, 375–388 (2012).

First, it is prescribed that all the treatment options in Slovenia should have been exhausted and that by this kind of treatment (also examination, audit) abroad, healing, improvement of medical condition or at least prevention of further deterioration of health condition could be reasonably expected. In this case the expenses of medical services are reimbursed to insured person in the amount of the actual cost of these services in the country in which they were received.

The second condition is attached to the fact of exceeding the maximum allowable waiting periods or reasonable time for waiting to treatment in Slovenia. It is also regulated by the Regulation (EC) No. 883/2004 of 29 April 2004 on the coordination of social security systems.[55] The expenses of medical services are reimbursed to insured person in the amount of the actual costs of these services but not in a higher amount that goes for their costs in the public healthcare network in the country in which they were received.

The third condition is based on the decision for treatment in other Member State of EU and is arranged in line with Directive 2011/24/EU of 9 March 2011 on the application of patients' rights in cross-border healthcare.[56] The decision for treatment is made by a doctor who issues the medical referral and refers the patient to foreign hospital or specialist outpatient medical services (that could also include the prescribed medicines and medical devices). It cannot only be done in case specialist outpatient medical services are available for the insured persons without a medical referral in public health network in Slovenia. The decision can also be made by an act of Health Insurance Institute of Slovenia regarding referral to health resort (spa) treatment, eligibility for medical device before the expiry of its service life and the right to complex medical device. The expenses of these medical services are reimbursed to insured person in the amount of their average price in Slovenia, but not more than that were the actual costs.[57]

The previous act of approval of Health Insurance Institute of Slovenia should be made in all of the fallowing cases (in order to receive reimbursement of expenses): hospital medical services, which include overnights; medical services that require highly specialized and expensive medical infrastructure or medical equipment. Insured person is not entitled to reimbursement of expenses for medical services in primary healthcare; for medical services in the field of long-term care, including

55. *See* OJ EU, L 166, 30 Apr. 2004 and also the following connected directives: Council Regulation (EU) No. 517/2013 of 13 May 2013 adapting certain regulations and decisions in the fields of free movement of goods, freedom of movement for persons, company law, competition policy, agriculture, food safety, veterinary and phytosanitary policy, transport policy, energy, taxation, statistics, trans-European networks, judiciary and fundamental rights, justice, freedom and security, environment, customs union, external relations, foreign, security and defence policy and institutions, by reason of the accession of the Republic of Croatia (OJ EU, L 158, 10 Jun. 2013); Regulation (EC) No. 987/2009 of 16 Sep. 2009 laying down the procedure for implementing Regulation (EC) No. 883/2004 on the coordination of social security systems (OJ EU, L 284, 30 Oct. 2009); Commission Regulation (EU) No. 1224/2012 of 18 Dec. 2012 amending Regulation (EC) No. 883/2004 of the European Parliament and of the Council on the coordination of social security systems and Regulation (EC) No. 987/2009 of the European Parliament and of the Council laying down the procedure for implementing Regulation (EC) No. 883/2004 (OJ EU, L 349, 19 Dec. 2012).
56. *See* OJ EU, L 88, 4 Apr. 2011.
57. For the detailed explanation, *see* Art. 44c of Health Care and Health Insurance Act.

non-acute hospital treatment and the treatment and care in social welfare institutions; for medical services in the field of gathering and transplantation of parts of human body; for medical services in the field of screening programmes; for coexistence of one of the parents in health institution with sick child until (and including) the age of five; for medical devices that are subject of renting for the needs of treatment, care and rehabilitation at home; for educated dog guide for which the blind person is entitled; for travel expenses and escort. In connection to cross-border healthcare there are also Article 77b and 77c of Health Care and Health Insurance Act, dealing with the national contact point for cross-border healthcare and also with control over appropriate use of funds for financing healthcare programmes.

55. The insured person exercises his or her right to healthcare services, medicinal products and technological medical devices with the selected personal physician. A patient with concluded social insurance can freely select such a physician, who is in turn obliged to accept him or her. Exceptions apply in cases, when an individual physician already reached the limit for the number of registered patients. A private patient (self-paying patient) can meanwhile select almost any health service performer.

56. An insured person can, apart from the personal physician, also choose a personal gynaecologist and a personal dentist. The personal physician can be changed without reason after a year. Prior to that, this can only occur if the trust between the insured person and his or her doctor has been damaged. The selected personal physician performs important guidance, coordinating and documentary services: he or she takes care of the health of the insured person, prescribes prescription drugs, manages and collects healthcare documents and refers the insured person to a specialist or a hospital. A referral is not necessary for check-ups and treatment at a specialist psychiatrist and at check-ups for tuberculosis and sexually transmitted diseases. This serves to protect the privacy of the patient and facilitates treatment of the more sensitive areas of human health without intervention by the chosen physician.[58]

57. As I have already mentioned, the rights of the insured person are by large decided by the chosen personal physician or, only in a few specific cases, a so-called appointed physician. These cases include spa treatment, justification of a request for a replacement of a medical device before its date of use has run out, right to more complex technological medical devices and right to treatment abroad. If the patient disagrees with the appointed physician's decision, he or she can file a complaint with the Institute's healthcare committee, which consists of two physicians and a lawyer.

58. All insured persons in the same or a similar health condition have the same right to access to all types of healthcare services. It is forbidden to discriminate them

58. *See* A. Bubnov Škoberne & G. Strban, *Pravo socialne varnosti* (*Social Security Law*) 299 (GV Založba 2010).

on the basis of personal circumstances. The only allowable measure for giving priority (and thus discriminate) between the insured persons is the urgency of the medical procedure. However, equal access without unfounded discrimination on the basis of personal circumstances, such as age and wealth of an individual, can only be guaranteed within the public healthcare network, as part of compulsory health insurance.[59]

59. A patient has the right to a second opinion, but the legislator distinguishes between the entitlements of private patients and the patients with health insurance. The right to a second opinion can be used without restriction by the former, of course if he or she is willing to pay for it. If the insured person disagrees with the physician's decision, he or she can file a complaint directly with the performer, i.e., a community health centre, hospital, private practitioner. The insured person also has the right to file a complaint with a competent supervisory body, such as the Medical Chamber, the Ministry of Health or the Institute, even if he or she is not acting as a client in the procedure.[60] The final decision of the competent physician, the healthcare committee and bodies of the Institute can be contested by filing an appeal at the Labour and Social Court.

ii. Voluntary Health Insurance

60. In accordance with the Health Care and Health Insurance Act, voluntary healthcare insurance can also be provided by other insurance companies, apart from the Institute. These insurance companies can define their scope and general conditions of voluntary insurance, but are at the same time obliged to include all who want to conclude an insurance policy that requires additional payments as well as respect the principle of equal treatment.[61]

61. Voluntary health insurance enables three additional insurance categories: insurance that includes supplementary payments for the services provided within compulsory health insurance, insurance that widens the scope of the rights and insurance that allows a higher standard of services.

62. The prevalent voluntary health insurance type in Slovenia is the supplementary health insurance for additional payments. As these payments can be quite high, an individual avoids this risk by concluding supplementary health insurance.[62] Supplementary top-up health insurance is currently offered by three insurance companies in the Republic of Slovenia.[63]

---

59. *Ibid.*, at 302.
60. *Ibid.*, at 303.
61. *See* Arts 61–62j of the Health Care and Health Insurance Act.
62. Data shows that such insurance has been concluded by a total of more than 90% of persons with compulsory health insurance. *See* https://www.e-zavarovanja.com 25 Dec. 2020.
63. These are the insurance companies which have to fulfil certain criteria from the Health Care and Health Insurance Act. In Slovenia, there are three such insurance companies: Adriatic Slovenica d.d., Triglav, zdravstvena zavarovalnica d.d. and Vzajemna zdravstvena zavarovalnica d.v.z.

As was already mentioned, several types of voluntary health insurance exist in Slovenia.

(a) Supplementary Health Insurance

63. This type of insurance covers the difference between the value of a healthcare service and the share paid for by compulsory health insurance or a part of the difference when the additional payment is used for the right to medicinal products and technological medical devices.

This is the main and the most widely concluded form of voluntary health insurance. Pursuant to the Health Care and Health Insurance Act, supplementary health insurance represents the public interest of the Republic of Slovenia. It is being carried out in accordance with the principles of inter-generational and inter-gender solidarity between all persons with voluntary insurance, which is why the act relatively extensively regulates obligations and restrictions for insurance companies regarding this special form of insurance.

An insurance company offering supplementary insurance must accept all individuals with compulsory health insurance who want to conclude this type of insurance. When concluding the insurance, all individuals must receive equal treatment. Such insurance must generally be concluded for at least one year. The insurance premium for supplementary health insurance must be the same for all insured persons of an individual insurance company, regardless of their age, sex or any other personal circumstances of the insured person. Insurance companies which offer supplementary health insurance take part in supplementary health insurance equalization schemes, which are used to equalize the differences in the costs of healthcare services. These differences stem from the different age and sex structure of insured persons at individual insurance companies. This means that health insurance companies with relatively younger insured persons and lower costs for healthcare will pay for the higher costs of insurance companies with older insured persons through the equalization scheme. By doing so, the state wanted to prevent the possibility of some insurance companies only concluding insurance policies with young and healthy insured persons and thus reaping higher profit, while others might be left with an ageing population and cash flow problems. This is also a way to enforce inter-generational solidarity and mutuality between all Slovenian insured persons, as all insurance companies offering supplementary health insurance must participate in equalization schemes.

(b) Substitute Health Insurance

64. This kind of insurance is meant for individuals, who cannot conclude compulsory health insurance in accordance with the legislation of the Republic of Slovenia. Such insurance covers the costs of healthcare services (accessories, medicinal products), at most to the extent of the standard compulsory health insurance.

(c) Additional Health Insurance

65. This type of insurance covers the costs of healthcare services, medicinal products and technological medical devices and includes monetary payments, which are not a part of rights under compulsory health insurance.

(d) Parallel Health Insurance

66. This type of insurance covers the costs of those healthcare services, which are included in compulsory health insurance, but can be carried out by the insured persons through different procedures and under different conditions as set in compulsory health insurance.

4. Private Healthcare Services

a. The Field of Activities

67. Private healthcare services were introduced in 1992 in addition to the existing public healthcare network. Private healthcare professionals (private practitioners) can choose from a relatively extensive choice of activities. The state excluded only the most delicate areas, which are reserved for public healthcare institutions, such as the provision of blood and blood products, removal and preservation of human transplant organs, epidemiological and health-related environmental activities, and pathological activities.[64]

68. This means that core healthcare services can be performed by private practitioners at the primary level. They can also perform healthcare activities at the secondary level, i.e., specialist outpatient services. Private practitioners with an appropriate concession can also open a pharmacy and supply prosthetic and other aides.

b. Conditions for Private Practice

69. A healthcare professional must fulfil certain conditions in order to carry out private practice. Apart from the required level of education, he or she must also have adequate facilities and equipment to perform a specific healthcare activity. Based on the activity, he or she must also provide proof of suitably trained and qualified co-workers and the like. In agreement with the nature of his or her activity, he or she must provide twenty-four-hour emergency medical aid, ambulance transport, laboratory and other diagnostic and therapeutic procedures. To this end, he or she can establish connections with the closest community healthcare centre or other healthcare institutions and/or private practitioners.

64. *See* Arts 35–44 of the Health Services Act.

70. The private practitioner must receive an approval by a competent chamber or professional association. After providing proofs for meeting all the required conditions, the Ministry of Health issues him or her with a decision that serves as an entry into the register of private healthcare professionals. He or she can open the private practice on the day of issuance of such a decision.

The register is managed by the Ministry of Health and contains data on the healthcare professional, his or her education, type, scope and location of performed healthcare services and the starting date for the activity. The Ministry of Health decides on entering or deleting an individual from the register. The reasons for deletion are as follows: a private practitioner fails to perform the activity within a year after being entered into the register, dies or cancels the performance of the activity, does not meet the conditions for performing the activity or performs it contrary to the entry into the register. There can be no appeal regarding the decision on entry or deletion from the register. A lawsuit is, however, possible at the Administrative Court of the Republic of Slovenia.

c. Concession

71. A private healthcare professional (foreign or Slovenian natural or legal entity) can, after fulfilling all the legislative conditions, request a concession for performing public service in the healthcare area. The concession for performing public service within the core healthcare area is awarded by the municipal or city administrative body, which is competent for health, after receiving approval by the Ministry of Health. The concession to perform public services in other healthcare activities is awarded by the Ministry of Health. The decision-making procedure includes an opinion by the Institute and the competent chamber or professional association, which has to be acquired by the above-stated bodies.

72. The concession agreement regulates the relationship between the concessionaire and awarding authority regarding the performance of the public service and the conditions applying to the concessionaire in performing it. The concession contract defines in more detail the type of healthcare activity, the scope of carrying out the public service, the starting date of the concession, the period for cancelling it and the means that are provided by the concessionaire in order to perform the service.

73. Should it be discovered that the concessionaire does not perform the public service in accordance with the regulations, the decision and the contract on the concession, the awarding authority sets a period in which these deficiencies must be eliminated. If they are not, the awarding authority revokes the concession with a decision. If a concession is revoked, the concessionaire must make sure that his or her patients are received for treatment under equal conditions by a different healthcare institution or private practitioner, performing public service.

74. And when is a concession, based on which private practitioners enter the public healthcare network and gain the ability to receive public funds, actually awarded? It is awarded in cases when the existing performers of public healthcare activities cannot perform healthcare services within the public healthcare network in the scope that is required by the needs of the patients. The sole aim of awarding concessions and public financing is to guarantee equal access to healthcare services. This also allows for the services to be carried out at an appropriate level and in a safe manner.

75. A concession gives the concessionaire only the right to perform the service in a public healthcare network. Availability to access public funds (and the amount) is decided at a later date. The concessionaire with a concession can bid at the Institute's public tender for the public funds, allocated for the specific programme that the concessionaire performs. The Institute then concludes a contract with the selected performers.

76. The launch of private practice improved the quality of healthcare services but not the scope of public healthcare activities, as the law limited the extent of public healthcare activities to the existing level. This means that a concession for private practice can only be awarded if the transfer of physicians and other healthcare professionals from the public network does not increase the scope of the public healthcare service. This resulted in the existence of private healthcare professionals without a licence (outpatient clinics with out-of-pocket pay) alongside private practitioners with concession.

C. Health Insurance in the Future

77. In Slovenia public and professional debate on crucial reforms is going on for several years now. It refers not only to health insurance, which would enable rationalization in implementing health services, but also to the long-term care and insurance for long-term care and to pension scheme.[65] The main focus is to manage financial challenges and cope with shortages of personnel.

78. The Government is aware of the problem of demographic changes and ageing of the population. Therefore, possible solutions for extending active life of the population and improving the quality of old age are under discussion. The modernization of the pension system and the implementation of active aging action plans are planned, with the aim of increasing the proportion of older workers in order to provide the long-term sustainability of public finances.[66]

79. One of the key priorities in Slovenian healthcare sector is the reduction of the number of patients waiting beyond the maximum established waiting times and then further shortening these. In order to achieve this goal, National Institute of Public Health (NIPH) made some improvements in co-ordination and management of the waiting lists, but it still has room for improvements in quality and in precision

65. The key aim of which is the long-term financial sustainability of the scheme and the adequacy of pensions: a secure old age for all generations. *See* https://www.eurofound.europa.eu, 27 Dec. 2020.
66. *Ibid.*

in order to provide a solid base for future planning of activities in managing waiting lists. The Government provided additional financial resources in order to tackle incentives for health professionals as well as for the increase in material costs for these patients. The plan on prioritization of the most important areas was made both by the number of patients waiting and the level of their objective urgency.[67]

80. In 2016 Slovenia accepted programme document titled *Resolution on the National Health Care Plan 2016-2025.*[68] In the document key priorities on the area are listed. Among them one of the most important goals is the improvement of healthcare and maintaining of its financial sustainability. Work is ongoing towards the implementation of a reform of the healthcare sector. The economic crisis, rising unemployment, insufficient financial resources and ageing population were main triggers for reforming the healthcare system.

81. In June 2013 the Ministry of Health opened a public debate on the new legislation proposal on healthcare. At the same time the proposal of the new public health services development strategy was launched for the public debate. The combination of compulsory and complementary health insurance, which are the main financial sources for financing healthcare, is found to be insufficient and not in line with the guidelines of social welfare policy.

82. Work was put into providing financial projections and scenarios of abolishing complementary health insurance and introducing other – alternative – ways of solidarity-based financing schemes. Changes are envisaged also in the field of healthcare provider network (mainly hospitals), their management, organizing structure and accountability. One envisaged reform is the broadening of contribution rates to certain new types of revenues with the aim of equalizing the financial burden and diminishing large differences in contribution rates among specific groups of insured persons or better balancing the burden of the insured persons based on the widest possible social consensus. Some steps in this direction were done in 2013 with the adoption of the amendments to the Health Care and Health Insurance Law. Contribution rates of some groups of the population (self-employed, farmers, etc.) were raised, so that partial broadening of contribution bases was introduced.

83. Plans for the future are that a special attention should be dedicated to the balance of healthcare professionals, by transferring certain competences and responsibilities between occupational groups and introducing new concepts in line with developments in medicine and other health professions. Based on the resolution, it was expected that the new Health Care and Health Insurance Act would be adopted in 2017, but it did not happen. Further planned changes concerning the management of waiting lists and on maximum allowed waiting times by health service were accepted in 2017 by changing and supplementing the Patients' Rights Act.[69]

67. *See* https://www.hspm.org, 27 Dec. 2020.
68. Resolution on the National Health Care Plan 2016-2025, OG RS, No. 25/2016.
69. OG RS, No. 55/2017.

84. Slovenian main challenges for the future improvement of the healthcare sector as such are: to continue increasing the efficiency of healthcare spending, promoting quality and integrated care as well as focusing on costs in view of the increasing healthcare expenditure, which is a challenge to the fiscal sustainability over the coming decades. To this end, the promotion of public procurement as a means to rationalize expenditure is needed. Slovenia has to improve the basis for more sustainable and efficient financing of healthcare in the future (e.g., considering additional sources of general budget funds), aiming at a better balance between resources and spending, as well as the number of contributors and the number of beneficiaries. This implies tackling the lack of sufficient in-built automatic stabilizers, especially in view of the need to reconsider the role of complementary health insurance as a driver of excess demand and avoidable costs. We will also have to tackle the excessive use of specialist and hospital care by strengthening the role of the primary care sector and family doctors as gatekeepers. The coordination and integration of care among different healthcare levels should be promoted, while ensuring adequate coverage in both urban and in rural areas. We should also promote the use of quality indicators and patient-oriented measures for healthcare procedures. Slovenia also has to further the efforts to shorten long waiting lists for some healthcare services by a more efficient allocation of human and capital resources between sectors and specializations, through active purchasing of services by public health insurance institute and by promoting day cases for surgical procedures. To this end, we will have to promote the use of ICT in the gathering, storage, use and exchange of health information.

85. In future, Slovenia has to foster the process of modernization, specialization and competition among hospitals, for example, by allowing for selective contracting of hospitals by health insurance funds, and extending legal possibilities for quality-based financing of hospital care services. We have to improve reimbursement mechanisms that create incentives to increase efficiency, including improving the current DRG system to better reflect actual costs. To this end, we will have to consider whether remuneration mechanisms of hospital staff and management could be better linked to performance, for instance, with the implementation of pay-for-performance (P4P) schemes. Gradually we have to increase the use of cost-effectiveness information in determining the basket of goods and the extent of cost sharing.[70]

II. Financing Healthcare

86. Healthcare in the Republic of Slovenia is financed from public and private means. Public funds include money from state and municipally budgets[71] and money collected through the compulsory health insurance system. Private funds

70. *See* the Resolution on the National Health Care Plan 2016-2025, OG RS, No. 25/2016.
71. Mentioned is a relatively modest public source of funding, accounting for 3.3% of health expenditure in 2014. *See* T. Albreht et al., *Slovenia, Health System Review*, 18(3) Health Systems in Transition, XVII (2016).

meanwhile include funds from voluntary healthcare insurance, part of the means from accident insurance, direct payments of inhabitants for healthcare services, medicinal products and technological medical devices. This category also includes funds from various charity organizations and donors.

87. In Slovenia, as much as in the majority of other European countries,[72] public funds provide the bulk of money spent on healthcare. The basic model of financing primary healthcare in Slovenia is the so-called capitation (financing per capita) and services model while secondary healthcare is financed by a system of a group of comparable cases.[73] This means that half of the annual value for the majority of core healthcare activities, carried out by personal physicians, is reimbursed according to the number of individuals who have chosen a certain personal physician (capitation) and the other half in accordance with the number of performed services by an individual doctor. The highest possible number of individuals, being treated at an individual physician, is taken into account when calculating the capitation. The number of such individuals also limits the amount of services that the Institute is bound to pay for to an individual performer. On the secondary level (stationary hospital treatment), Slovenia uses the model of financing, which is based on a programme developed in Australia. This is the so-called Diagnosis Related Groups – DRG model, which is based on the principle that the price for the same healthcare service is the same at all performers, regardless of the length of hospitalization or the type/status of the hospital. The DRG system groups patients into medically and economically comparable groups on the basis of medical criteria, demographic data and resource use. Financing outpatient treatment on the secondary level utilizes a service system, limited by the planned maximum available sum. Some services also have a set price.

88. In 2016, the Ministry of Finance rejected the proposal from the Ministry of Health to earmark tobacco tax for spending on health (with an estimated revenue from excise tax on tobacco of approximately EUR 450 million per year), but instead agreed to increase the budget for public health activities by about EUR 4 million in 2017, most of which is to be distributed to NGOs and not-for-profit institutions by public tender.[74]

89. For the implementation of public health services, the Ministry of Health contracts with the NIPH and the National Laboratory of Health, Environment and Food (NLHEF) on the basis of mutually agreed work programmes. Capital investments of these institutions are agreed by the Ministry of Health and covered from the state budget. For health promotion services in the workplace (under the Health and Safety

72. *See* M. Bužinel, *Prostovoljno zdravstveno zavarovanje v Sloveniji in izbranih državah EU* (*Voluntary Health Insurance in Slovenia and Selected EU Countries*) 43 (2006).
73. *See* B. Morovič & B. Simčič, *Nacionalna strategija razvoja financiranja zdravstvene dejavnosti* (2010–2020) (National Strategy to Develop Health Care Financing), 1 (2010) http://www.drmed.org, 5 Jan. 2021.
74. V. Kerstin Petrič & A. Maresso, *Slovenia*, in *Organization and Financing of Public Health Services in Europe: Country Reports* (B. Rechel et al. ed.), https://www.ncbi.nlm.nih.gov, 27 Dec. 2020.

at Work Act[75] as well as an annual plan) the Ministry of Health contracts with the Institute of Occupational, Traffic and Sports Medicine at the University Medical Centre of Ljubljana. This institute also generates additional financial resources based on annual contracts with the Health Insurance Institute.

90. One of the main challenges in the financing of public health services is that budgetary allocations to the NIPH and the NLHEF are done on an annual basis, resulting in considerable uncertainty and undermining long-term planning. Financing of NGOs is even more unstable and unpredictable.[76]

91. The Ministry of Health co-finances the participation of Slovenia's public institutions and NGOs in EU projects. Recognizing that cooperation in international research and development projects was contributing to building Slovenia's own capacities in specific areas of public health, a separate budget line was established for this purpose at the Ministry of Health. Involvement in EU projects and international networks is considered a bonus for NGOs and other institutions when bidding for funds from public tenders set out by the Ministry of Health.

92. Another important source of financing for public health services is EU financial mechanisms. The health priority financed through this source in the period 2007–2013 was the development of e-health. In 2014, public health was included in the operational plan within the budget line for social inclusion. The partnership agreement between Slovenia and the European Commission for the period 2014–2020 recognized that investments in the prevention of risk factors, the early detection of diseases and quality of care can help to reduce premature mortality; it puts an emphasis on health promotion, prevention, early detection of diseases, fostering a healthy lifestyle throughout the lifecycle and reducing health inequalities.[77]

93. Apart from EU resources, additional funding is provided to Slovenia through a financial mechanism from the Government of Norway, as part of the financial contributions from Norway to reducing economic and social disparities in the European Economic Area (EEA). A grant to Slovenia of approximately EUR 11.7 million was approved in 2013 for projects aiming to improve public health and reduce health inequalities, and for the promotion of gender equality and work-life balance. Of this total amount, EUR 2.35 million was allocated to the 'Together for health' project (2013–2016) that was implemented by the NIPH, while the remaining funds were distributed to public health institutions and NGOs through tenders in 2015.[78]

75. OG RS, No. 43/2011.
76. Glej V. Kerstin Petrič & A. Maresso, *Slovenia*, in *Organization and Financing of Public Health Services in Europe: Country Reports* (B. Rechel et al eds.), https://www.ncbi.nlm.nih.gov, 27 Dec. 2020.
77. *Ibid.*
78. *Ibid.*

§3. MEDICAL LAW

I. Definition and Functions of Medical Law

94. The most concise definition of Medical Law is that this special branch of law governs medical activity. It is a set of rules, which regulate medical activity, determine the status of individuals performing this activity and their relations with the users of their services. The rules of Medical Law regulate or define in more detail the human rights to health, healthcare and health insurance, liabilities and rights of physicians, other medical professionals and medical institutions. It deals with a specific and, due to the nature of relations between the participants, one could say, a very sensitive area which is regulated as a form of public activity of special social importance. Medical Law thus includes all legal aspects of healthcare activities, all subjects in the area, relations and procedures to which it binds appropriate legal consequences, i.e., individual rights and liabilities. It is a meeting point between law and medicine, both of which aim to protect the most highly safeguarded human rights such as life, body, health, dignity, and so on.

95. In its narrower meaning, Medical Law encompasses legal rules, which govern relations regarding the performing of healthcare or medical care activities. In its wider meaning, Medical Law also includes other regulations which are connected with but do not directly govern relationships regarding the performance of healthcare activities. These include regulations on sale and purchase of medicinal products, liability insurance in healthcare, medical equipment, transfusion activities, etc.

A. *Medical Law and Health Law*

96. Legal theory and jurisprudence also use the term 'Health Law'; however, several authors believe that this term is much wider than the term 'Medical Law' as it includes all rules and regulations connected with healthcare or health. Some authors furthermore think that Health Law is not only wider in scope than Medical Law but that the two deal with a different area of social/healthcare activities.[79] The term 'Health' is in itself wider and more inclusive than what we understand under the term 'Medical'. Healthcare is a specific form of a very important social activity for all societies, while medicine has its own specific and narrower connotation and meaning. The term 'Medical Law' is also narrower in scope because it principally governs relations between physicians and patients as a relation between two subjects, whereupon one provides or performs a medical activity and the other requires or receives it. Other healthcare personnel is only indirectly included into this relationship. This is why some authors believe that Medical Law is only one of the branches of Health Law.[80]

---

79. *See* V. Žnidaršič Skubic, *Civilno medicinsko pravo* (*Civil Medical Law*), Uradni list 36–37 (2018).
80. There are contrary opinions as well. *See* J. Čizmić, *Bioetika i medicinsko pravo* (*Bioethics and Medical Law*), 44(2) Medicina 175–176 (2008).

97. One way to help us distinguish between the terms 'Medical Law' and 'Health Law' is to look at historical course of events, as the situation today differs from the past. In the past, the relationship between the physician and patient held front stage with the physician self-evidently playing the dominant role. With the progress of medicine and ever-increasing amount of teamwork, other health and non-health (administrative) personnel have entered the area of healthcare or began providing various healthcare activities, causing the term 'Medical Law' to become limited in scope. It does neither cover nor explain all the relations between patients and healthcare professionals during the performance of health-related activities. That is why the prevailing opinion is that Health Law or Health Care Law has a wider scope of use, and in this (wider) scope supplants the term 'Medical Law'. The fact that Health Law is being used in EU regulations and directives can serve as a further indicator of this development.[81]

98. Health Law can also be defined as a set of rules, which govern the performance, and provision of suitable healthcare activities, expertly carried out by qualified healthcare professionals. Health Law in its narrower scope contains legal rules, which regulate the contents, manner of performance, scope and structure of carrying out healthcare activities by qualified healthcare professionals. These rules govern the contents, scope, performers and the manner of performing healthcare, dental healthcare, pharmaceutical and other activities. Health Law in its wider meaning also regulates issues that stem indirectly or directly from the procedures used when performing health care. Health Law has, the same as Medical Law, developed into a special branch of law and as such forms an established part of study programmes at numerous universities around the world.

99. As we can see, Medical Law theory gives somewhat differing answers to the questions regarding the meaning of terms such as 'Medical Law' and 'Health Law'. While the majority believes that the latter has a wider scope, not all share this opinion. Despite that we can safely say that both terms have become a sort of *terminus technicus* for labelling the ever-increasing number of legal practices, which deal with complex relations found in healthcare procedures, as well as of all those who are in any way connected to performing such procedures. Some authors also point out the fact that the scope of both terms is not all that important, as they are often used synonymously in practice.[82]

The scope of Medical Law or Health Law is very wide and has an explicit tendency of expansion. Healthcare activity as the subject of study of Medical Law is developing daily, causing an increase in the number of problems and issues stemming from it.

100. Medical Law can also be defined through its subject matter, whereupon we first have the subjects. We are primarily dealing with three categories of subjects:

81. *See* T.K. Hervey & V.J. McHale, *Health Law and the European Union* 13–19 (University Press 2004).
82. J. Čizmić, *Bioetika i medicinsko pravo* (*Bioethics and Medical Law*), 44(2) Medicina 176 (2008)

(1) patient and his or her fundamental rights, such as the right to healthcare, life, health, safety, and so on;
(2) physicians and other healthcare professionals; and
(3) hospitals and other healthcare institutions and the health system as a whole (its regulation and efficient functioning).

A specific subject of Medical Law is also health insurance. This deals with human rights based on health insurance and the right to financing of healthcare. The Health Care and Health Insurance Act states in Article 1 paragraph 3 that healthcare also includes the rights from health insurance, which ensure social security in case of illness, injury, birth or death.

The subject of Health Law can also be gained from the definition of a healthcare activity. The latter in accordance with Article 1 paragraph 2 of the Health Care and Health Insurance Act deals with the measures and activities for protecting health, preventing, diagnosing and treating patients or injured. These measures and activities are performed in line with the medical doctrine and with the use of medical technology by healthcare professionals and/or their co-workers.[83]

B. Medical Law in Slovenian Legal Practice

101. The term 'Medical Law' is well entrenched in the academic sphere in Slovenia and has been for many years the subject of special interest and studies by theoreticians. It was incorporated fifteen years ago in the postgraduate curriculum and soon thereafter in the undergraduate curriculum as a specific subject at the Faculty of Law, University of Ljubljana. The students are very interested in it, and their interest grows by the year. Medical Law is the topic of several periodical interdisciplinary conferences and meetings between legal experts, physicians and other healthcare professionals. It is increasingly used as a special legal discipline in court practice as well and defined as a special area, to which individual passed judgments are distributed to.

II. Sources of Medical Law

102. There is no general law outlining a framework in Medical Law in Slovenia. Medical interventions are generally evaluated within the general principles of law. However, there are laws and other documents, national and international, that serve as sources for Medical law.

83. *Ibid.*, at 171–185.

A. International Sources

103. In accordance with Article 8 of the Constitution of the Republic of Slovenia, ratified and published international treaties are applied directly. Laws and other regulations, i.e., various implementing regulations, have to be in accordance with generally valid principles of international law and with binding international treaties.

104. In the wider sense (when dealing with the enjoyment and protection of general human rights and freedoms) in the Republic of Slovenia, the source of Medical Law are the passed and ratified conventions and declarations on human rights. The most important ones are the following: European Convention for the Protection of Human Rights and Fundamental Freedoms,[84] Convention on the Rights of the Child,[85] European Convention on the Exercise of Children's Rights,[86] and the UN Universal Declaration of Human Rights.[87]

105. In a narrower sense, the international source of Medical Law is mainly the Convention for the Protection of Human Rights and Dignity of the Human Being with regard to the Application of Biology and Medicine (The Oviedo Convention)[88] and its four additional protocols. They are the Additional Protocol on the Prohibition of Cloning Human Beings,[89] the Additional Protocol on Transplantation of Organs and Tissues of Human Origin,[90] the Additional Protocol concerning Biomedical Research,[91] and the Additional Protocol to the Oviedo Convention regarding Genetic Testing for Health Purposes. [92] Slovenia has signed and ratified all of the mentioned protocols. The international legal sources named above present an important legal frame which our country used to draft some of its more important legal regimes in the area of Medical Law.

B. National Sources

1. Constitution

106. The Slovenian Constitution contains a number of general provisions, which are connected with the inviolability of the human life and body, human rights in general and their implementation, privacy, personal rights, etc. All of the mentioned general provisions are important and sometimes even deciding for Medical Law as well as other legal branches.

84. OG RS – IT, No. 7-41/1994, 33/1994.
85. OG SFRY – IT, No. 15/1990 and OG RS – IT, No. 9/1992.
86. OG RS – IT, No. 26/1999.
87. *See* http://www.un.org, 27 Dec. 2020.
88. OG RS – IT, No. 17/1998.
89. *Ibid.*
90. OG RS – IT, No. 20/2005.
91. *Ibid.*, 13/2006.
92. OG RS – IT, No. 62/2009.

In Slovenia, everybody is guaranteed the same human rights and fundamental freedoms, regardless of nationality, race, gender, language, religion, political or other leanings, wealth, birth, education, social status or any other personal circumstance. These 'other circumstances' unquestionably include an individual's health status. All are equal before the law (Article 14 of the Constitution of the Republic of Slovenia).

107. Human rights and fundamental freedoms are exercised directly on the basis of the Constitution. Laws can regulate the manner of exercising human rights when the Constitution so requires or when this is necessary due to the nature of an individual right or freedom. Human rights and fundamental freedoms are limited only by the rights of others and in cases set by the Constitution. The Constitution guarantees judicial protection of human rights and fundamental freedoms and the right to obtain redress for the violation of such rights and freedoms.[93] No human right or fundamental freedom regulated by legal acts in force in Slovenia may be restricted on the grounds that this Constitution does not recognize that right or freedom or recognizes it to a lesser extent (Article 15 of the Constitution of the Republic of Slovenia). The Constitution also protects everybody's right to personal liberty (Article 19), equal protection of rights (Article 22) and freedom of movement (Article 32). The last right may be limited by law, but only in case of specifically stated reasons. One of them is to prevent the spread of infectious diseases (alongside ensuring the course of criminal proceedings, protecting public order or if the defence of the state demands so).

108. In general and for the area of Medical Law, there is a special provision for protecting the rights of the children. In accordance with Article 56 of the Constitution, children enjoy special care and protection. They enjoy human rights and fundamental freedoms consistent with their age and maturity and are guaranteed special protection from economic, social, physical, mental or other exploitation and abuse. Regarding health, it is also prudent to mention the provision that guarantees the right to a healthy living environment (Article 72 of the Constitution).

109. More closely connected to the area of Medical Law are Article 17 of the Constitution, which states that human life is inviolable, and Article 18, which prohibits anybody being subjected to torture, inhuman or degrading punishment or treatment. Article 18 also states that conducting medical or other scientific experiments on any person without his or her free consent is prohibited. Article 34 of the Constitution gives everyone the right to personal dignity and safety, while Article 35 guarantees the inviolability of the physical and mental integrity of every person, his or her privacy and personality rights.

110. Collecting and processing data on patients is one of the more touchy subjects in the area covered by Medical Law. The Constitution itself guarantees basic

93. *See also* the novelty in our legal system, the collective action – in Collective Actions Act, OG RS, No. 55/2017. For more, *see* A. Vlahek, *Development of Consumer Collective Redress in the EU: A Light at the End of the Tunnel?*, 18, Baltic Yearbook of International Law 134–168 (2020).

personal data protection as it prohibits its use contrary to the purpose for which it was collected. It also guarantees the right for an individual to access collected personal data that relates to him or her and the right to judicial protection in the event of any abuse of such data (Article 38 of the Constitution). Article 46 of the Constitution guarantees conscientious objection for everyone (including physicians), but only in cases provided by law where this does not limit the rights and freedoms of others. A physician's right to conscientious objection in Slovenia is regulated more in detail by the Patients' Rights Act, Medical Services Act, Health Services Act and the Code of Medical Ethics.[94]

111. The right to social security for the citizens of the Republic of Slovenia is provided in Article 50 of the Constitution. The conditions under which the state guarantees such protection are regulated in more detail by legislation; however, the state is bound to provide for compulsory health, pension, disability and other social security measures, and shall ensure their proper functioning. The Constitution also specifically defines the right to healthcare for everyone under conditions provided by law. It moreover states that rights to healthcare from public funds shall be provided by law. Another important provision that supports the concept of a patient's autonomy is that nobody can be compelled to undergo treatment. Exceptions are provided by law (Article 51 of the Constitution). The provisions in Article 55 of the Constitution are important for the area of so-called reproductive law. These provisions guarantee the freedom of choice in childbearing. The state is bound to guarantee opportunities for exercising this freedom and creating conditions that enable parents to decide to bear children.

2. Legislation

a. General

112. Some of the most important acts that present the source for the Slovenian Medical Law are listed below:

(1) Health Care and Health Insurance Act – *Zakon o zdravstvenem varstvu in zdravstvenem zavarovanju*, Official Gazette of the Republic of Slovenia (OG RS), Nos 72/2006-UPB3, 114/2006-ZUTPG, 91/2007, 71/2008 Skl.US (Constitutional Court decision): U-I-163/08-7, 76/2008, 118/2008 Skl.US: U-I-163/08-12, 47/2010 Odl.US: U-I-312/08-31, 62/2010-ZUPJS, 87/2011, 40/2012-ZUJF, 21/13 – ZUTD-A, 91/13, 99/13 – ZUPJS-C, 99/13 – ZSVarPre-C, 111/13 – ZMEPIZ-1 in 95/14 – ZUJF-C, 74/2015, 61/2017, 64/2017, 36/2019.

(2) Health Services Act – *Zakon o zdravstveni dejavnosti*, OG RS, Nos 23/2005-UPB2, 15/2008-ZPacP, 23/2008, 58/2008-ZZdrS-E, 77/2008-ZDZdr, 40/2012-ZUJF, 14/2013, 88/2016, 64/2017, 1/2019, 73/2019, 82/2020, 152/2020.

94. *See* https://www.zdravniskazbornica.si, 27 Dec. 2020.

(3) Medical Services Act (official consolidated wording) – *Zakon o zdravniški službi (uradno prečiščeno besedilo)*, OG RS, Nos 72/2006, 107/2010-ZPPKZ, 40/2012 – ZUJF, 88/2016, 40/2017, 64/2017, 49/2018, 66/2019.
(4) Patients' Rights Act – *Zakon o pacientovih pravicah*, OG RS, Nos 15/2008, 55/2017, 177/2020.
(5) Mental Health Act – *Zakon o duševnem zdravju*, OG RS, Nos 77/2008, 46/2015, 44/2019.
(6) Communicable Diseases Act (official consolidated text) – *Zakon o nalezljivih boleznih (uradno prečiščeno besedilo)*, OG RS, Nos 33/2006, 49/2020, 142/2020, 175/2020.
(7) Act Regulating the Obtaining and Transplantation of Human Body Parts for the Purposes of Medical Treatment – *Zakon o pridobivanju in presaditvi delov človeškega telesa zaradi zdravljenja*, OG RS, No. 656/2015.
(8) Health Measures in Exercising Freedom of Choice in Childbearing Act – *Zakon o zdravstvenih ukrepih pri uresničevanju pravice do svobodnega odločanja o rojstvu otrok*, OG SRS, Nos 11/1977 and 42/1986; OG RS, Nos 29/1995-ZPDF and 70/2000-ZZNPOB.
(9) Infertility Treatment and Procedures of Biomedically-assisted Procreation Act – *Zakon o zdravljenju neplodnosti in postopkih oploditev z biomedicinsko pomočjo*, OG RS, Nos 70/2000 and 15/2017.
(10) Complementary and Alternative Medicine (CAM) Act – *Zakon o zdravilstvu*, OG RS, Nos 94/2007 and 87/2011.
(11) Healthcare Databases Act – *Zakon o zbirkah podatkov s področja zdravstvenega varstva*, OG RS, Nos 65/2000, 47/2015, 31/2018, 152/2020.
(12) Medicinal Products Act – *Zakon o zdravilih*, OG RS, Nos 17/2014 and 66/2019.
(13) Health Inspection Act (official consolidated text) – *Zakon o zdravstveni inšpekciji (uradno prečiščeno besedilo)*, OG RS, Nos 59/2006 and 40/2014.
(14) Pharmacy Practice Act – *Zakon o lekarniški dejavnosti*, OG RS, Nos 85/2016, 77/2017, 73/2019.
(15) Medical Devices Act – *Zakon o medicinskih pripomočkih*, OG RS, No. 98/2009.

Numerous implementing regulation acts were passed to support the acts above. These regulations provide more detailed way of using the legislation in practice and facilitate their implementation.

b. Civil Law

113. The general provisions of Civil Law form the basis of Medical Law in many ways. First, I would like to mention the unified concepts of Slovenian theory and jurisprudence, i.e., that the relationship between a patient and a physician falls under Civil Law, making it a contractual relationship. While a contract on treatment is not specially defined or regulated in Slovenian law, the theory and the jurisprudence see it as a work contract or a contract of undertaking,[95] lately also as a contract of mandate.[96] Based on the contract between the physician and the patient, a contractual obligation is created, which establishes mutual rights and obligations. This is valid regardless of whether the physician has a private practice or works for a public health institution. The patient's obligation is to pay for the performed healthcare service (by himself or herself or through health insurance funds), while the physician's obligation is to provide in full the agreed healthcare service. The physician's obligation is by the nature of things to strive to perform to his or her best potential and not (necessarily) to achieve the result (success). The physician therefore does not guarantee the success of the treatment (the patient being cured), but must perform with all due care (act *lege artis*). Exceptions from the above rule are some special procedures, such as cosmetic surgery, dental treatment, prosthetics, anaesthesia and the like, where a result can be required, based on the contract.

114. What follows from the above is that the Code of Obligations[97] is a key for dealing with a contractual relationship between a physician and a patient and between a health institution and a patient. If the contract is breached, appropriate Civil Law sanctions can follow in line with the Code of Obligations.[98] If a patient has been harmed, the physician or the health institution can be held liable.

115. If a contract was concluded between the performer of healthcare services and the patient, we are dealing with a contractual liability for damages. If that is not the case (such as when a physician acted as *negotiorum gestor* in an urgent case without the patient's consent), the liability is based on a delict. In such cases, we are dealing with breaches of a basic obligation law principle *neminem laedere*, which states that everybody must refrain from activities that could harm another person. However, the Slovenian Code of Obligations does not distinguish between regulating liabilities arising from legal or delict grounds, which is why we are talking about monism in Slovenian Tort Law.[99]

c. Criminal Law

116. Within Criminal Law, we deal with its specific subtype, termed by some as Medical Criminal Law. This is Criminal Law which specializes on criminal offences

---

95. For more on contract of undertaking, *see* D. Možina & A. Vlahek, *Contract Law in Slovenia* 218–225 (Wolters Kluwer 2019).
96. For more on contract on mandate, *see* D. Možina & A. Vlahek, *Contract Law in Slovenia* 260–263 (Wolters Kluwer 2019).
97. OG RS, No. 97/2007, 64/2010, 20/2018.
98. For further details on such sanctions, *see* A. Vlahek, *Zahtevki naročnika v primeru nepravilne izpolnitve podjemne in gradbene pogodbe* (*Remedies of the Ordering Party in Cases of Improper Performance of Contract for Work and Building Contract*), in X. dnevi civilnega in gospodarskega prava Institute for Comparative Law at the Faculty of Law in Ljubljana, 12–13 Apr. 2012, Ljubljana, 21–26.
99. A. Polajnar Pavčnik, *Obligacijski vidiki razmerja med bolnikom in zdravnikom* (*Obligational Aspects of the Relationship Between Physician and Patient*), Pravo in medicina, Cankarjeva založba, 95 (Ljubljana 1998).

where physicians or other healthcare personnel in lieu of their medical profession are the perpetrators and (mainly) the patients are the victims. This area specifically stresses the protective function of Criminal Law in the sense of protecting patients from unlawful actions by physicians and other healthcare professionals.[100] Criminal liability, stemming from performing various medical procedures, is regulated by the Criminal Code.[101] The code includes specific provisions dealing with breach of professional secrecy, abandonment of medical help, negligence in treatment, healer practices, unlawful transplanting of parts of the human body, specific (specifically determined) illegal actions in the area of fertilization with biomedical assistance and genetic testing, cloning and false issuance of physician certificates.

100. *See* D. Korošec, *Medicinsko kazensko pravo* (*Medical Criminal Law*), Pravna fakulteta and Cankarjeva založba 27 (Ljubljana 2004).
101. Criminal Code (KZ-1), OG RS, Nos 50/2012 (official consolidated text – 2), 54/2015, 38/2016, 27/2017, 23/2020, 91/2020.

Part I. The Medical Profession

Chapter 1. Access to the Medical Profession

§1. Medical Education

I. General

117. The Constitution of the Republic of Slovenia states that education and schooling are free. In accordance with the constitutional provisions, the state shall create the opportunities for citizens to obtain proper education (Article 57 of the Constitution). Primary education is compulsory and financed from public funds. Article 58 meanwhile guarantees autonomy of state universities and other institutions of higher education. The manner of their financing is regulated by the Higher Education Act.[102] Slovenia invests more in education and training than the whole of EU taken on an average.[103]

II. Historical Overview

118. Medical education in what is today of the Republic of Slovenia began with the establishment of 'Academia operosorum Labacensis', the 'Academy of hard-working people of Ljubljana'. Established in 1693, this was the first scientific academy in Ljubljana. Its initiators were doctors Marko Gerbec and Janez Gregor Dolničar, who were also active members of an academy in Vienna. At the time of its founding, the academy had twenty-three members: thirteen jurists, six theologians and four doctors. It held its first general assembly in 1701. The main idea behind the establishment was to practice and progress in literature. The academy's members investigated their own fields. It ceased functioning in 1725, after the death of J.G. Dolničar, who was its most active member. The academy was followed by a midwife school, while a first true predecessor of the Faculty of Medicine was the Department for Medical and Surgical Studies at the Ljubljana Lyceum. During the (French) Illyrian Provinces in 1809, the Lyceum grew into an 'Ecole Centrale', a

102. OG RS, Nos 32/2012 – UPB7, 40/2012 ZUJF, 57/2012, 109/2012, 85/2014, 75/2016, 61/2017, 65/2017, 175/2020.
103. In 2018, Slovenia spent 5.4% of its GDP on education, compared to the EU-27 average of 4.6%. *See* https://op.europa.eu, Publications Office of the EU (europa.eu), Education and training monitor 2020, 27 Dec. 2020.

type of university which also operated a medical department. This department is considered as the germ of the first faculty of medicine on the territory of Slovenia. Studies at the Ecole lasted for five years, which was more than at the inception of a medical faculty in 1919. As the French retreated and the Austrians returned, the higher studies were suspended, and the Ecole was first degraded and then abolished in 1848.

The modern Faculty of Medicine sprung into being in 1919 as part of the newly established University of Ljubljana. The faculty got its third year only in 1940, but the subsequent German occupation of Yugoslavia stalled its development. A complete Faculty of Medicine with a five-year and later a six-year programme was established in 1945. The dental medicine clinic, responsible for dental medicine, was also established then. It later grew into an independent dental medicine department, which was first called the 'Faculty of Dental Medicine' and is now the 'Department for Dental Medicine'. The Faculty of Medicine at the University of Maribor was established in 2003.

III. Medical Education Today

119. Slovenia currently has two medical faculties: the Faculty of Medicine at the University of Maribor and the Faculty of Medicine at the University of Ljubljana. The reasons for establishing the second medical faculty in the country – in Maribor, with the first students enrolling in the 2004–2005 academic year – were mainly pragmatic, as Slovenia is experiencing a severe shortage of physicians. According to data by the Medical Chamber of Slovenia, Slovenia is one of the countries with a small number of medicine doctors. Slovenia is lagging behind OECD average and also if we take into account the data of Eurostat, we are far behind the developed countries: in Slovenia there are only 3.1 medicine doctors per 1,000 inhabitants, whereas in Austria there are 5.18.[104]

A. *Undergraduate Studies*

1. General Practitioner

120. The Faculty of Medicine at the University of Ljubljana has a long tradition and carries out two study programmes – a uniform postgraduate medicine (master) programme of the second level and a uniform postgraduate (master) dental medicine programme of the second level. The studies last for six years (twelve terms) and can be attended by anyone who has completed the general matura examination (school leaving exam required for the completion of secondary education) after 1 June 1995 or finished any secondary school programme before that date. The students of the first year of medicine are between 18 and 19 years old on average. The professional title awarded to the graduates is Doctor of Medicine. The main aim of

104. *See* https://www.zdravniskazbornica.si, 27 Dec. 2020.

the unified medicine postgraduate study programme (at the Faculty of Medicine in Maribor as well as Ljubljana) is to train professionals, who are qualified to perform professional tasks in the area of medicine and give them the basis to continue their professional development as part of specialization or to continue doctoral studies.

The student graduates after meeting all the requirements in accordance with the study programme collects a total of 360 credit points.[105] A thesis or its equivalent written product is not required upon completing the studies.

121. Special conditions are set for transfers between study programmes. Students can transfer from other universities to the Faculty of Medicine at the University of Ljubljana only in second or third year, provided they had attended the same type of study programme. The transfer is only possible if the applicant meets all the general admission requirements and has passed all the exams in all the years at his or her original faculty with at least the average grade 8.5. The applicant must present its original faculty's study programme for review. If this programme is not in agreement with the programme at the Faculty of Medicine of the University of Ljubljana, the applicant must pass differential exams, as determined by the Commission for Students' Issues.

2. Secondment (Internship)

122. On 1 February 2018, the Medical Services Act introduced secondment into the system of postgraduate training of doctors. An individual who has acquired the professional title of a Doctor of Medicine or was issued an order on the equivalence of a title received abroad with the Slovenian professional title of a Doctor of Medicine may apply for secondment. The secondment is conducted in two separate parts: a compulsory part – internship, which ends with a professional exam (six months of the internship programme for the profession of medicine doctor) and elective part – rotation in various specialist fields lasting at least two months. The optional part of the secondment lasts up to a maximum of six months. Before starting to perform secondment, a doctor must register in the register of doctors.[106]

B. Postgraduate Studies

1. Physician Specialist

123. A licence for independent work can be obtained by the dentist after the successfully passing of expert exam and by the medicine doctor after the concluded specialization and successfully passed specialist exam.

124. Physicians or dental medicine doctors who have passed the expert exam can decide which area they want to specialize in. Specialization for physicians is a

105. *See* http://www.mf.uni-lj.si, 27 Dec. 2020.
106. *See* https://www.zdravniskazbornica.si, 27 Dec. 2020.

form of postgraduate professional training, which is required for an additional and in-depth acquisition of skills and knowledge in one of the areas of medicine or dental medicine. In the Republic of Slovenia, this area is regulated more in detail by the Rules on the Types, Content, Duration and Course of Specialization of Doctors.[107]

125. The programme for an individual specialization has to define:

(1) the scope of knowledge and skills that a specializing physician has to master by the end of specialization;
(2) contents and duration of individual parts of specialization (work at a department, outpatient clinic, laboratory, attending seminars, workshops, research activities);
(3) a list of compulsory training performed by the trainee during the specialization; and
(4) ways of real-time assessment of knowledge and performance of a specialist exam.

126. Specialization is performed at approved specializing workplaces in public healthcare institutes, departments at faculties of medicine and at other legal and natural persons with a concession. The specializing individual has to be guaranteed the possibilities to acquire the necessary scope of knowledge and skills for a specific area of medicine or dental medicine.

127. The Medical Chamber manages a register of approved specializations and a register of free and occupied specialized workplaces. In agreement with detailed procedures by the above-mentioned Rules, the Chamber performs a call for bids twice a year to meet the public healthcare service demands for specialists in the Republic of Slovenia. At the end of the tender procedure, the Chamber, on the basis of a proposal by a special selection committee, issues a decree on specialization for all applicants who have applied for specialization in a specific region. Based on this decree, the Chamber issues a decision to the applicant to whom specialization has been granted. The decision contains the date of beginning of specialization and the applicant's main mentor. The selected applicant at the same time receives instructions for performing specialization. The employer for the applicant is proposed by the Chamber.

128. Throughout the specialization, the specializing trainee has a main mentor as well as direct mentors at individual specialist workplaces. The period, defined as the length of the specialization in the programme, is the shortest amount of time in which specialization can be completed. Specialization can last for at most three additional months if the trainee did not gain the needed knowledge and skills in the scope of time that was originally devoted to this kind of specialization.

107. OG RS, No. 22/2018.

129. During specialization, trainees can individually perform the activities and services they are qualified for through their previously completed formal education (studies completed with an expert exam, a different completed specialization). The remaining services from the current area of specialization can only be carried out according to a prior written authorization by a mentor or under his or her direct supervision.

130. The part of the traineeship that conforms to the specialization programme can be included fully or in part in the trainee's specialization programme. The decision on this is passed by the Chamber upon proposal by the trainee's main mentor.

131. If the main mentor discovers that the trainee is failing to carry out his or her obligations according to the programme and has no valid excuse for doing so, the mentor must warn the trainee in writing and then propose to the Chamber that specialization is cancelled. Before the final decision the Chamber obtains explanations from the trainee.

132. The achieved level of a trainee's knowledge and skills is reviewed by mentors during specialization itself. Specialization is completed by a specialist exam, which should be done at latest in three months after finishing the prescribed programme of specialization. The specialist exam is generally taken at the authorized provider of the specialist activity where the trainee was working. The specialist exam is composed of a theoretical and practical part. The success of the trainee is marked by 'passed' or 'failed'. If a trainee shows exceptional knowledge, the exam committee can mark his or her exam with 'cum laude'. If a trainee fails the specialist exam, the exam committee can propose to the Chamber that specialization be extended and additional circulation for minimum three and maximum six months. The exam committee should name the professional areas on which it proposes the prolongation of specialization. The trainee who fails a second specialist exam loses the right to take this exam again in the running year. In total, trainee is allowed to access to the exam no more than three times. The trainee who passes the specialist exam is issued a certificate on the passed exam by the Chamber, which gives the trainee the title of a specialist for his or her field. Based on the certificate on the passed specialist exam and after the trainee submits an application, the Chamber issues a licence for performing his or her specialist activity. The title of specialist can be also recognized on the basis of work experience of a specialist[108] and on the basis of specialist title received abroad.[109]

a. Foreign Physician Specialist

133. A specialist title received abroad can be recognized in Slovenia in a special procedure, on the bases of an application. It is reviewed by associate expert in the field of specialization, appointed by the Chamber. The expert compares the scope,

---

108. *See* Arts 50–52 of the Rules on the Types, Content, Duration and Course of Specialization of Doctors.
109. *See* Arts 53–64 *ibid.*

time and the content of the foreign specialization with the Slovenian programme of specialization on the field (valid on the day of filing the application for recognition). His or her opinion can be positive (positive written opinion); he or she can suggest additional training or additional taking of proficiency test and also find out that the needed adjustment period for the applicant would be more than twelve months. Based on the mentioned opinions the Chamber issues a decision on a recognition of a foreign specialist study, a decision with additional conditions for the applicant to achieve the recognition or the decision on non-recognition of the title of specialization received abroad.

134. A foreign citizen can perform specialist activities in the Republic of Slovenia under the conditions and in line with the procedures set by law, implementing regulation acts and according to the programme that applies to the citizens of the Republic of Slovenia.

2. Doctoral Studies

135. Graduates of the Faculty of Medicine can continue their studies in several doctoral programmes offered by the faculties at the University of Ljubljana and University of Maribor. A special scientific (interdisciplinary) postgraduate study to receive the title of Doctor of Science in Biomedicine is run by the University of Ljubljana. The programme lasts for four years, is worth 240 credit points and is a third-level programme according to the Bologna system. The main focus of doctoral studies is on research, interdisciplinary studies and cooperation between internationally distinguished Slovenian and foreign experts. The doctoral programme allows postgraduates to gain the title of Doctor of Science in ten fields of science: Biochemistry and Molecular Biology; Pharmacy; Genetics; Clinical Biochemistry and Laboratory Biomedicine; Medicine-Clinical; Medicine-Basic; Microbiology; Neuroscience; Public Health; Toxicology and Veterinary Medicine.[110]

§2. Manpower Planning

I. General

136. Physicians and dentists are the core performers of medical activities everywhere, which is why determining the number of required professionals is one of the most demanding tasks in planning healthcare. The number is mainly influenced by the country's wealth, manner of performing healthcare and its organization.

137. While the use of some market mechanisms in healthcare is possible, they can only play a partial role. In Slovenia, these mechanisms are mainly in force for private practitioners, i.e., those who work outside of the public health network or have not received a concession. They must be listed in a register of private medical

110. *See* https://www.uni-lj.si, 27 Dec. 2020.

practitioners to be allowed to operate. Some authors meanwhile are talking about the existence of the so-called pure private sector, which presents an alternative to or amends the activities of public healthcare services. These additional healthcare services are available to those who can afford them, as they are paid for by the users themselves and are as a rule quite expensive. Such services are mainly present in Slovenia in dentistry and several other specialist (mainly outpatient) areas, where (public health) waiting lists are generally quite long or where private practitioners provide a much higher quality of services.

138. In the remaining cases within the framework of the public healthcare network, which is composed of public health institutions and private practitioners with concession, the number of providers is limited or planned. The reason for that is mainly that patients as users of healthcare services only have partial professional information about them and that a social state (as Slovenia declares itself to be in Article 2 of the Constitution) must strive to reduce social inequalities. These inequalities should not influence the accessibility of all patients to the core and most urgent healthcare services.

II. Legal Foundations

A. The Health Services Act and Health Care and Health Insurance Act

139. One of the legal foundations for planning within the framework of a public healthcare network are Articles 4 and 5 of the Health Services Act, which state that healthcare as a public service is performed within the framework of a public healthcare network. The rules for setting up a public healthcare network are set by the healthcare plan of the Republic of Slovenia and take into account:

- state of health, number, age and social structure of inhabitants;
- the equal conditions or possibilities for using healthcare services;
- the needed scope of an individual activity;
- the level of urbanization of areas, specifics of population density and accessibility in demographically endangered areas, and the level of pollution; and
- economic abilities.

140. On the primary level, the responsible body for determining the public healthcare network is a municipality or city, while the state takes over in demographically endangered areas and for student healthcare. The state also provides for and manages the public healthcare network on the secondary and tertiary level.

141. The public healthcare network is determined in more detail annually with the aid of the so-called General Agreement and Regional Agreements, which specify the implementation of the General Agreement. In accordance with Article 63 paragraph 1 of the Health Care and Health Insurance Act, the parties to the General Agreement are the Heath Insurance Institute of the Republic of Slovenia, relevant chambers, associations of healthcare institutions and other institutions and organizations that perform healthcare activities and the Ministry of Health. These stakeholders annually agree the programme of services of compulsory health insurance, define the required capabilities for their implementation and set the amount of money. On that basis, they then determine the starting points for performing the programmes and setting the prices for the programme/services as well as other bases for entering into contracts with healthcare institutions and organizations performing healthcare activities and private practitioners.

B. The Medical Services Act

142. The legal basis for the planning is also the Medical Services Act, as it defines the physician as the core performer of a health service. Healthcare service is performed at the physician workplaces within and outside of the public healthcare service network. The workplaces within the public healthcare service network are distributed according to areas and specialist fields in a way to allow the population as equal access to quality healthcare services as possible. Physician workplaces in the public healthcare service network are, according to specialist areas, allocated to public institutions, other legal persons with a concession and private practitioners with a concession. The distribution of workplaces in the public healthcare network is set by the Minister of Health. The task of the Medical Chamber of Slovenia is to monitor the occupancy of physician workplaces, give information on such workplaces to unemployed physicians and provide employers with information on unemployed physicians. The Chamber also gives opinion on awarding concessions to private practitioners as well as plans and approves specializations in accordance with the needs and the age structure of physicians of various types. The Chamber, it could be said, thus plays a key role in planning physician workplaces, especially in defining development issues, such as the network of specialist workplaces.

143. At the time of writing this monograph, the Resolution on the National Health Care Plan 2016–2025, entitled *Together for the Society of Health* was promulgated. In accordance with the plan of Resolution, the number of doctors should raise to one doctor for 1,500 patients. As of 8 August 2020 the number of doctors in Slovenia is 8,568.[111]

III. Planning the Number of Doctors in Practice (Restricting Admission to the Faculties of Medicine)

144. In Slovenia, the control over the number of physicians and dentists has been under relatively strict control for the past forty-five years. The supervision has

111. *See* https://www.zdravniskazbornica.si, 28 Dec. 2020.

been carried out mainly through the admission policy to the Ljubljana Faculty of Medicine (and to the faculty in Maribor after 2004). There was practically no need for any other drastic measures.

145. Admission to both Slovenian faculties of medicine is as a rule restricted. Every year there are many more applicants than available spots. In the 2019–2020 academic year, the applicants could apply for 150 spots for studying medicine and fifty spots for dental medicine at the Ljubljana Faculty of Medicine. A total of 313 candidates meanwhile applied to study medicine and 128 to study dental medicine. Because of the number of applicants, the following rules for admission were used in accordance with the admission rules of the Ljubljana Faculty of Medicine: general matura score was worth 35% of the admission points, the total of grades in years three and four of secondary school were worth 20% and the grades of three individual general matura subjects (mathematics, foreign language and a natural science subject – biology, physics or chemistry) accounted for 45% of the points. If the applicants completed their secondary school studies before 1 July 1995 (before the general matura exam system entered into force in Slovenia) criteria for the points was as follows: final exam score was worth 35% of the admission points, the total of grades in years three and four of secondary school were worth 20% and the grade of one of the subjects (biology, physics or chemistry) at the final exam or in the last year of secondary school when this subject was taught accounted for 45% of the points. The applicant for the Faculty of Medicine in Ljubljana in the 2019–2020 academic year had to have at least 90.05 points (out of 100).[112] There is currently no special admission exam required to study at the Faculty of Medicine, but several faculties within the University of Ljubljana, including the Faculty of Medicine, are considering the reintroduction of admission exams.

146. The main reason for restricting the number of students at both Slovenian Faculties of Medicine is the limited existing educational capacity, which has to be on a level that still guarantees a high level of knowledge and professional qualifications. The lack of doctors in Slovenia was for a time mitigated by increasing the number of available spots at both faculties (and even more so, as I have already stated, with the establishment of the Faculty of Medicine in Maribor), but the trend cannot be sustained. Research shows that in the future the core of active doctors will still mainly come from graduates at one of the two Slovenian Faculties of Medicine, that is the faculty of medicine in Ljubljana, with some 8% of the number being taken up by physicians coming from abroad.[113]

112. *See* https://www.mf.uni-lj.si, 28 Dec. 2020.

113. I. Grmek Košnik & T. Albreht, *Načrtovanje števila zdravnikov in zobozdravnikov v zdravstvu – metode, uporabnost, omejitve in odvisnosti* (*Physician and Dentist Workforce Planning Methods, Applicability, Limitations and Dependence*), No. 45 Zdravstveno varstvo journal 105 (2006).

IV. Reasons for Physician Shortage

147. The reasons for the lack of physicians in Slovenia are manifold. To a certain degree, the shortage was caused by the legislative changes, caused by Slovenia joining the EU, especially regarding the amount of allowed extra work outside of the regular working hours. This reduced the number of on-duty hours, while it was still mandatory to maintain a twenty-four-hour emergency service. About two-thirds of all physicians are women, which means that they can be absent from work for several years during their reproductive age. The duration of specialization for most of the areas has in recent years increased from four to six years. In accordance with the work code, physicians older than 50 years are exempt from night work or standby duties. Specialization in family medicine was changed, resulting in increased rotation and absence from work. The lack of physicians was also compounded with the larger number of physicians who found employment outside of the public healthcare network, as the opportunities to open private practice have improved, and the intensification of the 'drain' of physicians to various jobs of the newly established representative offices of foreign pharmaceutical companies.[114]

V. Specialization Planning

148. Short-term and long-term needs for new specialists in individual areas to meet the requirements of the public healthcare network are defined by the Medical Chamber on the basis of the planned strategy on specialist activities, actual data from the register of physicians and notifications from the providers of the public healthcare service. The specialist activities strategy deals with short-term and long-term forecasts of needs for specialist physicians and the network of specialist physicians for individual regions and the country as a whole. Certified providers of healthcare service inform the Ministry of Health and the Medical Chamber about the needs for new specialists once a year.

Based on the acquired data, the Chamber sets the number of new specializations for individual expert areas (following approval by the Minister of Health) while taking into account the number of free specialist workplaces. The number of new specializations is determined for the entire country and for every individual region.

VI. Experts Position

149. Some of the experts in human resource management in healthcare warn that planning the number of physicians in Slovenia relies too much on a method which defines the needs for physicians in the form of a quotient between the number of physicians and the number of inhabitants. They believe that disadvantages of such planning could be eliminated by using additional and functional parameters, such as the time needed for a patient, for a specific diagnosis, for the procedure, for specialty and so on. Planning the number of medical employees could most efficiently

114. *Ibid.*, at 104–105.

be carried out with the aid of clearly set rules (demographic, epidemiological and performance), efficient information sources with computer-aided data collection and with defined norms and standards as well as suitable rules for evaluating the performance and quality of services.[115]

115. *Ibid.*, at 97.

Chapter 2. The Practice of Medicine

§1. Authorization to Work as a Physician

I. Licensing General Practitioners, Specialist Physicians and Postgraduate Education

A. General

150. A licence must be acquired (in accordance with the prescribed procedure) by all physicians, who want to independently perform medical services in the Republic of Slovenia. The licence is governed by the Medical Services Act, the Health Services Act and set in more detail by the procedure for awarding, extending and revoking the licence, put down in the Rules on Medical Licences.[116]

151. The licence is a public document, which proves the physician's qualifications for independently carrying out healthcare services in his or her professional area. The Rules on Medical Licences set in detail the conditions and procedures for awarding, extension and potential revocation of a licence for providing independent healthcare or dental services. The licence must be acquired by all physicians, who want to individually perform healthcare services in the Republic of Slovenia.

152. The awarding, extension and revocation of the licence is usually governed by the rules of the general administrative procedure. The Medical Chamber of Slovenia decides on awarding and extending the licence, while the decision on a temporary or permanent revocation is taken by the Chamber's Arbitration Panel as prescribed in the Regulation on the Organization and Functioning of the Tribunal of the Medical Chamber of Slovenia.[117]

B. Conditions for Awarding the Licence

153. A physician who is named in the register of doctors should be granted a licence ex officio after he or she passed the specialist exam or after his or her specialist title, awarded abroad, was recognized or after he or she was awarded the specialist title on the basis of his or her work. A physician who performs complementary or alternative medicine services is not awarded the licence. A physician can individually perform healthcare services only for the area for which he or she holds the licence.

116. OG RS, No. 48/2015.
117. OG RS, No. 121/2004.

1. Licence Awarding Procedure

154. To be awarded the licence, a physician must submit a filled-in application with the Chamber. It is, however, true that a physician who has completed the specialist exam in the Republic of Slovenia (or in other two cases mentioned above) and meets all the criteria for receiving the licence as prescribed by law and rules receives the licence under official duty.

155. If a physician fails to submit a complete application, the Chamber notifies him or her that the document must be amended within a specified time. After this period, the Chamber issues a decision which can be appealed against. A physician can reapply for the licence, except in cases where this is expressly prohibited.

156. Should the physician who has applied for the licence fulfil all the prescribed conditions, the Chamber must issue the decision on awarding the licence within thirty days of receiving a complete application. When issuing licences under official duty, it must do so within thirty days from the completed specialist exam in the Republic of Slovenia.

The licence is generally awarded for a period of seven years, except where a different duration of the licence is prescribed by law.

An appeal can be filed against the decision on awarding the licence within fifteen days of receiving the written decision by the Chamber. The appeal is decided upon by the Ministry of Health.

157. A licence document is issued within eight days after the finality of the licence awarding decision. It includes the following data:

- date, place and licence number;
- name and family name of the physician;
- expert, scientific and specialist title of the physician;
- expert area for which the licence is issued;
- a clause that the licence is issued on the basis of the law which regulates medical service and Rules on Medical Licences, and that it is extended on the basis of a decision which is issued for the licence period; and
- signature by the President of the Chamber.

C. Extending a Licence

158. A licence can be extended for a licensing period of seven years on the basis of supporting documents regarding professional qualifications to continue work in his or her area. A physician who has received the title of councillor or senior councillor or an educational position at a faculty of medicine (assistant professor, associate professor, tenured professor) does not have to present supporting documents on professional qualifications when extending the licence. Such individuals, however, have to prove the necessary professional qualifications if they do not meet the prescribed conditions at the following habilitation and their title was not reconfirmed.

1. Continuous Postgraduate Education

159. Their professional duty requires physicians to continuously and actively train for the entire duration of their professional career. The Medical Services Act binds physicians to continue their professional education (this is also their right). This means that they have to continuously monitor the development of the medical profession, gain new knowledge, maintain, update, deepen and widen their professional knowledge as well as their attitude to the patient, the public and to their profession. The law also lists the obligations of a physician's employer to enable him or her professional education at least in the scope that allows the physician to extend his or her licence without the need to undergo another professional qualification exam.

160. Checking professional qualifications of a physician for the licensing period is ascertained through credit points that are acquired by the physician through continuous postgraduate additional training. If a physician fails to get the required number of credit points to extend the licence, he or she must pass a professional qualifications exam. A physician, who fails to pass this exam the first time or does not take the first exam within a specified period, must perform additional professional training in his or her area at his or her own expense. After completing additional professional training, the physician can once again take the professional qualifications exam.

161. In order to extend the licence, a physician must acquire at least seventy-five credit points during the previous seven-year licence period in line with the provisions of the Rules on Medical Licences. At least fifty points have to be gained on a professional field of existing licence and at least five from the area of patient safety and quality of medical treatment, ethics and communication. If a physician does not meet these requirements, he or she has to pass the test of professional competence. It goes the same for the doctor who did not perform his or her duties on the field of licence expertise in the last licence period or did not perform it in a sufficient extent to be adequately professionally competent. Physicians are advised to equally distribute continuous postgraduate training throughout the seven-year period in order to secure permanent and continuous professional training.

162. Continuous postgraduate training includes various professional meetings, self-training and training in medical and other institutions. These activities include lecturing or participation at professional meetings, publication of professional papers in a journal, collection of papers, book or monograph, self-training through multimedia programmes, studying professional literature with written answers to exam questions, study trips and attendance or participation at individual professional lectures.

163. The Chamber issues the certificate to those organizers of professional meetings, who want the meeting that they organize to be certified as continuous postgraduate training and that credit points are given for it. The certificate can be issued for organizing an individual professional meeting, for a set of professional meetings within a specified time period or for professional meetings which are organized periodically in (at most) a twelve-month period.

164. The organizer must prove that he or she is qualified to organize professional training and must meet the following conditions:

- have the organizational and professional (human) resources for organizing the meeting;
- has selected individuals responsible for carrying out the professional meeting's agenda;
- has established a system for recording attendance and checking the knowledge of participants;
- has the ability to archive the documents on participation at continuous postgraduate education and, upon request, send them to the education council; and
- at least half of the contents must fulfil the conditions set for continuous postgraduate training.

165. The organizer must submit the application for allocating credit points to the Chamber. However, if a physician attends a different type of continuous postgraduate training, he or she must submit the application for recognition of continuous postgraduate training and for receiving credit points to the Chamber by himself or herself. The application must include appropriate supporting documents. Every instance of continuous postgraduate training is allocated a certain amount of credit points. For example, one credit point is allocated for one hour of a lecture. Lecturers, as active participants of continuous postgraduate training, receive four points per lecture.[118]

166. Financing of continuous postgraduate training, which can be used for extending the licence, must be regulated in agreement with the standards for financial assistance and sponsoring of education activities, which are based on the ethical standards by the World Health Organization (WHO) for Medicinal Drug Promotion (dated April 1995) and the Code of Pharmaceutical Marketing Practice of the International Federation of Pharmaceutical Manufacturers and Associations (dated August 1994). A more precise manner of financing continuous postgraduate training and use of funds is set in special rules of Rules on Medical Licences.[119]

118. For more details, refer to Art. 11 of the Rules on Medical Licences.
119. *See* Arts 21–22.

2. Licence Extension Procedure

167. Two years before the expiration of his or her licence, the Chamber informs the doctor about the expiration date of a licence, about the number of points gathered until then and that it will initiate the procedure of renewing the licence ex officio two months before the expiration of the licence. The Chamber also informs the doctor that if he or she does not collect a sufficient number of points, he or she will have the opportunity to submit the missing evidence of professional competence in the process of licence renewal.

168. For a doctor who is entered in the register of doctors, the Chamber introduces the procedure of renewing the licence ex officio two months before the expiration of the licence. Upon initiating the procedure, the Chamber shall inspect the records not only of points collected by the doctor, information on the doctor in the register of doctors, but also of other information about the doctor at its disposal. The Chamber shall ex officio extend the licence of a doctor who, on the day of the initiation of the procedure, meets all of the above-mentioned conditions.

169. The Chamber invites a doctor who has not collected a sufficient number of points to submit the missing evidence of professional competence within fifteen days, or to indicate which evidence he or she expects until the expiration of the licence and when he or she will obtain it. If we are dealing with the doctor who did not perform his or her duties on the field of licence expertise in the last licence period or did not perform it in a sufficient extent to be adequately professionally competent, he or she is invited to submit a description of his or her professional work in the expiring licence period and any additional evidence of his or her professional competence. If the licence is not extended, the Chamber issues a decision ascertaining that the physician does not meet the conditions for performing medical services from a certain date onwards. The Chamber notifies the physician's employer and the Ministry of Health of this fact at least thirty days before the expiration of the licence. The physician can appeal the decision on extending/not extending the licence within fifteen days after receiving it in writing. The appeal is submitted to the body which issued the decision at the first stage and is decided upon by the Ministry of Health.

3. Professional Competence Test

170. The test of professional competence shall be performed in the professional field for which the doctor has been granted a licence. The test shall be considered as obtaining an expert opinion within the procedure of licence renewal. The performance of the test shall be ordered by a decision determining date and place of the test and the three-member commission. A member of the commission must be of the same profession as the doctor performing the test and should also meet the following conditions: for a test in the field of primary healthcare, ten years of experience in the profession or the title primarius; for a test in the field of hospital and specialist healthcare, ten years of experience as a specialist or the title of primarius, councillor or senior councillor or the title of higher-education teacher.

171. A commission, after the examination, obtains information on any professional deficiencies already identified at the doctor (except for those for which the Chamber has already performed another procedure during the licence period). It also interviews the doctor about the method of work, methods and course of treatment of patients (status, anamnesis, diagnosis, therapy). It assesses the professionalism of the doctor's work on the basis of the examined medical documentation and the interview. If we are dealing with the doctor who did not perform his or her duties on the field of licence expertise in the last licence period or did not perform it in a sufficient extent to be adequately professionally competent, the commission also inspects the description of the doctor's professional work in the expiring licence period and any additional evidence of his or her professional competence.

172. In case all of the abovementioned cannot be performed, the commission can (also by the proposal of a doctor himself or herself) perform competence test in the form of an oral or written examination of the doctor's theoretical knowledge, with additional practical part. This kind of examination of knowledge shall not be performed if the doctor agrees with the immediate referral to additional professional training.

173. The commission can pass two kinds of decisions. It can state in the report that the doctor has successfully passed the test and does not require additional professional training, or the opposite – the doctor has not successfully passed the test, so additional professional training is required. In that case the commission shall indicate the areas in which the doctor must receive additional professional training and also the needed duration of additional professional training. The commission may also propose the suspension of the doctor's licence.

174. If the doctor does not attend the examination without a justifiable reason, it shall be deemed that he or she has not passed it.

4. Additional Professional Training

175. Additional professional training shall be ordered by a decision determining: duration of training, the healthcare provider who will enable the training, areas of training, a doctor who will monitor and supervise the course of training (he or she must meet the conditions for a mentor to a specialist) and the date of retest. The training may last for a maximum of twelve months. Upon completion of the training, the mentor submits to the chamber a report on the course and observations during the training. If there are justified reasons for interrupting the training, the Chamber may postpone the date of the re-examination, but for a maximum of three months. In cases of sick leave or maternity leave or parental leave, in the form of full absence from work, for a maximum of the time of absence due to these reasons, extended for additional three months. A justifiable reason for discontinuing training is given only when, for the same reason, the doctor is unable to provide medical services.

5. Re-examination of Professional Competence

176. After completing the training, the doctor shall again perform a test of professional competence. On re-examination, the commission reviews the mentor's report, verifies that the training was conducted in accordance with the accepted decision, interviews the doctor and checks the professionalism of the doctor's work on the basis of the reviewed medical documentation created during the training. In the record of the re-examination, the commission shall state that the doctor has successfully passed the retest or the opposite – the doctor did not pass the retest.

D. Licence Revocation

177. The licence can be revoked temporarily or permanently.

178. The Chamber decides to temporarily revoke the licence for a period of up to five years in the following cases:

- if a physician has been instructed to attend additional professional training as part of the licence extension procedure and at the first professional competence test the commission proposes that the licence be revoked until the second proficiency test;
- if it is ascertained that a physician's activities pose a serious threat to the health or life of a patient;
- if a physician receives a court ruling which temporarily prevents him or her from performing an activity or job;
- if, after the licence has been granted, it is established that the doctor has not obtained proof of fulfilment of the conditions for independent work in a valid manner;
- if a physician is performing complementary or alternative medicine services; and
- if the doctor does not use language in his or her work with patients in accordance with Medical Services Act.

179. If the doctor does not successfully pass the re-examination of professional competence, the fourth paragraph of Article 35 of the Medical Services Act shall apply directly for the revocation of the licence. It namely states that after the second unsuccessful test of professional competence, or if the doctor does not respond to the invitation to take the test a second time, the Chamber revokes the doctor's permission to work independently.

180. A permanent revocation of the licence can be made due to large professional deficiency or error at work in cases where such activities by a physician caused lasting and severe damage to the patient or the patient's death. The licence is permanently revoked in cases and according to the procedure prescribed by the Regulation on the Organization and Functioning of the Arbitration Panel of the Medical Chamber of Slovenia.

E. Foreign Doctors

1. General

181. In the Republic of Slovenia, doctors and dentists who, in addition to the conditions determined by labour law and other regulations, also meet special conditions determined by the Medical Services Act, may independently perform the medical service. In order to perform the medical service independently, a doctor must have the appropriate education and training qualification, he or she should be written in the register of doctors and have a medical licence, that is a permit to independently perform medical services in a specific professional field. Pursuant to Article 11 of the Medical Services Act, all doctors performing medical services in the Republic of Slovenia are obliged to use the Slovene language. As already mentioned, physician must communicate in Slovene when carrying out his or her activities, as well as Italian or Hungarian in the bilingual areas of the country containing the Italian or Hungarian minority. The required level of knowledge of Slovene is set at level C1 of the Common European Framework of Reference for Languages. This applies to the doctors who provide medical services in direct contact with the patient. For doctors who do not provide medical services in direct contact with the patient, knowledge of Slovene is required at least at level B2 of the Common European Framework of Reference for Languages, or higher if the employer considers that higher knowledge of Slovenian is required. A professional qualification is a set of professional or university education and professional qualifications acquired by a doctor through education and training programmes, on the basis of which he or she acquired the right to perform his or her profession or professional activity. It is proved by a diploma, which confirms the successful completion of schooling, or by another proof of successfully completed specialization, and also includes any professional experience gained in performing the profession. In Slovenia the Ministry of Health is responsible for the recognition of a diploma obtained at a medical school abroad.

2. European Union

182. Doctors and dentists who have obtained a professional qualification in a Member State of the European Union should – as a first step – start the procedure for recognition of professional qualification in the Republic of Slovenia. Responsibility for conducting the procedure for the recognition of professional qualifications achieved in a Member State of the European Union is on Ministry of Health of the Republic of Slovenia.

183. After a recognized professional qualification in the Republic of Slovenia (issued by the Ministry of Health), a doctor should submit an application to the Medical Chamber of Slovenia for entry into the register of doctors, within which proof of knowledge of the Slovene language must be submitted. For a doctor, who has been issued a decision by the Ministry of Health on the recognition of qualifications for the regulated profession of specialist doctor (or a dentist/a dentist specialist) and was enrolled in the register of doctors, a licence shall be granted on the basis of an application. The application for a licence must be accompanied by the following supporting documents: signed accession statement for membership in the Medical Chamber of Slovenia; a decision on the recognition of a qualification for performing the regulated profession of specialist doctor in the Republic of Slovenia; certificate of goodwill, which may not be older than three months (certificate of goodwill is issued by the competent authority of the state; the certificate shows that a doctor is not in disciplinary, criminal or other proceedings which would result in a ban on performing medical service); curriculum vitae describing work experience with a bibliography (focusing on the last seven years). All evidence must be translated into Slovene (court-certified translation).

3. Third Countries

184. Status and recognition of qualifications for physicians, who have been educated or have received their professional title in a third country, i.e., a country which is not a member of the EU, EEC or the Swiss Confederation, is regulated by the Act on Recognition of Professional Qualifications for Medical Doctors, Specialist Doctors, Doctors of Dental Medicine and Specialist Doctors of Dental Medicine.[120] The precondition for entering the procedure under this law is that the physician received an offer to work in the Republic of Slovenia. Otherwise, he or she is treated under the normal procedure of recognizing the professional title, which is performed by the Ministry of Education, Science, Culture and Sport.

185. The procedure under the above-mentioned law is shorter and less complicated as well as carried out by the Ministry of Health. The candidate must submit an application, which has to include supporting documents on completing studies at a medical faculty abroad, supporting documents on content and course of the study programme abroad, offer to work in the Republic of Slovenia, other supporting documents of education, professional training and experience, curriculum vitae and proof of reputation. Proof of reputation is in the form of a certificate by a competent body from the third state, which states the registration of the physician with the competent body and confirms he or she is not involved in a disciplinary, criminal or other procedure, which would result in prohibiting the physician from performing the job. The application is ruled upon by a special expert committee, which can issue the decision on recognizing the vocational qualification, or decide on a case-by-case basis that a physician must fulfil additional conditions (traineeship, additional final exam and the like).

120. OG RS, Nos 107/2010 and 40/2017.

186. The procedure for recognizing a specialist title obtained abroad (not in a case mentioned above or in next chapter) is prescribed by the Rules on the Types, Content, Duration and Course of Specialization of Doctors.[121] In the process of recognizing a specialist title obtained abroad, a comparison of specialist programmes is performed, with the aim of bringing the knowledge and qualifications of an applicant closer to the level of a specialization programme recognized in the Republic of Slovenia. The comparison of a specialization performed abroad with a specialization programme in the Republic of Slovenia is performed by an expert in the field of specialization of the applicant. When the procedure requires the acquisition of expertise which is not available to the official expert conducting the procedure, in accordance with Article 189 of the General Administrative Procedure Act,[122] an evidence is performed with other experts or obtained by an expert opinion.

The expert examines the written documentation submitted by the applicant and compares the scope and duration of the programme of specialization performed abroad with the specialization programme in force in the Republic of Slovenia on the day when the applicant submitted the application for recognition of a foreign specialist title. He or she also compares the content of the specialization programme completed abroad with the content of the specialization programme used in Slovenia. When preparing a written opinion, the expert also takes into account the work experience and additional knowledge that testify to the qualification of the doctor. In the event of any discrepancies between the specialization programmes in an individual professional field, the expert proposes the conditions under which the applicant may unify the specialization programme performed abroad with the programme in the Republic of Slovenia.

After a detailed and comprehensively explained comparative analysis of specialization programmes, the expert concludes a written opinion. There are three options.

He or she can assess that the specialization programme completed abroad and any work experience and additional knowledge do not fully correspond to the specialization programme according to which the comparison is carried out, or that the applicant's qualifications are not sufficient. In its written opinion, depending on the circumstances of the case, it proposes that the applicant meet at least one of the following additional conditions: complete three to twelve months of professional training with an authorized provider with the final opinion of the mentor (the so-called adaptation period) or to pass a test of professional competence.

If the expert assess that the specialization programme completed abroad and any work experience and additional knowledge fully correspond to the specialization programme according to which the comparison is made, or that the applicant's qualifications are sufficient, he or she issues a positive written opinion for recognition of the specialist title obtained abroad.

If the expert assess that the recognition of a foreign specialist title requires an adaptation period of more than twelve months, he or she has to explain the decision in a written opinion and state the reasons for it.

---

121. OG RS, No. 22/18.

122. OG RS, Nos 24/2006 – official consolidated text, 105/2006-ZUS-1, 126/2007, 65/2008, 8/2010, 82/2013, 175/2020.

The Medical Chamber of Slovenia issues a decision on the recognition of a foreign specialist title to the applicant if it is established that the programme of specialization performed abroad and possible work experience and additional knowledge fully correspond to the Slovene specialization programme or when the applicant submits proof of successfully completed imposed supplementary conditions. After that a doctor is enrolled in the register of doctors and as such, granted an ex officio licence.

4. Countries of the Former Socialist Federal Republic of Yugoslavia

187. Due to once having been a part of the same country, a specific regime is in force for physicians who have received their professional qualification prior to 25 July 1991[123] in one of the republics of the former Socialist Federal Republic of Yugoslavia (SFRY). Article 1 of the Constitutional Act Implementing the Constitution of the Republic of Slovenia[124] states that diplomas issued in the republics of the former SFRY before 25 July 1991 in accordance with the then valid regulations in the area of education are valid in the Republic of Slovenia without the need for recognition. Diplomas or certificates on passed specialist exams, issued in the republics of the former SFRY before 25 July 1991, do not have to be accredited, so this law is not used for those, who have received their professional qualifications in the republics of the former SFRY before 25 July 1991.

§2. The Practice of Medicine

I. General

188. The following laws play the key role in regulating medical practice in the Republic of Slovenia: the Medical Services Act, the Health Services Act, the Act on Recognition of Professional Qualifications for Medical Doctors, Specialist Doctors, Doctors of Dental Medicine and Specialist Doctors of Dental Medicine.

II. Legal Conditions for the Practice of Medicine

189. The Medical Services Act prescribes that a physician can individually perform healthcare service if he or she, in addition to requirements set in contractual and other regulations, meets the following conditions: has suitable education and qualifications to be listed in the register of physicians, has the permission for independent performance of healthcare service in a specific professional area – i.e., has a suitable licence.

123. The day when the Republic of Slovenia became an independent country.
124. OG RS, Nos 33/1991, 42/1997, 66/2000, 24/2003, 69/2004, 68/2006, 47/2013, 75/2016.

A. Entry into Register

190. A physician can perform healthcare service after being entered in the register of physicians, managed by the Medical Chamber. The entering procedure is prescribed in more detail by the Rules on the Register of Physicians.[125] Entry is made on the request of the physician who meets all the required conditions, regardless of whether he or she is a citizen of the Republic of Slovenia or a foreigner.

1. Temporary Entry

191. A specialist physician, who is a citizen of an EU Member State, European Economic Community or the Swiss Confederation, who carries out his or her duties in accordance with the regulations of any of the stated countries, can be temporarily listed in the register if he or she wants to occasionally perform healthcare service in the Republic of Slovenia. The temporary entry must by no means mean that the services by such a physician can be obstructed in any way or incur additional costs.[126] A physician who is temporarily listed in the register has the same rights and obligations as registered physicians, but is however, also bound by the provisions on providing healthcare service. Such a physician must also act in accordance with the discoveries of medical science and use professionally tested methods as well as act in accordance with the rules of the Code of Medical Ethics. The entry is carried out on the basis of a notification by the Ministry of Health. The regulations above mean that Slovenian legislation is now in line with the Directive by the European Parliament and Council 2005/36/EC dated 7 September 2005 on recognition of vocational qualifications.[127]

2. Regular Entry

192. The following individuals must be listed in the register of physicians: trainee physicians, specialist physicians, physicians with a valid licence for performing healthcare service. The same is true for physicians who have requested to be given a medical licence, but the Chamber, due to their failure to meet the conditions, stated that they must fulfil specific conditions; physicians, whose licences have been revoked for a set period of time and were instructed to attend additional training (or are in training according to their own wish); and physicians, who are citizens of other EU Member States and who have received a decision on the recognition of professional qualifications in the Republic of Slovenia.

---

125. OG RS, Nos 35/2000, 57/2000, 43/2004, 31/2010.
126. For further details on the plausible consequences of breaching these rules, *see* A. Vlahek, *Kakšne kazni lahko doletijo Slovenijo zaradi kršitve skupostnega prava?* (*What Sanctions May Be Imposed on Slovenia for Breaching Community Law?*), No. 8 Podjetje in delo 1796–1828 (2007).
127. OJ EU, L 255, 30 Sep. 2005.

193. The following people can be listed in the register: students of medicine or dental medicine; physicians, whose licence has been revoked for a set period, but who were not instructed to attend additional training; physicians, whose licence was permanently revoked; retired physicians without a licence to perform healthcare services and physicians who were named honorary Chamber members.

194. The following physicians' data is being kept in the register: personal data; citizenship; title and address of the workplace; the manner of performing medical service; personal number; place and date of the diploma; date of the expert exam; date and type of completed specialization; date, type and duration of the awarded licence; date and type of acquired additional knowledge; date and areas of acquired scientific titles; acquired professional and pedagogic titles; membership in Slovenian and foreign medical associations; statement on the use of the right to conscientious objection; and other data required to carry out tasks and public powers by the Chamber. For private practitioners, the following data is kept additionally: date of start and end of performing in a private practice; area and place of performing private practice; date, area and duration of the awarded concession; date of concluding and duration of the contract with the Health Insurance Institute of Slovenia and the area and scope of programme for which the contract has been concluded with the Institute.

195. The Chamber decides about the entry into the register in an administrative procedure. The same is also true for decision on removal from the register of physicians. Based on a (complete) application of a physician or a notification by the Ministry of Health, the Chamber must within thirty days issue a decision that forms the basis of entry into or removal from the register. The decision can be appealed within fifteen days of receiving the decision in writing. The appeal is decided by the Ministry of Health.

B. Removal from the Register

196. The removal of a physician from the register is carried out:

(1) if a physician states in writing that he or she no longer wants to be listed in the register;
(2) if the registration is not obligatory (for those physicians who can be entered, but do not have to – as explained above);
(3) after completing a temporary or ad hoc healthcare service;
(4) if a physician does not fulfil the conditions as a Chamber member, based on the decision by the Executive Council;
(5) upon request by the Chamber's Arbitration Panel; and
(6) upon the physician's death.

The removal is carried out on the basis of an application by the physician or according to official duty. The latter is used for reasons listed in items (3)–(6) above. After being removed from the register, a physician can no longer perform healthcare services.

C. Entry and Removal of a Private Practitioner

197. The Rules on the Register of Physicians specifically deal with the registration of so-called private practitioners. A physician can be registered as a private practitioner if he or she meets the following conditions:

- has a licence to perform healthcare services in a specific professional area;
- is not in a working relationship with another employer;
- has not been prohibited from performing healthcare services by a final (legally effective) court decision; and
- has provided for suitable facilities and equipment.

Regarding the last condition, the rules specifically state that a physician is considered to have suitable facilities also if he or she rents the facilities of a healthcare institution or a hospital where he or she has up to then performed healthcare service. The same is also true if a physician rents suitable facilities at another private outpatient clinic.

198. A physician must be registered as a private practitioner by the latest on the day when he or she begins performing the service as a private practitioner. The registration application must also include adequate supporting documents on meeting the above-mentioned criteria. The decision on registration of a private practitioner includes general data about the practitioner; type of healthcare service or the area of work; type of the entry; address of the practice and other data, necessary for performing private healthcare service. An appeal can be filed against the decision with the Chamber within fifteen days of receiving the decision. The appeal is decided by the Ministry of Health.

199. The removal of a private practitioner from the register is carried out:

- if he or she states that he or she has stopped performing private practice;
- if a final (legally effective) decision prohibits him or her from performing such practice;
- if he or she performs the practice contrary to the entry into the register; and
- if it is discovered that he or she no longer meets the prescribed conditions for performing medical service.

III. Illegal Practice of Medicine

A. *Quackery*

200. Should the healthcare or complementary or alternative medicine services be offered by a person lacking the required qualifications, we speak about so-called quackery. In accordance with Article 180 of the Criminal Code, quackery is considered a criminal offence. It is defined as an activity that can be provided by a person performing healing or complementary or alternative medicine services, even though such a person does not have the required qualifications, and his or her activities discourage a patient from seeking timely medical help. In such a case, the perpetrator is punished with a prison sentence of between six months and five years. If a 'quack' causes the death of a patient, he or she can be sentenced to between one and ten years in prison. If performing such activity on a person who did not want to consent to it or was incapable of consent causes dangerous damage to a person's health, the 'quack' can receive between six months and eight years of prison.

201. The Medical Services Act lists as a misdemeanour to start performing healthcare services without meeting all the required criteria (prescribed in Article 10 of the Medical Services Act). A physician who makes such a misdemeanour can be fined between EUR 650 and EUR 1,200, while the healthcare institution, a different legal person holding a concession, a company or a private practice which employs such a physician can be fined between EUR 6,000 and EUR 20,000. A fine of EUR 800 to EUR 1,200 is handed for the same misdemeanour to a private practitioner with a concession, while the person responsible in the legal entity is fined between EUR 1,000 and EUR 4,000.

202. A trainee doctor or a specializing doctor who performs healthcare services for which they are training or specializing without management and supervision of a mentor are fined between EUR 650 and EUR 1,200. Exception to this is the case when a specializing physician performs those tasks and services during specialization for which he or she has acquired suitable knowledge, experience and skills, as confirmed by the mentor by signing the specialist registrar's form. The same fine is also handed out if a physician begins performing his or her duties without being listed in the register of physicians or if he or she performs complementary or alternative medicine services. In Slovenia, physicians, who wish to perform such activities, must return their medical licence. Performing healthcare and CAM services is not compatible in Slovenia. This position by the legislator has been often criticized by theoreticians, but the regulation currently remains unchanged.[128]

In accordance with the Health Services Act, a fine of between EUR 3,000 and EUR 50,000 is handed to a legal person who performs healthcare activities without authorization. The same range of fines can also be levied on the healthcare institution, which has entered into a contract for temporary or ad hoc healthcare services

128. They are referring to regulations in comparative law, where different solutions have mainly been adopted. For example, refer to Š. Kogovšek Sajovic, *Pravna ureditev zdravistva* (*Legal Regulation of Complementary and Alternative Medicine*) 250 (2020).

with a service provider who has not applied for or extended the written application. The same is also valid in the case when a healthcare institution expands or alters its activity or stops work without agreement by the competent body or when it tasks a medical employee with an activity for which he or she is unqualified or lacks suitable equipment.

B. Complementary and Alternative Medicine

203. CAM had to be legally defined in Slovenia as the large growth of such activities in practice required the area to be regulated by law. The Complementary and Alternative Medicine Act[129] is primarily intended to provide protection to all potential users of such methods as well as clearly and doctrinally separate this kind of treatment from classical medicine.

204. The Act defines the types of CAM, their performers, manner of performance, CAM Chamber and supervision over carrying out such practices. It defines CAM as an activity that can be performed by healers with the aim to improve the health condition of the users of the service. It lists measures and activities, based on CAM systems and methods, and defines that they have to be carried out in a way that does not harm health. Healers are persons of age with at least a completed secondary medical education or at least a secondary professional education and who have passed an exam on health topics prescribed by the Minister of Health. They must also hold a valid licence, acquired in agreement with the Complementary and Alternative Medicine Act. Homeopathy, chiropractic and osteopathy can only be performed by persons with a degree from a medical faculty, knowledge from the fields of homeopathy, chiropractic or osteopathy and a valid licence.

205. Should an individual use complementary or alternative systems or methods for healing a user of services without obtaining a requisite licence, he or she can be fined up to EUR 1,200. A fine of between EUR 400 and EUR 20,000 is meanwhile levied on a company which does not employ a healer and still carries out CAM activities or which carries out such activities without a suitable permit. A fine of between EUR 400 and EUR 2,000 is also handed to the person responsible of such a company.

129. OG RS, Nos 94/2007 and 87/2011.

Chapter 3. Control over the Practice of Medicine

§1. Professional Liability

I. Civil Liability

A. General Introduction

206. In the Republic of Slovenia, liability for damages for physicians (and other healthcare professionals) is governed by the general provisions of Civil Law – i.e., by the provisions of the Code of Obligations. Two key principles of the law of obligations provide the basis for liability for damages – *neminem laedere*, the principle that prohibits causing damages and from which we deduce the non-contractual liability for compensation, and the principle of diligence, which is used for contractual liability for compensation.[130] Discerning between liability due to a breach of contract or a wrongful act is not of key importance in Slovenian law, as substantial differences among the two do not exist. The liability for damages in Slovenia is a practically unitary institution. This kind of general principle is also accepted in the Slovenian Code of Obligations.[131]

B. Legal Grounds for Liability

207. Liability claims against physicians can be made on the grounds of two different legal bases, depending on the nature of the relationship between a physician and patient, which can be contractual or non-contractual. This means that contractual or delict legal grounds are possible, which are used in ascertaining a physician's contractual liability or delict liability.

1. Contractual Liability

208. A contract on healthcare service can be concluded directly between the patient and the physician or between the patient and the healthcare institution. The first case is typical for the private sector and makes the physician directly liable to the patient, as the contract was concluded directly between the two. In the second case, when we are dealing with healthcare institutions, liability is ascertained according to rules on responsibility for employees and rules on the responsibility of the healthcare institution for its own activities.

---

130. Refer to V. Žnidaršič Skubic, *Civilno medicinsko pravo* (*Civil Medical Law*), Uradni list 81 (2018).
131. Refer to A. Polajnar Pavčnik, *Obligacijski vidiki razmerja med bolnikom in zdravnikom* (*Obligation Relations Between Physician and Patient*), Pravo in medicina, Cankarjeva založba, 96 (Ljubljana 1998).

209. The legal relation between a patient and a physician has always been defined as a contractual relationship in Slovenia, even though socialist legal systems usually listed such relationships as public law relationships. Slovenian theoreticians, similar to their German counterparts, define a treatment contract as a labour contract, but lately also as a mandate agreement. Such a contract binds the physician to try his or her best, but does not bind the physician to succeed. The physician, entering into a contract, binds himself or herself to treat the patient and act in the manner of *lege artis*, i.e., with all due professional care, but without guarantee of successfully treating the patient. Exceptions to that are some specific types of medical contracts, where the result could be considered a necessity, like plastic surgery, prosthetics, anaesthesia, etc.[132]

210. The liability for contract violation is based on a breach of contract, as concluding a contract between a patient and a physician creates a relation under the law of obligations, thus establishing their mutual rights and obligations. The physician's obligation is to fulfil the agreed healthcare service with all due care, while the patient is required to pay for the service. As has been explained above, direct payments for services are not common in practice, as a patient's obligation to pay for such services is regulated by the compulsory and voluntary healthcare insurance system. If a patient is treated by a private practitioner without a concession, the patient pays for the service directly to the treating physician. At contractual liability for the damages, the client claims repayment of the damage that occurred because of a breach of contract as the physician failed to perform his or her duties with all due care.[133]

2. Delict Liability

211. The relationship between the patient and the physician can also be defined as a non-contractual liability relationship or a civil delict. The consequence of breaching this relationship is non-contractual or delict liability. The latter appears if the physician and patient were not in a mutual legal relationship before the incident. Non-contractual liability arises due to encroaching on a foreign area, and this happens on the basis of legislation.[134] It stems from the breach of the general liability principle, which states that everybody is obliged to refrain from activities that could cause harm to others (Article 10 of the Code of Obligations).

212. If a patient does not consent to undergo a medical procedure, such a procedure is deemed inadmissible, apart from exceptional cases. Every unauthorized

132. Refer to A. Polajnar Pavčnik, *Obligacijski vidiki razmerja med bolnikom in zdravnikom* (*Obligation Relations Between Physician and Patient*), Pravo in medicina, Cankarjeva založba 94 (Ljubljana 1998).

133. Refer to A. Polajnar Pavčnik, *Varstvo ustavnih človekovih pravic med zdravljenjem* (*Safeguarding Constitutional Human Rights during Treatment*), Nos 6–7 Podjetje in delo 1271 (1998).

134. Refer to B. Strohsack, *Odškodninsko pravo in druge neposlovne obveznosti* (obligacijska razmerja II) (*Tort Law and Other Non-Trade Obligations. Obligation Relations II*) 18 (Uradni list RS 1996).

breach of a patient's body integrity causes damage to the patient for which the physician must be held responsible. In case of excluding the inadmissibility of a medical procedure, the procedure is not unlawful. Therefore the grounds for claiming liability are lost. Unlawfulness can be excluded according to the principle of *volenti non fit iniuria.* If a patient consents to a medical procedure and the physician performs it *lege artis*, no grounds for claiming damages from the physician exist. The medical procedure is, even if the patient does not consent to it, allowed in cases when consent cannot be received due to the patient's condition, while the physician needs to take immediate action to remove a threat to the patient's life. In such cases, the physician acts as a manager without explicit orders or a *negotiorum gestor*, and there can be no civil delict.

3. Liability Assumptions

213. The following criteria must be cumulatively met for liability for damages to exist:

(1) unlawful damaging act, event or behaviour;
(2) inadmissible damages;
(3) causal association (causality) between unlawful activities and inadmissible damages; and
(4) the existence of liability of the perpetrator of the damages.

Should one of the four criteria be unfulfilled, the injured party will not succeed in his or her claims for damages.

(a) Unlawful Damaging Act, Event or Behaviour

214. An unlawful damaging act is an unlawful activity by an individual, which causes damage. A medical procedure is unlawful when the impairment of health is a consequence of incorrect or unprofessional activities by the physician. These are cases that we commonly refer to as medical errors. A medical procedure is also unlawful when the physician's treatment was professionally beyond any reproach, but was illegal because of the lack of the patient's consent or because the consent was not given of free will and was as such invalid.[135]

The unlawfulness of a physician's actions can therefore be excluded by respecting the rules of the profession and the rules on informed consent. Even if the expected treatment results were not achieved or the patient's health condition worsened, the physician who carried out the procedure *lege artis* and had appropriate patient consent cannot be held liable.

135. Refer to S. Sivec, *Odškodninska odgovornost zdravnika* (*Liability for Damages of a Physician*) 21 (Graduation Thesis, Ljubljana, 2008).

(b) Inadmissible Damages

215. Damages are any deprivation that arises due to an encroachment on human rights or legally protected interests. The Code of Obligations discerns between material and non-material damages. Damages can mean a diminution of property (material damage), prevention of the appreciation of property (lost profit), and inflicting bodily or mental distress or encroachment upon the reputation of a legal person (non-material damage). Only damages that meet the criteria, listed in the Code of Obligations, are legally recognized damages and can be dealt with under property law. Other potential irks and unpleasant events that an individual could see and feel as damages are not sanctioned by law (no right to reimbursement).[136]

216. The consequences of inadmissible medical intervention can take the form of material damage, but even more common is non-material damage. It is in the latter where numerous issues arise in practice, especially regarding the existence of such damages and ways to prove it. Damage must be real, and there must be no doubt regarding its existence. Non-material damage appears in the form of any kind of health impairment, suffered mental or physical pain, deformations, fear, injuries, death. Pain plays a role in ascertaining liability of the physician only in cases when such pain is the consequence of a physician's inappropriate action and not any general unease, which the patient suffers due to the disease itself.

(c) Causal Association (Causality) between Unlawful Activities and Inadmissible Damages

217. Causal association (causality) is defined in theory as the connection between an event, caused by the client, and the consequences of the said event that constituted damage.[137] The injured party (patient) must prove that the physician's unlawful (unprofessional) activities damaged his or her health. This link can be difficult to prove in practice, which is why the patient's position is facilitated by Slovenian law in the way that he or she does not have to definitely prove the existence of causal association, but a proof of probability suffices.[138] The Slovenian case law mainly uses two theories on causality: one is the *ratio legis* theory and the other the theory on adequate causality. The first states that only those causes are considered by law that at the same time also violate legal norms and are seen by the legal norms as causes.[139] More prominent, however, is the theory on adequate causality, which states that out of the numerous circumstances that are linked to the appearance of

136. Refer to B. Strohsack, *Odškodninsko pravo in druge neposlovne obveznosti, Obligacijska razmerja II* (*Tort Law and Other Non-trade Obligations. Obligation Relations II*) Uradni list RS 31 (1996).

137. S. Cigoj, *Teorija obligacij: splošni del obligacijskega prava* (*Theory of Obligation: General Part of Law of Obligation*), Uradni list RS 222 (2003).

138. Refer to L. Koman Perenič, *Odškodninska odgovornost zdravstvenih delavcev, Kako odloča Vrhovno sodišče RS* (*Liability for Damages of Medical Professionals – History of Supreme Court Decisions*), Javna uprava, year 42, No. 2/3, 541.

139. Refer to B. Strohsack, *Odškodninsko pravo in druge neposlovne obveznosti, Obligacijska razmerja II* (*Tort Law and Other Non-trade Obligations. Obligation Relations II*), Uradni list RS 34–35 (1996).

damages, typical circumstances are the ones that are considered as their cause. These circumstances are those that led to damages in the due course of events. This theory also eliminates all non-typical and unusual damages.[140]

(d) The Existence of Liability of the Perpetrator of the Damages

218. The perpetrator of damages must be guilty and of sound mind to be declared responsible for the damages. The Slovenian law of damages, including the area of damage liability in health, uses the basic principle of guilt responsibility. This means that Slovenian law states that whoever causes damages to another person needs to pay for it, unless it is proven that damages arose without his or her guilt (Article 131, paragraph 1 of the Code of Obligations).[141] Exceptions to this rule are the cases of the so-called strict (objective) liability for damages, where the individual is charged regardless of the guilt. This could only be applicable to healthcare when a medical activity or carrying out a certain medical procedure would be assessed as extremely dangerous or if a medical device would be excessively dangerous by itself. The damages, caused by a dangerous object, are the responsibility of the object's owner, while damages arising from hazardous activity are in the domain of the person carrying out the activity (regardless of the guilt).[142]

C. Liability of Employees

219. Liability for damages in healthcare is also linked to the principle of responsibility for the activities of others, where one of the manifesting forms is the responsibility of employers for the activities of the employees. This means that a healthcare organization or an institution could be responsible for damages caused by its employee (physician) while performing his or her activities or in connection with his or her activities regarding the patient, unless the organization manages to prove that the employee (physician) acted as he or she should under the given circumstances (Article 147, paragraph 1 of the Code of Obligations). If a healthcare organization therefore wants to waive its responsibility, it must prove that the physician in a specific case acted in accordance with due care that is required by the employer. This is especially important when the employer is an expert in the area that he or she performs in, while the employed physician is not. The patient reasonably expects that the service will be performed with due care that is expected from a healthcare institution, so a different regulation would not be appropriate.

140. Refer to A. Polajnar Pavčnik, *Obligacijski vidiki razmerja med bolnikom in zdravnikom (Obligation Relations Between Physician and Patient)*, Pravo in medicina, Cankarjeva založba 98 (1998).
141. The culpability is acknowledged if the injuring party causes harm on purpose or from negligence. The physician must use the manner of diligence that can be expected from an average physician of his status.
142. The court decides on a case-by-case basis whether the situation was dangerous to a degree that requires the special – objective – liability for the damages. This is how the court adds contents to the legal standards.

220. The notion of responsibility of employers is very important in healthcare, as the healthcare organization holds responsibility for the activities of a physician who failed to act in accordance with *lege artis*. This is the case because such organizations as more powerful economic subjects have larger economic power and ability to pay higher damages than an individual physician. Such regulation also lessens the physician's burden while performing his or her activities and thus allows him or her to carry them out with more self-initiative and in a more relaxed manner.

221. The injured patient has the right to request damages to be paid directly by the perpetrator of the injuries, i.e., the physician, if the latter caused the damages on purpose. The healthcare institution can meanwhile institute proceedings for recourse against the physician who has deliberately or due to serious negligence damaged the patient's health.

II. Criminal Liability

A. General

222. Physicians as well as other healthcare professionals around the world daily invade the patients' body integrity. From a Criminal Law standpoint, we could thus say that they en masse fulfil the essence of criminal offences regarding bodily harm. This is most obvious in various surgical procedures or in introducing different types of medication into the patient's body. But still healthcare professionals, within the frame of performing their medical activities, are not in principle held responsible for such acts. The reason lies in the exclusion of unlawfulness of their actions.

223. In Slovenia nowadays, the modern position prevails that sees Criminal Law increasingly resisting the recognition of a special status to healthcare activities while a patient's agreement at the same time takes an important place in the so-called Medical Criminal Law.[143] The adoption of the Patients' Rights Act, with its detailed regulation of the institute of patient's consent to undergo medical treatment and similar notions, has greatly influenced the adoption of the newer Article 125 of the Criminal Code (KZ-1). The latter states that causing slight physical injuries is not unlawful if the injured party gave his or her consent. But KZ-1 specifically excludes the existence of unlawfulness in cases of grievous or particularly grievous bodily harm if such was caused during medical treatment or complementary/alternative treatment if the consent was given in the form and under the conditions prescribed by law. It thus expressly recognizes that the patient's will is the key element in excluding unlawfulness of such medical body violations and not the general social utility of healthcare, as was the case in the past.

The physician is otherwise responsible for any criminal offence, caused intentionally or through negligence, during his or her work with patients in accordance

143. L. Bavcon et al., *Kazensko pravo, splošni del* (*Criminal Law, General Part*), Uradni list RS 241 (2009).

with the general rules of Criminal Law. In specific cases, his or her criminal liability, as we will see below, is somewhat more strictly regulated due to the special social role that the physician plays. It is linked to the specifically confidential nature of the relationship between the physician and the patient. In certain cases, a criminal offence is created that can only be performed by a physician (or perhaps by a healer or another healthcare professional) if specific preconditions are met.

B. Negligent Treatment

224. One of the specific criminal offences that can only be performed by a physician (or a healer or another healthcare professional) is negligent medical treatment (Article 179 of the KZ-1). This is a criminal offence caused by negligence, which cannot be carried out with intent, neither according to its notion nor according to the nature of things. The law states that a physician who in the course of performing medical activities does not act in conformity with the relevant code of professional conduct, thereby causing a substantial impairment of a patient's health, shall be sentenced to imprisonment for not more than three years. If such activities cause the death of a person, the perpetrator shall be sentenced to imprisonment between one and eight years. The same goes for sentencing other healthcare professional or a healer.

225. The described criminal offence cannot, even in theory, be carried out with intent. Should a physician intentionally act without due care in treating a patient and caused the patient's health to visibly deteriorate, it is possible to invoke the provisions regarding grievous or particularly grievous bodily harm (Articles 123 and 124 of the KZ-1). In the first case, the perpetrator can receive a prison sentence of between six months and five years, while in case of the patient's death, the sentence can be between one and ten years. In case of particularly grievous bodily harm, the perpetrator is sentenced to between one and ten years in prison or between three and fifteen years if the patient later dies due to the perpetrator's activities. If intentionally negligent treatment resulted in the death of the patient, it is possible to talk about manslaughter, i.e., deprivation of life without aggravating circumstances (Article 115 of the KZ-1) or even about murder, which is defined as a more serious form of taking a life (Article 116 of the KZ-1). Manslaughter is punishable with five to fifteen years in prison and murder with a minimum of fifteen years in prison.

1. Structure of a Criminal Offence of Negligent Treatment

226. Theory warns that negligent criminal offences, including negligent treatment, are structured differently than 'ordinary' criminal offences. The fundamental elements of such criminal offences are:[144]

144. Refer to L. Bavcon et al., *Kazensko pravo, splošni del* (*Criminal Law, General Part*), Uradni list RS 282–284 (2009).

(1) The act itself constitutes a breach of the rules of the medical science and profession. This means that the notion of the due procedure is of deciding importance, as the ascertained violation represents the social and ethical foundation of the criminality of such acts. Violating due procedure includes 'non-lawfulness' or 'unlawfulness' and danger of performing a criminal offence out of negligence. Violating due procedure can be intentional or unintentional, reflecting a larger or smaller level of contemptibility of the perpetrator's actions, which has to be taken into account when deciding on the sentence.
(2) The damaging consequence forms the vital part of the structure of such criminal offences committed out of negligence. This consequence states the level of danger of the act (violation of due procedure by the physician).
(3) The causal relationship between the violation of the due conduct and the resulting damaging consequences must be treated differently than with typical intentional criminal offences. The following limitations must be taken into account:
   - An objective predictability of the damaging consequence must be stated; if it cannot be objectively predicted, there is no causal relationship between the current violation of due procedure and the resulting illegal damaging consequence.
   - If an illegal damaging consequence would also happen in the case when the defendant would have done everything due procedure required, then there is no causal relationship. This means that the established violation of due procedure cannot be the cause of the consequence, if the same result would have occurred had the perpetrator followed due procedure.
(4) Two basic rules have to be stressed regarding guilt: it is impossible to ask of anyone to do more than what he or she is able (*ultra posse nemo tenetur*), and it is obligatory to demand as much as he or she can do and not less. These are the cases when a court would ascertain that a certain physician has specific abilities, but has not used them even though he or she was obliged to do so.

C. *Failure to Render Medical Assistance*

227. One of the criminal offences that a physician (or another healthcare professional) can commit is failure to render medical assistance (Article 178 of the KZ-1). Should the physician, contrary to his or her professional duty, fail to help a patient or anybody else whose life is in danger, he or she shall be sentenced to up to one year in prison. This is not the case when the physician suspends a specific method of treatment, surgery or medical procedure upon an expressed written request by a patient who has the capacity for self-determination. Another important circumstance is that the treated individual continues to refuse assistance even after being told about its importance and of the possible consequences of rejection and even after the physician again tried to persuade the individual to change his or her mind.

D. Individual Areas of Medicine

1. Reproductive Medicine

228. Illegal encroachments into pregnancy are dealt with in Article 121 of the KZ-1. The perpetrator of the criminal offence is not necessarily a physician but anyone who would in contradiction with medical conditions and the manner of artificial termination of pregnancy, as prescribed by law, perform an abortion (begin to perform or provide assistance in performing it) on a pregnant woman with her consent. The perpetrator of such acts shall be sentenced to between six months and one year in prison. Should an individual terminate the pregnancy without the pregnant woman's consent, he or she shall spend between one and eight years in prison.

229. Criminal offences in the area of fertilization with biomedical assistance can as a rule be made only by physicians (or other healthcare professionals), but that is not always the case. This is why incrimination is general in this area as well, as it states that whoever affects the selection of gender of the future child by using the method of fertilization with medical assistance, unless in order to avoid severe hereditary disease connected to gender, faces a sentence of up to three years in prison. The same sentence can be levied for unlawfully performing the procedure of fertilization with biomedical assistance due to surrogate maternity as well as trade in sperm cells, unfertilized egg-cells and early human embryos.

Should an particularly grievous bodily harm be caused to a woman in case of performing the above-mentioned activities (abortion or BMAP procedures), the perpetrator shall be sentenced to between one and ten years in prison. In case of the woman's death, the sentence shall be between three and fifteen years.

Article 181 of the KZ-1 also prescribes the question of unlawful extraction of sex cells, illegal activities regarding such cells or violating the anonymity of the donor of such cells. The perpetrator in such cases shall be sentenced to imprisonment for between six months and five years.

2. Transplants

230. Organ transplants are quite a sensitive/delicate area of medicine, and the dangers inherent in it are relatively very high. This is why they should be granted special criminal law protection, also in the form of a specific criminal offence. Article 181 of the KZ-1 states that in case of unauthorized transplant of parts of a patient's body a physician who, for the purpose of performing a transplant removes a part from the body of a patient or who transplants a part of the body of a patient even though such actions are deemed unjustified according to the rules of the medical science and profession, shall be sentenced to imprisonment for between three months and five years. The same sentence is levied on a physician who, with the intent of performing a transplant, would remove a part of the human body before the donor's death has been ascertained in the prescribed manner.

231. A physician who, in order to perform a transplantation removes a part from the body of a patient or who transplants a part of the body of a patient without having obtained prior consent from the donor or the recipient of the part of the body (or their legal representatives) faces a prison sentence of between three months and five years. The same sentence is also levied in cases where the physician would contrary to the prescribed procedures, store or use the removed part of the human body for some other purpose than the one for which it was removed for.

3. Genetics, Experiments and Research on Humans

232. A physician can also be the perpetrator of a criminal offence of changing the human genome. This means that he or she performs or attempts to perform a procedure with an aim to change the human genome, which is not carried out for preventive, diagnostic or therapeutic reasons or when the aim of such procedure is to introduce changes to the offspring's genome. For such cases, the Criminal Code prescribes a prison sentence of up to five years.

233. Physicians, especially specialists in the areas of gynaecology and obstetrics or infertility treatment and experts from the area of fertilization with biomedical assistance (as well as biologists and other experts from the field of biomedicine), are (the main) possible perpetrators of illegal creation of human beings. It, however, needs to be stressed that the Criminal Code does not limit the possibility of perpetrating such criminal offences only to the above-mentioned experts, but rather includes everybody (Article 114 of the KZ-1).

234. Whoever manufactures or participates in manufacturing or attempts to manufacture or crossbreed human beings or other species, which is harmful for the humankind and banned according to the regulations and international law, shall be sent to prison for between five and fifteen years. If the above acts concern creation of a human being, who is genetically identical with another living or dead human being (cloning), creation of human embryos for research, industrial or commercial purposes, or exchange of important human body parts or organs, the perpetrator shall be sentenced to a prison sentence of between ten and fifteen years.

235. A fine or sentence of imprisonment for not more than three years is handed to whoever performs genetic research, which could forecast hereditary diseases or enable determination of carrying the gene responsible for the disease, or identify genetic predisposition or susceptibility to a disease, but the research is not performed exclusively for medical purposes. The same sentence is handed to anybody who, in conducting research, abandons appropriate genetic consultancy or violates regulations in conducting research in the field of biology and medicine, which are banned according to regulations and international law. A fine or imprisonment for up to three years is also prescribed for anyone, who endangers the integrity or life of a human embryo during research on human embryos.

236. Criminal liability is also prescribed for individuals who provide financing or in any other way enable manufacture or crossbreeding of human beings or other species, cloning, creation of human embryos for industrial or commercial purposes or replace important human body parts or organs. Such enabling activities include providing buildings, devices or material to create or crossbreed living beings or recruiting co-workers and carry a prison sentence of between three and ten years.

4. Other Criminal Offences

237. A physician can also be sentenced for issuing a false medical certificate. If a physician knowingly issues such a certificate, he or she shall be imprisoned for up to three years.

238. If initiated by a private action, the unlawful disclosure of a professional secret (Article 142 of the KZ-1) can also be prosecuted. If a physician unlawfully discloses a secret, about which he or she has learned while performing his or her duties, he or she can be punished with a fine or a prison sentence of up to one year. The physician shall, however, not be penalized if he or she commits such acts for the general good, the benefit of the public, or some other person's benefit. However, in the last case, the no-penalty clause is valid only if the good or benefit therein is greater than that of withholding the secret or if the disclosure is mandated by law.

239. The section which deals with criminal offences against sexual integrity also regulates the sexual assault on a person under 15 years of age (Article 173 of the KZ-1). This article states that whoever has sexual intercourse or performs any lewd act with a person of the same or opposite sex under the age of 15 years shall be sentenced to imprisonment for between three and eight years. If such an act is committed by a physician, who is entrusted with treatment of such an individual, the abuse of the confidential nature of the relationship between a physician and a patient is punishable by imprisonment for between three and ten years. A physician could possibly also serve as an assistant in suicide (for a terminally ill person, who would ask him or her to do so). In case of specific mitigating circumstances when performing such an act, the physician could be sentenced to up to three years in prison.

III. Vicarious Liability

240. Obligatory liability insurance for the medical profession was introduced to Slovenia in 1999. Its introduction was to a large extent caused by the increasing number of liability claims filed against physicians and the rise in the amounts claimed.[145] The Medical Services Act states in Article 61 that a physician who is working directly with patients must be insured against liability for damages that could arise during his or her work. The amount of insurance differs for individual

145. M. Pavliha, *Analiza obveznih individualnih zavarovanj v Sloveniji* (*Analysis of Compulsory Individual Insurance in Slovenia*), Podjetje in delo, year XXV, No. 6, 1355 (1999).

expert areas. The amount is set every year by the Medical Chamber of Slovenia after approval by the Minister of Health. An employed physician is insured by the employee, i.e., the community healthcare centre, hospital, etc. Insurance companies allow making insurance policies against the physician's liability for damages, but not against the criminal liability for an unlawful procedure.[146]

IV. Quality Assurance

A. General

241. Measuring the quality in healthcare systems is a relatively complex and therefore ungrateful task. Experts warn that there exists a relatively large number of quality indicators, as well as the methodologies to perform such tasks, and the latter are far from being unified. One of the possible ways of understanding quality in health is to divide quality into three categories: professional quality (measured through the highest possible results in the profession), economical quality (shown in the best relation between the quality and amount invested) and social quality (measured as the largest possible satisfaction of the users of healthcare services).[147] All three categories hold equal importance in all healthcare systems.

242. The tasks of the healthcare system are (roughly) divided into direct health policy (on a national and local level), performers (healthcare institutions) and the payer (the Health Insurance Institute of the Republic of Slovenia). As all the participants in the healthcare system are responsible for monitoring quality in health services in their own areas, a comprehensive assessment of quality of healthcare in Slovenia can only be arrived at by joining the results and findings of all the participants.[148]

243. The legal regulation of the healthcare system is reasonably well regulated in Slovenia; however, a framework act and implementing regulation acts on comprehensive quality management in the healthcare system have not yet been passed. The professionals in the area have been calling for such an act for a long time as they believe that the state should adopt a policy of quality, define strategic resources and the means to achieve them in order to establish a comprehensive quality management system.[149] However, positive steps towards that goal have been made recently. The Ministry of Health thus includes a separate sector for Quality and

146. Refer to S. Sivec, *Odškodninska odgovornost zdravnika* (*Liability for Damages of a Physician*), Graduation Thesis 37 (2008).
147. Refer to M. Pajntar, I. Verdenik & B. Leskovšek, *Kakovost v zdravstvu Slovenije* (*Quality of Health Care in Slovenia*), https://vestnik.szd.si, 29 Dec. 2020.
148. J. Kersnik, *Kakovost v zdravstvu* (*Quality in Health Care*) 101–102 (Association of Family Physicians, Zbirka PIP 2d ed. 2010).
149. J. Kersnik, *Kakovost v sistemu zdravstvenega varstva v Republiki Sloveniji, Pregled stanja, Poročilo za WHO* (Quality of the Healthcare System in Slovenia, Overview, Report for the WHO), available at http://www.drmed.org, 29 Dec. 2020.

Safety of the Health Care System, which has drafted the 'National Strategy of Quality and Safety in Health (2010–2015)'. Among the numerous measures that are to lead towards a systematic quality and safety management as well as the development of culture in the field, the document also envisages the setting up of a national body for healthcare quality and safety.[150]

244. The successfulness of the healthcare system is measured by the relation between the achieved results and the maximum possible achievable results, while taking into account available resources. The research results show that the allocated funds for healthcare are not being spent entirely rationally, and that cheap and effective healthcare measures are not being implemented.[151] However, we must not overlook the immense heritage of the socialist healthcare system, which brought a widely spread network of healthcare institutions on the primary and secondary levels, easy accessibility to healthcare services, universal health insurance, and provided for a relatively stable development of the medical profession. The conservative nature of healthcare politics in allowing private initiatives to enter the area, a rich tradition of the organization of the solidarity healthcare insurance model as well as the inclusion of all partners in the talks on distributing the funds for performing healthcare activities, allow for a stable financing of the healthcare activity.

B. *Responsible Institutions*

1. The Government

245. The quality of healthcare in the Republic of Slovenia is principally under the responsibility of the Government, and its (competent) Ministry of Health. To that effect, a Health Inspectorate, functioning within the Ministry, performs various tasks, including inspecting the minimum hygiene/health conditions in public health institutions, at legal and natural persons who perform healthcare activities, and ensuring compliance with the legislation in implementing the rights of the patient in the area of mental health and medical services.

2. The Health Council

246. The Health Council, which works within the Ministry of Health, drafts the contents of healthcare programmes from the viewpoint of their feasibility, uniform development of all areas and the principle of equal accessibility. It can request from various extended professional collegiums to adopt their professional doctrine to the economic capabilities of the state or to propose the provision of programmes according to priorities and in a limited scope. Apart from the proposals by the

---

150. Refer to https://core.ac.uk, 29 Dec. 2020.

151. Refer to J. Kersnik, *Kakovost v sistemu zdravstvenega varstva v Republiki Sloveniji*, Pregled stanja, Poročilo za WHO (Quality of the Healthcare System in Slovenia, Overview, Report for the WHO), available at http://www.drmed.org, 29 Dec. 2020.

extended professional collegiums, the Health Council also deals with proposals by other nominators when such proposals impact the contents and scope of healthcare, including health policy and financing of healthcare. When the nominators of new healthcare programmes are not the extended professional collegiums, the proposal must first gain the approval of the relevant extended collegium before being discussed by the Health Council. The Health Council by itself does not determine the professional contents of healthcare programmes and services, but can request amendments and additional expert opinions for proposals it deals with.

3. The Extended Professional Collegiums

247. The extended professional collegiums are the highest expert bodies for individual medical areas. They represent the highest autonomous expert body for a certain area, which is bound in its decisions by scientific discoveries, professionally tested methods and the development of the profession, while taking into account public healthcare interests. They are formed at clinics, institutes and other healthcare institutions as determined by the Minister of Health upon proposals by clinics, professional associations and higher-education institutions that carry out programmes for healthcare professionals. The extended professional collegiums include councillors, senior councillors, faculty teachers and other renowned experts in the area of healthcare. Their task is to coordinate proposals by the clinics, professional associations and chambers, higher-education institutions, healthcare institutions and individual professionals. They draft the professional doctrine on improving health, prevention, diagnosing, treatment, healthcare and rehabilitation of the sick, injured and people with body or mental disorders. The expert proposals, presented by the extended professional collegiums, which impact the contents and scope of healthcare and, by doing so, the health policy and financing of healthcare, are discussed and confirmed by the Health Council, as the highest professional/coordinating body in the area of healthcare.

4. The Professional Chambers

248. Several chambers (the Medical Chamber of Slovenia, the Nurses and Midwives Association of Slovenia, etc.) are active in Slovenia to carry out joint interests and ensure quality implementation of tasks and public authorizations as prescribed by law. An important task of the chambers is professional supervision of their members, which is carried out under public authorization. Those professionals in the area, who currently do not have a chamber, are under the professional supervision of the Ministry of Health.

5. Association of Health Institutions of Slovenia

249. Another organization that should be mentioned is the Association of Health Institutions of Slovenia, a voluntary organization of performers of healthcare activities. One of the Association's more important tasks is partnership talks with the Ministry of Health and the Health Insurance Institute of Slovenia, which serve to determine the total scope of healthcare services and the necessary means to pay for the programme on a national level. The result of the partnership talks is a written agreement, which presents the legal grounds for entering into contracts with public healthcare institutions and private practitioners. The Association organizes training for its members and places a lot of attention on implementing and establishing suitable information systems, which facilitate links within the sector and ensure quality information, thereby improving the quality of healthcare.[152]

6. The National Institute of Public Health and the National Laboratory for Health, Environment and Food

250. The National Institute of Public Health (NIPH) is a public institute, established for execution of tasks defined by law in the field of public health. For the fields of health, environment and food a special public institute was established: the National Laboratory for Health, Environment and Food (NLHEF).[153]

NIPH is the main national institution whose basic purpose is to study, to protect and to improve the level of health of the country's inhabitants. This is carried out by measures of raising their awareness and also by other preventive measures. Besides its central role in the field of public health, NIPH's activities cover also its participation in various international projects covering different fields of health and general public health problems of the inhabitants. NIPH also represents the expert level for a support to decisions that are accepted by the state at a national or local level and have a direct or indirect impact on health.[154]

NLHEF is the central and the largest laboratory for public health, dealing with hygienic and health-related ecological activities, environment protection problems, microbiological diagnostics and chemical analyses of samples of different kind and research activities. In the laboratory, the services for governmental needs are executed, first of all for monitoring and official inspection and supervision from the competencies of the Ministry of Health, Ministry of Agriculture, Forestry and Food and Ministry of the Environment and Spatial Planning, free capacities are offered to customers on the open market. In cooperation with other institutions in Slovenia and abroad, the NLHEF cooperates in national and international research, applicative and advisory projects.[155]

---

152. Refer to https://zdrzz.si, 29 Dec. 2020.
153. *See* Art. 23 of Health Services Act.
154. Refer to https://www.nijz.si, 29 Dec. 2020.
155. *See* https://www.nlzoh.si, 29 Dec. 2020.

7. Legislation on Physician's Licence

251. The systemic laws, i.e., the Health Services Act and the Medical Services Act are also key in judging the quality of the performance of the core provider of healthcare activities – the physician. As has already been explained above, a specific system of appraisal is planned which will serve as the grounds to award, extend or revoke licences for independent performance of activities. The licence needs to be renewed every seven years. Tasks relating to that are entrusted to the Medical Chamber of Slovenia. In case of proven professional deficiencies, the ultimate measure is a permanent revocation of the licence, which prohibits the physician to perform public healthcare service in the area of the Republic of Slovenia.

8. Medical Ethics Committee of the Republic of Slovenia

252. Another body for ensuring quality healthcare and compliance with the law in the area is the Medical Ethics Committee of the Republic of Slovenia (presented in more detail below), which has the power to decide on medical and ethical questions regarding everyday work and biomedical research.

V. Review Boards

253. Healthcare activities are monitored by a variety of authorities. The Health Services Act prescribes the following types of supervision (Article 76):

(1) internal professional supervision, which is carried out by healthcare professionals and their co-workers through self-supervision and by those responsible for the quality of work at an institution;
(2) professional supervision with a qualified opinion, performed under public competence by the competent chamber or professional association in cooperation with clinics, clinical institutes or clinical departments and other institutions;
(3) administrative supervision carried out by the Ministry of Health;
(4) supervision carried out by the Health Insurance Institute of Slovenia:
   (a) Internal professional supervision is carried out pursuant to a general legal act of a specific healthcare institution.
   (b) Professional supervision with a qualified opinion is carried out by the competent chamber or professional association in cooperation with clinics, institutes and other institutions and in accordance with a specific programme, adopted by the chamber or a professional association after approval by the Minister of Health (more on that below). Should serious deficiencies be discovered in the line of such professional supervision, the competent chamber must demand additional professional training for those of the institute's employees for whom a lack of training is discovered and notify the Ministry of Health. In such a case, the Ministry can issue suitable decisions such as the demand to remove organizational,

resource and other deficiencies that cause the lack of quality or professionalism of the activities. The Ministry can also temporarily (until the discovered deficiencies have been eliminated) prohibit a specific institute, its department(s) or healthcare professional(s) from performing its activities. If individual professional groups of healthcare professionals do not work under the umbrella of a chamber or a professional association with a public authorization for performing such activities, the Ministry of Health is responsible for carrying out such supervision.

(c) Administrative supervision over the legality of work by healthcare institutions and private practitioners is carried out by the Ministry of Health on the basis of a programme or upon proposal of a patient, his or her relative or caretaker, healthcare institution, employer, the competent chamber or according to its own judgment. The Health Minister sets the manner for carrying out administrative supervision. If irregularities are discovered in performing the supervision, the Ministry of Health issues a decision in which it sets the measures and due dates for eliminating them. An official who performs administrative supervision can as an exception issue a temporary order to prevent direct danger for the health of people or for the health conditions. The healthcare institution or a private practitioner can appeal the decision within eight days at the Ministry of Health; however, the appeal does not delay the decision's implementation. If supervision uncovers a healthcare professional or an institute co-worker or a private practitioner who is unable to carry out the entrusted tasks, the competent chamber and the employer must be notified.

(d) The authorization to the Health Insurance Institute of Slovenia to, among other things, define its supervisory function in its statute,[156] is provided by Article 76 of the Health Care and Health Insurance Act. The Act moreover states (Article 77 and 77a) that the Institute supervises the implementation of contracts with performers of healthcare activities, the issuance and costs of medicinal products and equipment and the manner and procedures of implementing health insurance in accordance with the law and the Institute's statute. Should the authorized supervisors (the Institute's physicians or pharmacists) during the above-mentioned supervision discover professional or other irregularities regarding the work of healthcare service performers or unlawful activities, the Institute must inform the Ministry of Health within the next fifteen days. Should professional errors occur, the Institute must inform the competent chamber. Supervision over the legality of the functioning of the Institute and the correct use of means for financing healthcare programmes and services is carried out by the Minister of Health. If the supervision uncovers irregularities, the Minister is obliged to determine measures for their elimination.

156. Refer to Statute of the Health Insurance Institute of Slovenia, OG RS, No. 87/2001 (1/2002 amend.).

Professional supervision is financed from the national budget. If it uncovers irregularities, the cost of the supervision is transferred to the healthcare institution or the private practitioner, where irregularities were discovered.

§2. Disciplinary Organizations

254. Disciplinary misdemeanours are part of a wider set of penal offences. Disciplinary responsibility in a healthcare organization is an instrument to safeguard the interest of the employer versus the inadmissible activities of the employee. Equally important is the opposing view, i.e., regulating disciplinary responsibility in order to protect the employees' interest from abuse of disciplinary power by the employer. The latter can manifest itself in repressive or inadmissible encroachments into the personal, statutory and pecuniary position of individual employees.

I. Responsibility to Professional Organizations

A. *Medical Chamber of Slovenia*

255. Physicians associate in the Medical Chamber of Slovenia, which represents their professional, social and economic interests, maintains the reputation and honour of the medical profession and the fulfilment of obligations by the physicians. The Chamber is a legal person. Supervision over the legality of the Chamber's activities in carrying out public authorizations is performed by the Ministry of Health.[157]

1. Professional Supervision

256. The medical profession has certain obligations towards the competent bodies of the Chamber, which the physicians are bound to join by law. One of the Chamber's main tasks is to perform, among other things, certain public functions, such as awarding (and revoking) a licence, maintaining the public register, performing postgraduate training and education and performing a supervisory/preventative role. The Chamber performs so-called professional supervision with a qualified opinion.

157. It is performed also by other responsible authorities: for example, in October 2012, the Competition Protection Agency issued a decision finding that the Medical Chamber of Slovenia breached Slovenian and (as of 1 May 2004) European antitrust by setting in its rules the standards for valuation and calculation of dental and medical services and the supervision of its members in the implementation of such rules during the period of 1995–2012. For more details, *see*: A. Fatur, K. Podobnik, A. Vlahek, *Competition Law in Slovenia* 99–100 (Wolters Kluwer 2020).

257. Professional supervision is carried out in accordance with the Rules on Professional Supervision with a Counselling,[158] adopted by the Chamber. Professional supervision is performed by an expert committee, composed of two to five members, i.e., supervisory physicians. They are appointed by the Chamber's Executive Committee upon proposal by the Board on Professional-Medical Issues.

There are three types of professional supervision in Slovenia: regular, extraordinary and expert supervision with a qualified opinion.

258. Regular professional supervision is carried out on the basis of an annual programme and is as a rule performed once for an individual physician during his or her licence period.

259. Extraordinary expert supervision is carried out outside of the abovementioned programme. The Chamber can perform such supervision on its own initiative, following a proposal by the Minister, the payer of health services or somebody else who orders it.

260. Expert supervision with a qualified opinion can be carried out on the basis of a decision by the Chamber President, the Chamber's Committee on Professional-Medical Issues or the President of the Chamber's Panel of Arbitration. It can be carried out as part of the regular annual programme or as expert professional supervision. The procedure is performed so that the supervisory commission holds a talk with the supervised physician, which relates to some general issues of performing healthcare activities. Its task is also to check the data which are noted in the questionnaire that has been sent to the commission along with the order for expert supervision. The committee checks the professional level of the activities by the physician on the basis of checked medical documentation, carries out a conversation on its findings and on respecting the Code of Medical Ethics as well as provides advice to the physician. Upon the completion of expert supervision, the committee must compose a declaratory minutes, which is forwarded to the supervised physician, his or her employer or a private practitioner, the Ministry of Health and the Chamber's Committee on Professional-Medical Issues. In the case of extraordinary expert supervision, the findings are also forwarded to the body, which proposed the said supervision. The supervised physician can file his or her objections to the declaratory minutes, which are then decided on by the Committee on Professional-Medical Issues.

261. Based on the list of findings, the Chamber's Committee on Professional-Medical Issues assesses the work of the physician and, if necessary, proposes appropriate measures. If larger professional deficiencies have been discovered in the physician's work, the Chamber's competent body can:

- issue an admonition;
- request additional professional training or set the due date for eliminating the discovered irregularities;

158. Refer to OG RS, Nos 35/2000 and 64/2017.

– temporarily or permanently revoke the physician's licence;
– propose other measures to the Minster of Health;
– submit a proposal to the Chamber's Arbitration Panel to start proceedings if the Panel is authorized to deal with the irregularities; and
– decide on other measures in accordance with the Chamber's regulations.

A recommendation or a compulsory guideline can be issued to the physician in case of smaller professional deficiencies.

An appeal against the measures by the Committee on Professional-Medical Issues is dealt with by the Chamber's Executive Committee.

262. Should a temporarily listed physician violate his or her obligations as prescribed by Slovenian legislation, implementing regulation acts or the Code of Medical Ethics, the temporarily listed physician can be removed from the register and can also be served a suitable sanction, including the sanctions prescribed in the legal acts of the Medical Chamber of the Republic of Slovenia.

2. Code of Medical Ethics of Slovenia

263. In accordance with Article 13 of the Statute of the Medical Chamber,[159] its duties also include the adoption of the Code of Medical Ethics. The Chamber drafted the Code, which includes the activities which mean its violation. The Chamber is authorized to maintain the observance of the Code, check on the activities of physicians and take action if the Code is violated. The Chamber must strive to prevent the performance of medical service in an unauthorized manner. For this purpose, the Chamber includes specific bodies such as the Chamber Prosecutor and the Arbitration Panel.

264. The Chamber Prosecutor is an independent body of the Chamber with the right and duty to file a request with the Arbitration Panel to start proceedings to determine the violations of the Code of Medical Ethics, the Chamber's statute and its other acts and due to any irregularities in performing medical duties.

265. The Chamber's Arbitration Panel is an independent body which decides on the responsibility for any of the above-mentioned violations by physicians if requested to do so by the Chamber's Prosecutor, Assembly President, Chamber President or an individual Chamber member. The panel has two levels: level I and II.

a. General

266. The Code of Medical Ethics of Slovenia and the guidelines and statements by the World Medical Association and the World Dental Association are obligatory for all physicians in the Republic of Slovenia. Physicians are required to know these

159. OG RS, Nos 64/1996, 22/1998, 113/2000, 30/2001, 23/2008.

principles and act in accordance with them when carrying out their daily duties. International humanitarian principles are also obligatory for physicians performing their professional duties in prevention, treatment and rehabilitation.

The duties of the Slovenian Medical Chamber, the medical faculties and other medical educational institutions and institutes as part of performing their activities include informing the physicians of the documents adopted by the UN, the World Medical Association and other international professional associations and their bodies.

267. The introduction of the Code of Medical Ethics shows us that the highest norm of doctors' conduct is to protect and recover health and to prevent and ease the suffering. The very important duty is also to safeguard the secrets which are confided to them. They must not permit any discrimination on the basis of sex, race, genetic factors, lifestyle, sexual orientation, religion, nationality, political views or social status. The doctors promise to respect human life from the conception onwards, and that even under threat, they will not use their medical knowledge against the laws of humanity.

268. The content of the Code is divided into six main subtitles, each of them showing the needed responsibility of a doctor. First responsibility is devoted to the patient, then to the society, to profession, to medical team, to public and at the end also to doctor himself or herself.

b. Responsibility Towards the Patient

269. Under the title of responsibility towards the patient, there is a general rule of doctors' duty to regularly educate themselves and to do everything in their power to perform high-quality and safe treatment of the patient. They also have the right to conscientious objection, but it is not acceptable in cases of emergency – in these cases they have the duty to help everyone. The physicians may never use the patients for their own interests. They should also recognize the limits of their knowledge and work. Whenever needed, they should recommend or seek additional opinion or help.

270. Alternative procedures of healing, as a replacement of established diagnostic and treatment procedures, are not permissible. Outside of emergency medical treatment, physicians have the right to refuse the patients who, despite being warned, do not adhere to their obligations and instructions or are being aggressive and offensive towards the physician or other members of the medical team.

271. The physician has to be understanding and compassionate towards the patient and his or her family and relatives. The physician should provide his or her patients all the information they need in an accessible manner in order to make decisions about the suggested treatment. He or she should respect the right of every patient with decision-making capacity to accept or refuse a medical procedure. The physician should recommend only those diagnostic or therapeutic procedures that he or she considers to be beneficial to the patient and others. If a measure is recommended in order to protect others, for example as with public health measures, the physician shall inform the patient about this and shall act in line with his or her legal duty. When making medical decisions, the physician shall consider minors' decision-making capacities and the role of their family. The physician shall respect the autonomy of the minors who are capable of decision-making, but also do everything to protect the health and life of children or other persons who are not capable of decision-making. The physician should also respect the patient's right to seek a second opinion an also his or her written or oral expression of advance directives. If these are unknown, the physician will, in consultation with the patient's close relatives, propose treatment that is most beneficial for the patient. If the consultation procedure results in disagreement, a medical council shall decide on the patient's greatest benefit and shall inform the patient's close relatives about the decision. If the disagreement is not resolved at that point, the physician is not bound to comply with the relatives' divergent opinion.

272. The physician is obliged to safeguard the patient's health-related and personal records but he or she should enable inspection of medical documentation if the patient requires so. This does not apply to cases in which the physician can reasonably consider that the information contained in the documentation can have detrimental effects for the patient and others. The physician should not mention the patient's name in public in such a way as to jeopardize the patient's anonymity. The patient's personal health records can only be disclosed with the patient's consent with the exception of cases in which confidentiality could lead to serious harm for third persons. In such cases, the physician shall inform the patient within a reasonable scope that the principle of confidentiality will be violated.

273. Physicians should respect human life from the conception onwards and through their counselling they shall convey such outlooks to the wider community. Physicians should not propose the abortion as a method of family planning. The decision to terminate pregnancy must never be influenced by the interest to use the foetus for specific purposes. Sterilization is admissible only on the basis of medical, genetic, social, or personal reasons and shall be performed after giving preliminary information and obtaining written consent. In cases of reduced fertility, the physician shall offer counselling and reasonable use of biomedical treatment procedures to those affected. Surrogacy is not admissible. The use of fertilized ova, embryos, foetuses or stem cells for commercial purposes is prohibited. Under exceptional circumstances and with explicit consent by the National Medical Ethics Committee, the use or taking of tissue from a fertilized ovum, embryo, foetus or a stem cell is permissible only for therapeutic, diagnostic, or research and scientific purposes.

274. Organ and tissue transplantation is performed for medical purposes when other treatment modes are comparatively not effective. Organ and tissue transplantation must be performed according to professional norms and duties. Organ trafficking is inadmissible.

275. When performing diagnostic and therapeutic procedures in terminally ill patients, the physician should consider the quality of patient's life and his or her wishes. The physician should not introduce or withhold measures when these are futile or when the burden of treatment outweighs the benefits. Withholding or withdrawing of palliative care is ethically unacceptable. The physician should reject euthanasia or physician-assisted suicide.

276. Clinical trials can only be led by a physician, expert in the investigated domain, who knows the principles of good clinical practice and the methodology employed in the trials, and who can ensure adequate conditions for conducting the trials in a safe and scientifically valid manner. During planning, execution, analysis and reporting stages of clinical trials, the physician should refrain from biases that could lead to subjective or misleading conclusions. The research must be scientifically and ethically sound, in line with the Helsinki Declaration and the Convention on Human Rights and Biomedicine (the Oviedo Convention) and approved by the National Medical Ethics Committee. The patient must give informed written consent for participating in the researches, with the exception of some non-interventional trials, where the Committee can rule that the patient's informed consent is not required. When patients have limited autonomy, the consent is signed by a legal representative. The physician information on clinical trial must be communicated comprehensibly and must include the goals, benefits, risks, and the burden of the researches, a statement about the protection of confidential personal records collected during the trials, patient's insurance in cases of adverse treatment effects, the possibility of treatment outside clinical trials, and a statement of the patient's right to stop the trial at any point without any negative consequences for his or her medical treatment. If during the trials a conflict of interests develops, the benefits of the individual patient shall always take precedence over the interests of the trial.

c. Social Responsibility

277. The Code obliges the physician to contribute to public health concerns by participating in educational activities and by proposing measures that improve the health and well-being of individuals and the community. He or she should be professionally independent from their employers or clinical trial sponsors when estimating the environmental and occupational risks or occupational safety. The physician should promote equal healthcare for minorities and other vulnerable groups in society and should always strive for a fair access to healthcare resources. Physicians are bound to collaborate as medical experts, within the limits of their abilities and possibilities, in event of large-scale accidents, epidemics, natural disasters or war. The physician should refuse to participate or support activities that violate human rights.

d. Responsibility Towards the Profession

278. The physician should transfer knowledge to students, trainees in specialty, colleagues and workers in other professions. In the medical profession, there shall be no room for personal resentments that could influence treatment and could damage the reputation of colleagues. On suspicion of a colleague's misconduct, the physician should react promptly and discuss the situation with the colleague. If the situation is not sufficiently resolved, the physician should report his or her observations to those in charge. A public discussion is admissible only in cases in which the patient or his or her relatives decide to discuss the conflict in public on their own initiative or on suspicion of a criminal act.

279. Relations in the medical team must be based on mutual trust and must strive for the benefit of the patient. The physician is responsible for medical treatment; however, the physician shall also respect the expertise of his or her colleagues and their powers by means of which they accept their share of professional responsibility. Professional hierarchy must be respected; however, there must also be a continuous two-way exchange of information and experience. Whenever novel medical procedures and guidelines are introduced, these should be thoroughly presented and harmonized with the entire medical team. The physician can transfer a part of his or her powers for communication with patients and relatives to his or her co-workers; however, the physician retains the key responsibility.

The physician's relationship to healthcare-related business activities must not undermine his or her professional independence. The physician must not receive any remuneration or rewards in return for prescribing, using or purchasing medications medical accessories or other medical products.

280. The physician should not endorse public acknowledgements or praise of his or her own successes in the general public. For the physician, any abuse of public powers and means for personal gains is dishonourable. Public presentation of professional achievements and advancements must be balanced and conveyed without sensationalism or enthusiastic conclusions. The physician should not be involved in the advertisement of medications or medical products or professionally and scientifically objectionable diagnostic or therapeutic procedures. In cases of public accusation, physicians have the right and duty to defend their own reputation and the reputation and good names of colleagues. In cases of public accusation, the physician has the right to disclose those personal records that are crucial for an objective evaluation of the contentious act.

e. Responsibility Towards Oneself

281. The physician should safeguard and maintain his or her own health and should also attempt to recognize and control the stress factors in his or her professional and private life. The physician shall seek help from colleagues and other competent persons in cases of disease or personal difficulties that could have unpleasant consequences for his or her health and work.

B. Slovenian Medical Association

282. The Slovenian Medical Association works in the public interest. Its membership is voluntary. Established in 1861, it is one of the oldest medical organizations in Central Europe. The Slovenian Medical Association is an independent, professional, peer-based and non-party association of physicians, dentists and final year medical faculty students in the Republic of Slovenia. It can be joined also by Slovenian physicians and dentists living abroad and individual foreign physicians, who are closely linked to medicine in Slovenia.

283. The main aim of its activities is the transfer of professional discoveries and contemporary medical doctrine to Slovenian physicians and connecting Slovenian medical science with the world. The Association is a member of the World Medical Association, European Forum of Medical Associations and WHO, while its professional associations, societies and sections are members of Union Européen des Médecins Spécialistes (UEMS).

284. The Association operates a regional network, which guarantees a uniform and rapid transfer of professional doctrine and knowledge throughout Slovenia. It has also a professional superstructure, which connects experts in individual narrower specialties in sixty-five professional sections, associations and societies which form the Association's sub-units. The above-mentioned professional associations are organized in a manner that allows them to cover the areas of individual basic specializations in Slovenia in accordance with UEMS requirements and allow for the transfer of knowledge for those multidisciplinary sectors that do not yet have their own specializations.[160]

285. An Honorary Arbitration Panel is one of the Association's bodies in accordance with its statute.[161] The Panel rules on cases where association members or bodies acted contrary to the Code of Medical Ethics of Slovenia, the Statute, the Rules of the Association or the Guidelines of the World Medical Association. In accordance with the Rules on the Organization and Activities of the Honorary Arbitration Panel of the Association,[162] it also tries to achieve honourable arbitration between individual association members. Anybody can apply to the Panel to start proceedings. An arbitration procedure by the Panel can result in: settlement, expressing of opinion of the Panel, admonition, reprimand or a proposal for temporary or permanent removal from the Slovenian Medical Association.

160. Refer to http://www.szd.si, 29 Dec. 2020.
161. *Ibid.*
162. *Ibid.*

§3. The National Medical Ethics Committee of the Republic of Slovenia

286. The Committee was established pursuant to the Health Services Act, which authorizes the Ministry of Health (Article 60) to form a medical ethics committee, composed of renowned experts and healthcare professionals. The composition of the Committee, the manner of appointing its members, the area of its activities, its competencies and responsibilities are set in more detail by the Rules on the membership, responsibilities and working methods of the Commission for Medical Ethics.[163]

The Committee consists of a President, two Vice-Presidents and has altogether eighteen members. Its members are experienced and renowned experts in the areas of medicine, healthcare, pharmacy, psychology, legal affairs, sociological and humanistic fields and medical deontology. Member of the Committee could be also a representative of a lay community.

287. The Committee studies and deals with problems in the area of medical ethics and deontology and provides opinion and explanations on individual issues in this field. The Committee performs its activities on the proposal of the Minister of Health, the Health Council, chambers, health institutions or individuals. Especially important are the issues regarding the rights of individuals and their safety during treatment or research that is carried out on people, in connection with safeguarding professional secrecy and personal data of patients and healthcare professionals. The Committee gives approval to science and research projects in the area of healthcare as well as approves the testing of untested methods of diagnosing and discovering diseases and injuries, treatment and rehabilitation. It also provides approval for testing of medicinal products and performance of other biomedical research.

288. In its activities, the Committee uses the Code of Medical Ethics, the legislation of the Republic of Slovenia, the recommendations and conventions of the Steering Committee on Bioethics at the Council of Europe (especially the Oviedo Convention and its additional protocols), as well as the valid documents by the World Medical Association (especially the Helsinki Declaration on Bio-medical Research Involving Human Subjects) and several documents of the EU, alongside the guidelines of Council for International Organizations of Medical Sciences (CIOMS) and WHO. If it deems it necessary, the Committee can request expert opinions from the selected experts in order to issue its assessment or consults experts in Slovenia and abroad by itself.

289. The Committee's decisions generally cannot be contested. However, should the Bioethics Committee of the Council of Europe or the competent body of the WHO reach a different conclusion from the one arrived at by the Committee, the Committee must again discuss the issue.

---

163. OG RS, No. 11/2020.

Part II. The Physician-Patient Relationship

Chapter 1. General Description

§1. Rights and Duties of Physicians and Patients

I. The Law on the Rights of Patients

A. National Legislation on Patient Rights

290. In Slovenia, on 29 January 2008, the Patients' Rights Act has been accepted. This Act forms the key legal document in the field. It lays down the rights of a patient as a user of healthcare services at all providers of such services, the procedures to enforce these rights when they are violated and the obligations stemming from these rights. The purpose of the Act is to enable equal, adequate, solid and safe healthcare of a required standard that is based on trust and respect between the patient and the doctor or any other medical professional or medical collaborator.

291. Apart from the Patients' Rights Act, the Health Services Act also provides an additional legal basis in the field of the patients' rights. The Health Services Act lays down the measures and activities that shall be carried out by the medical professionals in safeguarding health, preventing, diagnosing and treating patients and the injured. The Act lays down the nature and the course of medical treatment, the public healthcare service and the links between healthcare organizations and medical professionals in chambers and associations. Functioning of the whole system is namely very important for the realization of patient's rights.

292. The Health Services Act lays down individual obligations by medical professionals that can be also viewed as the rights of patients. Special mention should go to the obligation to carry out health services in accordance with the valid medical doctrine and the Code of medical ethics or with other professional and ethical codes. In a similar fashion, the patients also implicitly have the right to equal treatment by the medical staff (originating from the constitutional principle of equality before the law, Article 14 of the Constitution). The Act lays down that the medical staff need to consider the patient's constitutional and legal rights, and that the only criterion for precedence lies in the urgency of medical treatment. By passing the Patients' Rights Act, the much shorter list of these rights, included in Article 47 of the Health Services Act, was annulled.

293. In a sense, the Patients' Rights Act amends and upgrades the Health Care and Health Insurance Act that lays down the rules for the healthcare and health insurance system and the manner for exercising the rights of patients stemming from health insurance. Individual rights of patients are also dealt with separately by individual acts for specific (specialist) areas, such as: the right to freedom of choice in childbearing (Article 55 of the Constitution), the Health Measures in Exercising Freedom of Choice in Childbearing Act and in the Infertility Treatment and Procedures of Biomedically-assisted Procreation Act; the rights regarding transplants in the Act Regulating the Obtaining and Transplantation of Human Body Parts for the Purposes of Medical Treatment; the rights in the field of contagious disease protection in the Communicable Diseases Act; the rights regarding the transfusion of blood in the Blood Supply Act,[164] etc.

294. Among relevant legal regulations, the Medical Services Act should be mentioned too. It (indirectly) lays down the rights and duties of patients through the introduction of the rights and obligations of a doctor and through laying down the manner in which doctors perform their services. The chapter entitled 'Interpersonal Relations' (between the doctor and the patient) requires special attention as there the Act deals directly with the interaction between the doctor and the patient, their rights and duties.

B. General Principles

295. The Patients' Rights Act lays down the basic principles that have to be considered in implementing the rights of patients under this Act:

(1) the principle of respecting all individuals as human beings and the respect for their moral, cultural, religious, philosophical and other personal beliefs;
(2) the principle of respecting physical and mental integrity and security;
(3) the principle of considering the greatest health benefit for the patient, especially a child;
(4) respect for privacy;
(5) respect of independence in deciding whether to undergo treatment; and
(6) respect of the individual's personality and dignity by making sure that nobody gets socially ostracized for his or her health situation or background, consequences and circumstances of his or her condition or healthcare that the individual was given because of such reasons.

296. The provisions of the Act do not encroach on patient's rights, as defined by other laws and international treaties binding for the Republic of Slovenia. This means that the Act also does not encroach on the scope of rights from the Oviedo Convention. The Act binds all of the providers of healthcare services to exercise patients' rights within the scope of modern medical doctrine, professional standards

164. OG RS, No. 104/2006.

and norms, and the level of development of the healthcare system in the Republic of Slovenia. Several provisions of the Act required coordination with the Health Care and Health Insurance Act, as the Patients' Rights Act lays down patient's rights which are at the same time linked to the health insurance system. It is decided that they should be enforced within the framework of the regulations from the field of healthcare insurance.

297. The Patients' Rights Act also includes a special provision on limiting patient's rights. These rights could be restricted by laws dealing with public security and public health and in cases where rights of others could be threatened.

C. The List of Patient's Rights

298. Article 5 of the Act lays down the list of patient's rights that is composed of fourteen items:

(1) right to access to health care and provision of preventive services;
(2) right to equal access and treatment in health care;
(3) right to free choice of the physician and the provider of healthcare services;
(4) right to an adequate, quality and safe health care;
(5) right to due consideration of the patient's time;
(6) right to being informed and to cooperate;
(7) right to make independent decisions on the course of the medical treatment;
(8) right to consider the previously expressed wishes of the patient;
(9) right to prevent and alleviate pain;
(10) right to a second opinion;
(11) right of insight into medical files;
(12) right to privacy and personal data protection;
(13) right to launch proceedings in case of violation of patient's rights; and
(14) right to free assistance in exercising patient's rights.

D. The Patient's Obligations

299. Despite the title and the basic purpose of the Act – i.e., to provide for the patients' rights – the Act also states the patient's obligations (Article 54). Without the obligations or cooperation of the patient with the doctor, it is impossible to provide for quality and safe healthcare. The Act expressly lays down the following obligations of the patient:

(1) The patient must actively participate in safeguarding, strengthening and recovering his or her health.
(2) At the time of sickness, the patient is obliged to act in accordance with the received instructions and treatment plans, to which he or she agreed to in writing or verbally.

(3) The patient is obliged to provide to the doctor in charge and to other medical professionals all necessary and truthful information regarding his or her health condition that he or she is aware of and which are important for continuing treatment. This is especially important for data on his or her current and past injuries, illnesses and treatment thereof, illnesses in the family, any allergies and medicine that he or she is taking.
(4) The patient is obliged to inform medical professionals of sudden changes to the health condition that could arise during treatment.
(5) The patient must be considerate and respectful to the right to privacy and to other rights of his or her fellow patients and medical professionals.
(6) The patient is obliged to act in accordance with the schedules, house rules and valid organizational procedures of the providers of healthcare services.
(7) The patient must notify in due time the provider of healthcare services on potential inability to attend a medical examination or treatment.

E. Human Rights Ombudsman

300. The Act also lays down the powers of the Human Rights Ombudsman in the area of patient's rights. Based on Article 55, the ombudsman has the duty to monitor the situation in the field of enforcement of patient's rights in accordance with his or her powers. On the basis of such monitoring, the ombudsman can request the responsible national bodies, local community bodies and holders of public powers to provide the conditions for effective enforcement of this act. The ombudsman appoints one of his or her representatives to act in the field.

F. Special Patient's Rights

1. Right to Access to Healthcare and Provision of Preventive Services

301. This right is stipulated in a relatively general form, as it states that the patient has the right to access to healthcare in accordance with the regulations in the area of healthcare and health insurance. Exercising the right to access to healthcare is the precondition for exercising all other rights in the Patients' Rights Act. What is important is that the Act guarantees (as part of the above named right) the absolute right to urgent healthcare service, which is universal and unconditional and cannot in any way be conditioned by payment or a referral. In connection with the right to provide preventive healthcare services, it has to be stressed that this is a programme norm, as the Act does not allow for its direct management. Preventive services are a factor of the high standard of the health system and exercising this right is mainly dependent on the medical profession standards, financial means available to the healthcare system and definition of preventive services outside the scope of the Act.[165]

2. Right to Equal Access and Care in Healthcare Treatment

302. This provision of the Patients' Rights Act guarantees equal treatment to all patients, regardless of their sex, nationality, race or ethnic origin, religious or other beliefs, disability, age, sexual orientation or any other personal circumstance. This right is a specific expression of the constitutional provision of equality before the law (Article 14 of the Constitution of the Republic of Slovenia). The principle of equality means that the state must provide public healthcare to all patients under equal terms and conditions. If that is not possible in certain cases, for example, if medical personnel or equipment is not available, it is necessary to primarily take care of patients with a life-threatening condition, followed by those who could suffer irreparable or grievous damage if medical aid is not provided. Only then is it possible to treat the remainder of patients. Rules on non-discrimination also apply to such professional-medical triage issues.[166]

3. Right to Free Choice of a Physician and Provider of Healthcare Services

303. The patient is guaranteed the right to free choice of a physician, but this is not an absolute right as it is linked in practice to the capabilities and norms within a healthcare network. The right to free choice of a physician is exercised by the patient on the primary level, where he or she can select a general practitioner (family doctor, paediatrist, gynaecologist and dentist), and on the secondary level, where the patient can select a specialist working in the public healthcare system. The physician is as a rule bound by the patient's choice. The physician can only reject the choice (never in emergency cases) in specific and well-grounded cases. These include cases when treatment would likely be less successful or impossible, for example, the physician exercising his or her right to conscientious objection or in a case of a breakdown of trust between the physician and the patient. The patient has the right to be adequately informed of the physician's decision and referred to a different physician. The reasons for rejection must be given to the patient in writing and within eight days after the patient selected the physician.

4. Right to Adequate, Quality and Safe Healthcare

304. The patient has the right to adequate, quality and safe healthcare in accordance with medical doctrine.

---

165. *See* J. Balažic et al., *Zakon o pacientovih pravicah s komentarjem* (*Patients' Rights Act Including Commentary*) 70–71 (GV Založba 2009).

166. *Ibid.*, at 71–72.

The Patients' Rights Act states adequate care as responsive to the patient's needs and in line with the capabilities of the Slovenian healthcare system. It must employ simple, transparent and user-friendly administrative procedures, which serve to establish a trusting and cooperative relationship with the patient.

Quality healthcare is meanwhile such that it consistently achieves treatment results which can be compared to standards or best practices. It has to consider the fundamental principles of quality, such as successfulness, safety, timeliness, continuity, efficiency, equality and focus on the patient.

Safe healthcare must prevent treatment-related damage to the patient and physical damage related to the safety of residing at the provider of healthcare services.

305. The patient has the right to a medical procedure or any other healthcare service paid out of public funds only if such procedure is necessary according to the rules of the medical profession and is expected to benefit the patient according to contemporary medical doctrine. In the worst-case scenario, the expected benefits for the patient must outweigh the risks and (financial) burden.

306. In case of stationary care (mainly in hospitals but also in social security centres), the Act binds the performer of healthcare services to provide the conditions for fulfilling the patient's right to adequate spiritual care in accordance with the Freedom of Religion Act.[167] This Act states that patients in hospitals (and other occupants) have the right to regular individual and collective spiritual services. The exercise of religious freedom in hospitals and similar institutions is detailed in the Rules on the Organization and Provision of Spiritual Care in Hospitals and other Healthcare Service Providers.[168]

5. Right to Due Consideration of the Patient's Time

307. The patient's right to due consideration of his or her time is relatively extensively stipulated in the Patients' Rights Act. It first includes the question of waiting times and periods. Emergency medical assistance must be provided to the patient immediately, regardless of the circumstances. For other types of medical assistance, which cannot be performed immediately, the performer of healthcare services must place the patient on a waiting list. When doing so, the performer must consider expert standards regarding the degree of urgency, which has to be separately documented on the waiting list. The degree of urgency is gauged in accordance with the patient's maximum health benefits and in a manner that prevents grievous damage to the patient's health.

308. The Act tasks its performers to ensure the shortest waiting times possible, while balancing between the available finances and the (reasonable) waiting period.

167. OG RS, Nos 14/2007, 46/2010, 40/2012, 100/2013.
168. OG RS, No. 100/2008.

309. If the patient can provide a valid excuse for not being able to appear at the scheduled date of the healthcare service, its performer must set a new date for its performance. This date must be set as soon as possible. But if the patient failed to arrive at the scheduled date and has not excused himself or herself within fourteen days after the date, the performer of healthcare services can remove him or her off the list. The patient is also struck off the list after the healthcare service had been performed.

310. The patient can only be placed on one waiting list at one public healthcare service provider for the same healthcare service. If the patient is entered into several such lists, he or she is called upon to state on which list he or she would like to remain. If the patient does not respond, he or she is kept on the list to which he or she applied first.

The performer of healthcare services must provide for telephone and electronic means of applying for the service and be organized in a way that the patient does not wait for longer period than necessary. The manner of applying must be published in a visible spot, which is accessible to the patients.

311. Waiting lists are in place at the primary, secondary and tertiary levels. Exceptions are the general practitioners that the patient had selected and paediatricians. The list includes the patient's personal data, the date of the scheduled and performed healthcare service, the level of emergency, the performer who placed the patient on the list and the one who carried out the healthcare service. The processing of data on the waiting list is mainly carried out to ensure patients get informed about the schedule and respect it, to provide information about waiting times and to guarantee fast and equal access to healthcare services.

312. The patient has the right to be informed about the reasons for the waiting time and its duration and the right to inspect, transcribe or copy the waiting list. This right, naturally, excludes personal data of other patients, but leaves the patient free to check his or her personal data. The longest admissible waiting times for individual healthcare services, provided by the public healthcare network, are set by the Minister of Health.

313. The NIPH manages the national waiting list for the purpose of informing the patients, exchanging data with healthcare service providers and managing the healthcare system. The institute moreover publishes statistical data on waiting times.

314. The Patients' Rights Act specifically stipulates the respect for the patient's time in case of specialist outpatient check-ups. The patient has the right to a timely examination by a specialist physician, while the specialist physician has the obligation to issue a written expert opinion. The latter must include proposals for continuing treatment, alongside diagnostic data. The written expert opinion must be published by the physician after the completed check-up or at the latest within three days after the completed check-up. In emergency cases, however, the specialist physician must write and communicates the opinion to the patient immediately.

6. Right to a Second Opinion

315. A second opinion can be given by a doctor at all levels of healthcare at the request of the patient. The doctor should have at least five years of work experience in the field for which a second opinion is required. The request for obtaining a second opinion for the patient must not have negative consequences during further medical treatment by the attending physician. Regardless of the content of the second opinion, the attending physician retains independence and responsibility in making professional decisions.

The doctor issues a second opinion on the basis of the submitted medical documentation, but may also perform an examination of the patient or perform or propose additional medical services. The medical documentation which is the basis for the second opinion may be provided to the doctor who will give the second opinion at the request of the patient by the treating doctor or by the patient himself or herself. The exercise of the right to a second opinion in the network of the public health service is determined by the law governing healthcare and health insurance.[169]

7. Right to Informed Consent

a. General

316. The basic right to informed consent can be found in constitutional material and the same goes for the Republic of Slovenia. The right to informed consent, which is expressly laid down by law, is based in the general and abstract provisions of the Slovenian Constitution that determine the right to personal dignity (Article 34) and the inviolability of the individual's physical and mental integrity and rights of personality (Article 35). Article 51 of the Constitution, which lays down the right to healthcare and, *inter alia*, determines the voluntary nature of medical treatment, is stressing the fact that no one may be compelled to undergo medical treatment except in special cases, provided by law.

317. The fundamental principle is that any medical procedure (treatment, examination) requires the patient's consent. The provision of the Patients' Rights Act lays down the right to consent to healthcare as part of a more extensive right to freedom to decide on undergoing treatment (Articles 26 and 27).

The Act also determines the principle of the patient's right to a free decision on treatment under the conditions set by the Act. The Act forbids any medical treatment or healthcare to be administered to a patient with disposing capacity without his or her free and wilful consent, made on the basis of received explanations, except under cases determined by law. The patient has the right to actively participate in selecting the method of treatment after being presented with the necessary explanations on the treatment.

169. Until this question is arranged, the regulation in Patients' Rights Act applies. *See* http://pisrs.si, 1 Jan. 2021.

318. The principle of free and wilful consent is also valid for several special procedures that the Act expressly defines and in which the patient participates, such as: taking part in education, especially in the presence of other people during the administering of healthcare; the use of health data for purposes that do not represent treatment; for acquainting third parties with medical files; for communicating information on a person's medical condition to third parties; for taking part in medical research; for carrying out research on biological material that was obtained from the patient; for the use of the body or its organs after the patient's death for medical training and scientific research; for donations of organs, tissues or cells during life or after death.

319. The right to informed consent is also mentioned in the Slovenian Code of Medical Ethics (as presented above).

b. Contents of Information Preceding Informed Consent

320. Consent to medical treatment is a declaration of will that amounts to exercising the right to free decision-making by an individual regarding the encroachments into his or her rights of personality. Legally valid consent can be given after the doctor informs the patient prior to the treatment in an adequate and comprehensible way on the illness or condition, explains the possibilities for treatment, potential dangers and the anticipated success rate.

The Patients' Rights Act lays down the patient's right to be informed and to take part in the treatment. This right is dealt with extensively, taking up seven articles of the Act (Articles 19–25).

321. The patient has the right to be addressed by medical professionals and other collaborators in Slovene or, in the areas populated by the autochthonous Italian and Hungarian minorities – where Italian and Hungarian are also used as official languages – in the official minority language.

322. According to Article 20 of the Act, the patient has the right to be informed of his or her medical condition and the likely course and consequences of the illness or injury, on the purpose, type, manner of implementation, likelihood of success and the expected benefits and the outcome of the proposed medical treatment. The doctor must moreover inform the patient on the potential risks, side effects, negative consequences and other inconveniences of the proposed medical treatment, as well as on the consequences of foregoing the treatment. The patient is also entitled to information on potential alternative treatments as well as the procedures and the methods of treatment that are not available in the Republic of Slovenia or do not fall under the scope of the rights from compulsory health insurance.

323. The attending physician must give all of the above-mentioned explanations directly to the patient. The explanations must be comprehensive, timely, considerate, provided in a comprehensible manner and in accordance with the patient's ability to understand them.

Surgical or other medical treatments linked to greater risks or burdens must be explained to the patient verbally or in writing by the doctor who is to carry out the procedure. If this is not possible, another doctor who is trained to carry out such procedures should provide the necessary explanations.

324. The patient has the right to ongoing and detailed information on the course of treatment and on the results of the treatment or potential complications after the completion of the treatment. If a patient lacks disposing capacity, he or she can still exercise the rights regarding the doctor's obligation to provide the above-mentioned information in accordance with his or her abilities of comprehension.

325. Article 23 of the Patients' Rights Act lays down that the patient has the right to know who is treating him or her and who is taking part in his or her treatment. The consulting room, surgery, outpatient clinic or other places where medical treatment is provided, must display in the waiting room or other frequented location the name and the professional and/or scientific title of the medical professional and other collaborators and his or her office hours. The medical and other professionals who is in direct contact with the patient, must wear a name tag and the professional and/or scientific title in a visible place as well as introduce himself or herself in person to the patient. The rooms where healthcare services are provided must contain in a visible place the title of the legal or natural entity with which the provider of healthcare services has contracted for performing laboratory and other services.

326. Slovenian case law states that foregoing the obligation to explain the potential consequences of the treatment represents the omission of professional treatment and could result in liability for damages.[170] This means it is not only important whether a doctor breaches the rules of professional provision of a certain treatment, but also that the patient was not adequately informed of it. This gives the obligation to explain an important position in ascertaining a doctor's liability for damages.[171,172] Slovenian case law expands the notion of the obligation to explain also to cases when no illness is involved, but relations still exist between a doctor and a patient (e.g., pregnancy and childbirth).[173] The doctors must carry out their obligation to explain also in cases when the patient decides to undergo treatment which the doctor does not recommend.

c. Form of Informed Consent

327. The Patients' Rights Act states that the patient can give his or her consent verbally or by performing an act from which it can be deduced with certainty that

170. Refer to Supreme Court decision, Pž 281/70, http://www.sodisce.si, 1 Jan. 2020.
171. Refer to V. Žnidaršič Skubic, *Civilno medicinsko pravo* (*Civil Medical Law*) Uradni list 81–82 (2018).
172. An overview or more important case law in the field can be found in K. Brulc, *Odškodninska odgovornost za zdravniško napako* (*Liability to Damages for Medical Errors*), Master's Paper 65–71 (2007).
173. Refer to Supreme Court decision, II Ips 306/95, http://www.sodisce.si, 1 Jan. 2020.

it means acquiescence. The consent can also be submitted in writing when determined so by the Act. Consent can be given for several individual medical procedures at the same time if they represent a functional whole within the course of treatment. Surgery or other medical treatments, linked to greater risk or strain, require written consent by the patient in a special form that the Act lays down in Article 27.

328. In case the patient is unable to provide the written consent, he or she can also acquiesce verbally in the presence of two witnesses of legal age. This has to be specifically documented in the special form (Article 27), including the cause of the inability. If the patient consents to the medical procedure but does not want to provide a written statement of consent, the fact and potential reasons for that must be documented in the form and confirmed by the signature of two witnesses of legal age.

329. The consenting form (Article 27) includes the following data:

(1) basic data on the provider of the health service;
(2) description of the medical treatment or healthcare including the major potential complications and the expected benefits and a summary of other explanations that were given to the patient;
(3) the name and the signature of the doctor who carried out the obligation to explain or the doctor who carried out the medical treatment or healthcare services;
(4) the statement of consent or rejection and the statement on the reception and comprehension of the explanations as well as the statement on the cancellation of the consent or the rejection of the treatment;
(5) the name and the Health Insurance Institute number or other personal data that can serve to identify the patient;
(6) the name and other data that allows the identification of the witnesses, the persons who gave the consent and the persons who gave consent on behalf of the patient without full disposing capacity;
(7) names, contact information and relations towards the patients of those persons that the patient sets as part of his or her consent as persons who are allowed to receive data on the patient's condition or are acquainted with his or her medical files, and the manner and scope of exercising this right;
(8) the time and date of the submitted statements;
(9) the list of reasons and the circumstances why the patient cannot provide a written consent or the reason why the patient agreed to the treatment but does not want to give the written consent;
(10) the signature of the patient, except in cases provided by the Act, and the signatures of other people, when necessary; and
(11) other components that are necessary in accordance with the nature and the circumstances of the consent or lack thereof or are laid down in a different act.

The Minister of Health determined the form in more details in an executive act.[174] A photocopy of the filled-out and signed consenting form is given to the patient.

330. Until the Patients' Rights Act was accepted, Slovenian legislation did not define the special form of expression of patient's will and the same was true for the scope, time and place for submitting such a will or statement. A patient's consent for entering a certain medical procedure did not require special formal confirmations, but rather rested on the patient's oral expression of consent. The expression of will could therefore also have been conclusive, meaning that the will was expressed through other everyday behaviour and through certain actions that allowed the inference on the nature of the will thus expressed to be made.[175]

331. It often happens in practice that patients sign special forms, but signing them does not mean that the doctor completed his or her duty to explain in its entirety. The explanatory forms are often the most extensive in cases of invasive procedures into the patient's body or in procedures that carry a high degree of risk.[176]

332. Special forms of expressing informed consent are laid down by individual laws that govern individual medical areas, due to performing highly sensitive or dangerous and more invasive medical treatment. For example, the Act Regulating the Obtaining and Transplantation of Human Body Parts for the Purposes of Medical Treatment sets down that a transplant can only be carried out on the basis of express written consent by the recipient. The consent by a living donor only has to refer to the planned treatment. It must be submitted in writing and be an expression of the donor's free will. The consent can only be submitted by a person who is of legal age and has full disposing capacity. The consent can be linked to the condition that the organ is transplanted to a specific person. The Infertility Treatment and Procedures of Biomedically-assisted Procreation Act also requires written consent of the couple (spouses or cohabiting partners), which underwent the BMAP procedures.

d. Exceptions to the Requirement of Informed Consent

333. The Patients' Rights Act lays down in Article 28 that in cases where the patient does not have disposing capability, emergency medical treatment is administered without his or her consent. Article 29 of the Act lays down when non-essential medical treatment can be administered to a patient without his or her consent, as well as when other procedures than operations or medical procedures

174. *See* Rules on forms for written healthcare directives (*Pravilnik o obrazcih o pisnih izjavah volje pacienta*), OG RS, Nos 82/2008 and 84/2008.

175. Refer to K. Brulc, *Odškodninska odgovornost za zdravniško napako* (*Liability to Damages for Medical Errors*), Master's Paper 40 (2007).

176. Refer to V. Flis & J. Reberšek Gorišek, *Pojasnilna dolžnost – kako obsežna in v kakšni obliki* (*Obligation to Explain – What Is Its Scope and What Form Should it Take*), Medicina in pravo 295 (2004).

entailing great risk or strain for the patient can be also carried out without his or her consent. This can be done in cases where the patient does not have disposing capability or when the doctor does not or could not know that the patient or his or her authorized representative is opposed to the treatment, and when consent cannot be obtained in a reasonable time and proceeding with the treatment at this time would be in the best interest of the patient's health.

334. Theory and case law in Slovenia favour the view that, in emergencies, the doctor should offer medical treatment to the patient even if he or she is not able to consent to this. The actions of the doctor in such cases are not considered to be unlawful, but he is rather viewed as *negotiorum gestor.*[177] If the doctor were to fail to administer medical treatment, resulting in harm or even death, he or she would be liable for dereliction of assistance.[178]

e. Refusal and Withdrawal of Consent

335. The patient has a right to freely decide on his or her physical and mental integrity and his or her privacy and personality rights (Article 35 of the Constitution of the Republic of Slovenia). This means that he or she can freely accept and also refuse medical assistance without specifying a reason.

336. The Patients' Rights Act deals with the right to refuse medical treatment in Article 30. A patient with full disposing capacity has the right to turn down proposed medical treatment or medical care unless this would threaten his or her life or the lives of others. In cases where the attending doctor deems that the decision of the patient is against his or her health interests or that refusal of treatment could threaten his or her life or result in irreparable damage to his or her health or cause a grave worsening of his or her condition, the doctor must attempt to convince the patient of the need to proceed with treatment. If the doctor deems it necessary, he or she can turn to the patient's immediate family for assistance or can propose to the patient to seek a second opinion.

337. The refusal of medical treatment or medical care should not affect the relationship between medical staff and the patient. In case of operations or other procedures entailing great risk or strain for the patient, rejection of treatment must be documented on a special form (Article 27).

338. Withdrawal of consent or refusal of medical treatment is dealt with in Article 31 of the Patients' Rights Act. In line with this article, the patient has the right to withdraw his or her consent to medical treatment or refuse medical treatment at any time.

---

177. Refer to S. Cigoj, *Teorija obligacij, Splošni del obligacijskega prava* (*Theory of Obligation: General Part of Law of Obligation*) Uradni list RS 180 (2000). *See also* A. Manohin et al., *Dileme v zvezi z bolnikovim zavračanjem transfuzije krvi* (Dilemmas Connected to the Patient's Refusal of Blood Transfusion) No. 1 *Isis* 21–23 (2011).
178. Refer to Art. 161 of the Code of Obligations and Art. 130 of the Criminal Code of the Republic of Slovenia.

339. Individual laws dealing with the medical questions contain special provisions on this issue. For example, the Infertility Treatment and Procedures of Biomedically-assisted Procreation Act determines that either spouse (or partner in cases of a civil union) can withdraw consent for or refuse BMAP procedures at any stage until the sperm or eggs cells or foetus is not introduced into a woman's body. The institution carrying out the treatment must register this act in writing and issue a report. The law also determines that the doctor must make sure before introducing sperm or egg-cells or the foetus into the woman's body that consent has not been withdrawn (Article 23). The donors can also withdraw their written consent to the use of their sex cells in BMAP procedures. Notification of withdrawal must be made in writing. In such cases, the institution carrying out the treatment must immediately destroy the sex cells and, if it is the wish of the donor, issue written confirmation that the donation has been withdrawn.

The act dealing with transplantation sets down that living donors can renounce their donation until the procedure for transplantation is started.[179]

f. Previously Expressed Wishes

340. The Patients' Rights Act deals with the right to consider previously expressed wishes in a special chapter (Articles 32–34). The law initially deals with the issue of the patient's authorized representative. A patient who is of legal age and has full disposing capacity may assign a competent person who shall be entitled to exercise the right to consent and refusal in his or her name in the event that he or she is unable to decide on medical treatment or other rights stemming from this Act. The patient's authorized representative in this case must be of legal age and have full disposing capacity. The representative has the right to be acquainted with the patient's health record and his or her state of health as well as to obtain all information that may be relevant in deciding on whether to consent to treatment.

341. A patient can name an authorized representative with a written authorization. The signature on the authorization must be notary verified. In the written authorization, the patient can set down instructions or guidelines for his or her representative or set down limitations to the access to the medical files or information on his or her medical condition. The patient can withdraw in writing his or her authorization at any time. Similarly, an authorized representative can withdraw in writing from his or her role, save in cases where this could result in serious harm to the health of the patient. The name, birth information and contact details of a patient's authorized representative is contained on his or her health card or in his or her main medical files.

179. Some view this to be contentious in cases of bone marrow transplants, where the recipient's own bone marrow begins to be destroyed approximately a week before the transplantation procedure is carried out, meaning that he or she would face certain death if the donor were to withdraw his or her consent at this stage of the treatment. Refer to Z. Krušič Mate, *O pravici do zasebnosti v medicini* (*On the Right to Privacy in Medicine*), Master's Paper 142 (2007).

342. Along with the right to an authorized representative, a patient also has the right to decide to exclude persons who would otherwise be entitled to take decisions on treatment on his or her behalf. Patients can exclude or limit the powers of such persons in writing, given that they have full disposing capacity and are of legal age. Information on such wishes is contained on the health card or main medical files of the patient.

343. Article 34 of the Patients' Rights Act deals with an important aspect of previously expressed wishes (so-called living will). The provision in question sets down that every patient with full disposing capacity has the right to have his or her will regarding rejection of treatment heeded if he or she should be in a position where he or she is incapable of expressing his or her will for cases where:

(1) he or she should suffer from grave illness, which given the ability of modern medicine would lead to death in a short period of time in spite of medical treatment or medical care, or for which treatment or care would not lead to an improvement in health or the alleviation of his or her suffering but rather only to the prolonging of his or her life; and
(2) his or her life would be prolonged by medical treatment or care, but he or she would end up being in a state where, due to the graveness of his or her disability, he or she would lose physical and mental ability to take care of himself or herself.

The patient's previously expressed wishes regarding treatment related to the first case (1) is binding for the attending doctor, whereas in the second case (2) the patient's wishes are considered by the doctor as a guide in deciding on the course of procedure.

344. The patient's previously expressed wishes must be considered in all such situations, save in cases where there are reasonable grounds to suspect that the patient would have retracted his or her wishes. The patient's previously expressed wishes must be registered on a special form (Article 27).

345. The patient's personal physician or his or her authorized representative should remind him or her of the consequences of his or her decisions in expressing wishes regarding future treatment. The special form containing a patient's previously expressed wishes regarding treatment must contain information on whether the person fulfils the conditions for informed consent (full disposing capacity, legal age) and basic explanations regarding the decision, as well as the patient's signature, name of his or her personal doctor and authorized health representative (Article 27).

346. The written statement regarding a wish for future treatment can be withdrawn by the patient in writing at any time. An attending doctor obtains information on a patient's previously expressed wishes regarding treatment on his or her medical card or in main health records.

8. Right to Information about the Patient's Health

a. General

347. The right to information about his or her health is a fundamental right in healthcare, guaranteed in the Republic of Slovenia not only on the basis of the provisions of the Convention but also in its legislation. The Patients' Rights Act makes reference to the right to be informed and does not differentiate between the right to informed consent and the right of a patient to information about his or her health. Under Article 20 of the Act, the patient has the right to be informed about his or her state of health and the likely evolution of a disease or injuries, as well as on the aims, type, method, success rate, expected benefits and outcome of the proposed medical treatment. The attending physician must provide all explanations to the patient first hand, in whole, in a considerate and timely manner, and in a way that can be understood by the patient in view of his or her abilities.

348. The patient has the right to be informed of the progress in treatment in a timely and detailed manner and also the right to be informed of the outcome of the treatment and possible complications. A patient without full disposing capacity can nevertheless exercise his or her right to information about his or her health – in this case the doctor is bound to explain in a way that can be understood by the patient.

349. In line with Article 23 of the Patients' Rights Act, the patient has the right to know who the attending doctor is and who else is involved in treating him or her. The name and title of medical professionals and other collaborators and their working hours must be displayed in a visible place in the waiting areas of consulting rooms, dispensaries and other places where healthcare services are provided. Medical professionals (and others) who are in direct contact with patients must have a name tag displayed in a visible place and must introduce themselves to patients.

350. The patient also has the right to general information and specific information upon discharge. The providers of healthcare services must explain the organizational aspects of the treatment to the patient in a comprehensible way. They must also acquaint the patient with the details of access to services such as waiting periods, waiting times and waiting lists and the methods of payment of the services in the programme of compulsory health insurance. Every provider of health services must also avail the patient of written information on the contents of the Patients' Rights Act and general information on the provider and the health services that the provider offers. The patient must be informed of the house rules and the accommodation when being admitted to the institution. When discharged from the hospital or a different institution, the patient has the right to be given a written report on the diagnosis, treatment and healthcare as well as to the instructions for further treatment until his or her first visit to the family doctor, including the necessary medication or medicinal products.

351. Article 25 of the Patients' Rights Act lays down the right of knowing the costs. In case the health service is paid for by the patient in total or in part, the provider of health services must previously give the patient information on the assessed cost of the health services in writing. After the service is completed, the patient must be invoiced for the provided health services, the medications and medicinal devices used.

If a patient does not pay for the health service from his or her pocket, the provider of health services delivers the end invoice to the patient after performing the service. The invoice must be itemized according to individual health services, medications and medicinal devices. If requested by the patient, the provider of health services is required to explain the invoice.

b. Right Not to Know

352. The right not to know about one's health condition is set down in the Patients' Rights Act, which states that the doctor must respect the patient's wish that he or she does not wish to be provided with information on his or her health state. An exception to this is when not informing the patient of his or her health state could pose a serious health risk to other persons. The patient's wish not to be told of his or her state of health must be registered in the medical file (paragraph 2 of Article 22).

c. Therapeutic Privilege

353. Slovenian legislation regulates the therapeutic privilege; it is set down in paragraph 1 of Article 22 of the Patients' Rights Act. The article determines that the doctor may, in exceptional cases, suppress information from the patient if he or she deems that, in the given circumstances, disclosure could have serious harm for the patient's health. This does not apply if a patient with full disposing capacity expressly demands that he or she wants to be informed in full of his or her state of health. Doctors must document the reason for suppressing information from a patient in the medical file.

9. Patient Rights Regarding the Medical File

a. Right to a Medical File

354. Slovenian legislation does not expressly deal with the right to a medical file, although this right is indirectly provided for in several regulations. The Health Services Act requires from health institutions and private medical professions to lead a medical file and other records in line with a specialized regulation. The same obligation is set down in Article 50 of the Medical Services Act, which states that the doctor must document the state of health of the patient and conduct other records in line with a specialized law. To this end, health institutions and private medical professionals are included into a common information system.

The Patients' Rights Act provides the patient with a right to be informed of his or her medical file (Articles 41 and 42), which in effect implies a right to a medical file.

b. Contents of the Medical File

355. This issue is dealt with in the Healthcare Databases Act. In the special annex, the Act determines which databases contain personal data and which do not contain such data. Among the former are listed basic medical documentation, health cards and registers from various medical fields (register on basic healthcare, database on preventive health of adults and children, register of accidents at work, etc.). Among the latter, the Act lists the register on the activities of a dental clinics, the register on the activities of a specialist outpatient service, the register of hospital activities and many others.

356. A standard medical file must contain the following information:

(1) Unique personal identification number.
(2) Health insurance policy number.
(3) Name and surname.
(4) A genogram.
(5) Marital status.
(6) Education.
(7) Profession.
(8) Address.
(9) Telephone.
(10) Diagnosis.
(11) Date of contact.
(12) Planned contacts.
(13) Doctor's identification number.
(14) Treatment.
(15) Referral.
(16) Reason for sickness leave.
(17) Cause of death.
(18) Insurance status.
(19) Reason for initial examination.
(20) The family's health history.
(21) Plan of medical treatment.

c. Right to Access the Medical File

357. This area is dealt with primarily in the Patients' Rights Act. The Act deals in particular with the right of insight into a patient's medical file (Articles 41 and 42). Article 41 determines how a patient can obtain access to his or her medical file: the patient has a right to access and transcribe without hindrance medical documentation related to him or her, but under the condition that this is done in the presence of a doctor or healthcare worker. The patient also has a right to independent access to his or her electronic medical file and information contained on his or her health insurance card, where the system allows this.

358. The patient or other persons with the right to access the patient's medical files should be given access to the medical file under the condition that they identify themselves and demonstrate legal grounds for accessing the file. The healthcare institution must enable the patient or his or her authorized representative access to the medical file within five days of receiving a request. The patient can request access to medical files related to him or her from the same health institution twice a month at the most. The patient can also request basic explanations regarding the contents of medical files and save in cases when he or she has already received detailed explanations from the doctor (Article 20). However, the patient can request extensive verbal explanations about medical files if he or she had not been provided any explanations by the doctor (Article 20).

359. Persons who are authorized to decide on consent or refusal of treatment on behalf of the patient may access the patient's medical file only in cases when this is required for a decision on treatment and only to the extent required to decide on treatment.

360. A patient with full disposing capacity can issue written authorization to any person to access his or her medical file provided that they fulfil the following conditions: have full disposing capacity and are of legal age (paragraph 7 of Article 41 of the Patients' Rights Act). The Patients' Rights Act states in this respect also that this right is exercised to the extent limited by the respect of the right to therapeutic privilege and the right of the patient not to know about his or her state of health (Article 22).

361. A patient has the right to nominate persons who have access to his or her medical documentation and persons who are prohibited access to his or her medical documentation, provided that this does not contravene any laws. The Act also determines instances when authorization is not required to use or otherwise process personal data, be it for medical or non-medical reasons:

(1) if this is for the purpose of epidemiological or other research, education, medical publications or other purposes from which the patient's identity cannot be ascertained;
(2) if this is used as a means of monitoring the quality and safety of healthcare, where the patient's identity cannot be ascertained;
(3) if legislation requires that the patient's condition be disclosed;
(4) if information is forwarded to the other healthcare provider for the purposes of administering treatment; and
(5) if this is determined in a specific law.

362. The Act also determines legal remedies for cases where the patient's right to access his or her medical file is violated. The patient or his or her authorized representatives may in this case file a complaint with the Information Commissioner.[180]

180. The role and powers of the Information Commissioner is dealt with in the Information Commissioner Act, OG RS Nos 113/2005 and 51/2007. The Information Commissioner is an independent state body, which is, among other, responsible for deciding on complaints against decrees with

363. The right to access data from a person's medical files usually belongs only to the person for whom the data applies. But the Medical Services Act determines that, in exceptional cases, where the attending physician concludes that this would benefit the patient, the doctor may provide the patient's immediate family or guardian or his or her cohabiting partner the information without prior approval from the patient (Article 53). Only the attending doctor (and not any doctor or other medical staff) can provide the immediate family members of legal guardians with information about a patient's state of health.

d. Right to Copy the Medical File

364. The Patients' Rights Act provides the patient with the right to photocopy, transcribe or otherwise copy his or her medical documentation. This possibility must be provided by the healthcare provider. The healthcare provider is only obliged to provide an authentic copy of visual documentation which is not in electronic form if it disposes with the technical equipment for this. The healthcare provider may charge for the costs of copying and dispatching of documentation in line with regulations governing the protection of personal data.

365. Like the Patients' Rights Act, the Personal Data Protection Act,[181] which regulates the right to access to personal data, expressively permits, besides the insight of the data, also the transcription or copying of personal data. The Act also allows the copy of personal data to be forwarded to an individual on his or her request if they are included in the collection and are referring to him or her.

e. Post-Mortem Access by Relatives

366. The Patients' Rights Act deals in Article 42 with the issue of the rights of relatives to be acquainted with the health files of a patient after his or her death. The provisions grant access to these files to persons authorized for this by law or for those whom the patient issued consent in written form. The right to be acquainted with a patient's health file after his or her death is held by the patient's spouse, cohabiting partner, same-sex partner, children or adopted children, or, if the patient has no such relatives, by his or her parents. They are given the right to access only the data that are necessary for the accomplishment of the legal intention of getting acquainted with those data. The aforementioned persons who want to be granted post-mortem access to the medical files generated while the patient did not have full disposing capacity, in cases where this state lasted until his or her death, must demonstrate legal grounds for this.

367. Others persons who are able to demonstrate legal grounds can access a deceased person's medical file, limited to the data for which they have legal grounds

---

which a state body violated the right of access to public information as well as oversight over the implementation of the law. The body also deals with inspections related to the implementation of the law and other regulations which touch on the protection and processing of personal data.

181. OG RS, Nos 94/2007 (UPB1) and 177/2020.

to obtain. The request of a spouse, cohabiting partners, same-sex partner, children or adopted children, or – in cases where the deceased did not have such relatives – the parents are rejected in part or in whole where the law determines this, or if the patient expressly prohibited access in writing or verbally in the presence of two witnesses. Regardless of a deceased patient's request to prohibit access to his or her medical file, parents, descendants, spouse, cohabiting partner or a same-sex partner, siblings and other persons who may have been in a special relationship with him or her (which they must be able to prove beyond a doubt) are granted access in parts that may be significant for their health. The access is obtained through a patient's personal doctor or an attending doctor. If this cannot be done, the healthcare provider determines a doctor who enables access to the data.

368. The healthcare provider has fifteen days to answer requests for access to medical files. If the request is turned down in part or in whole, the requesting party has the possibility to complain to the Information Commissioner.

369. A patient has the right to nominate persons who will have access to his or her medical documentation and persons who will be prohibited access to his or her medical documentation after his or her death. The ban to access the file shall be registered in the central health records register.

370. Post-mortem protection of personal data is set down also in more general act, that is, the Personal Data Protection Act. The Patients' Rights Act holds the status of *lex specialis* and *lex posterior*, meaning it has precedence over the Personal Data Protection Act. Nevertheless, a short summary of the latter follows. The Personal Data Protection Act determines in Article 21 that the healthcare provider can only provide information about medical records to those authorized for handling personal information, as set down in other laws. Yet, the doctor can hand over the health-related data on a dead person only to the person that is, by law of inheritance, his or her legal heir of the first or the second grade. The latter includes the descendants of the deceased, his or her adopted children, spouse, cohabiting partner, parents and their children (brothers and sisters of the deceased person). These persons can be informed of the health condition of the patient if they show the legal grounds[182] for this. Moreover, the medical staff must verify that the deceased did not prohibit in writing access to his or her file. In any case, the health file and other documents cannot be handed over, since health institutions in Slovenia are bound to keep this information. In the case of medical files and detailed information on disease, the institutions are tasked with keeping records for at least ten years.

f. Right to Correction, Erasure or Demolition

371. The Patients' Rights Act sets down a special right held by the patient to request that his or her remarks be added to his or her medical file (line 5 of Article 41). The procedure to amend, correct, block or delete such data is also governed by

182. For example, a filed lawsuit, researching root causes for death, etc.

Article 32 of the Personal Data Protection Act. The Act determines that the individual can demand that the administrator of personal data – i.e., the healthcare institution – amends, corrects, blocks access to or deletes personal data, referring to an individual, for which the individual can prove that they are incomplete, incorrect, out-of-date, or that it was collected or processed in violation of the law. Based on the demand of the individual, the healthcare institution that administers the individual's health data must inform all users of personal data and contracted processing entities to which it forwarded the individual's personal data, on the demand for amending, correcting, blocking or deleting if it had forwarded the said data before the demand by the individual was received. The institution is not required to do so only in case if informing the above-mentioned would cause extensive costs, disproportionate efforts or require a lot of time. The costs for carrying out the above activities are paid for by the personal data administrator.

372. The procedure to amend, correct, block or delete the data is governed by Article 33 of the Personal Data Protection Act. The healthcare institution or the doctor himself or herself can also determine that the personal data is incomplete, incorrect or out-of-date. In such a case, the administrator can amend or correct the data and inform him or her of the change.

10. Right to Medical Secrecy and Confidentiality

373. In this area, too, the Patients' Rights Act sets the fundamental standards. The law deals with personal data in Article 44 and with physician-patient confidentiality in Article 45.

The patient has a right to have his or her personal data kept confidential, which includes data about visits to the doctor and other details of his or her treatment. Medical workers must handle a patient's personal and other data in line with the principle of confidentiality and with respecting the regulations dealing with personal data.

Health and other personal data can be used and processed for use in treatment if this is done on the basis of approval from the patient or the person who is authorized to consent or refuse treatment on the patient's behalf where the patient does not have full disposing capacity. Health data can be used and processed for purposes outside of healthcare only with the approval of the patient or his or her authorized representative. Following the patient's death, access to such medical files can only be granted by his or her immediate family members, but only if the deceased did not prohibit such access in the first place. Regardless of this, the use of a patient's medical file outside of use for healthcare purpose is determined separately in the law.

374. Medical professionals and all other staff who handle such data are bound to protect as the professional secrecy of everything they find out about patients as part of their jobs. This applies foremost for information on the patient's state of health, his or her personal, family and social circumstances as well as information related to treatment and monitoring of disease or injury.

375. The duty of protecting the information on health condition of patient of all of the health workers can be abolished if the patient decides this way. Besides the patient, the same opportunity goes to patient's parents if he or she is younger than 15 years of age and also to parents of children older than 15 years of age in cases where information is needed for effective execution of parental rights or guardianship (and the child did not ban the giving of the information). The same right goes also to court and the person who had the right to consent to medical treatment for the incapacitated patient but only regarding the health information that are connected with the medical procedure to which this person consented.

A doctor can decide to release information about the state of a patient if he or she concludes that this is needed to save lives and to prevent grave damage. The doctor is obliged to report a possible criminal act regarding injuries, criminal act against sexual inviolability and criminal acts against marriage, family and the young where a child was the (or one of the) injured party.

376. The law expressly lays down that in the case of the use of therapeutic privilege or if the patient requests that data on his or her state of health are not to be communicated to him or her, the aforementioned people do not have a right to acquire more data than the patient would be able to acquire. The only exception to this case is if a patient would decide otherwise by himself or herself.

377. The provider of healthcare services must inform the immediate family members in a proper manner on the death of a patient and its causes, regardless if the patient prohibited his or her medical data to be communicated. If the provider is unaware of any such persons, he or she should inform on that to a competent state body.

378. Under Article 51 of the Health Services Act, medical professionals and other collaborators are obliged to treat as a professional secret data on the medical condition of the patient and the causes, circumstances and consequences of the condition.[183] Such data must also be treated as a professional secret by persons who have come across it due to the nature of their work, meaning all other healthcare staff. The Health Services Act also adds on the topic that the obligation to secrecy does not expire after the death of the patient (last paragraph of Article 52). In case the patient is transferred or moved or if he or she selects a different doctor, all medical files must be handed over to the doctor that is to continue the treatment.[184]

---

183. The Medical Services Act lays down only the doctor's obligation to treat as professional secret data on the medical condition of the patient and data on the causes, circumstances and consequences of such situation (Art. 51).
184. Article 54 of the Medical Services Act states a similar thing.

11. Right to Privacy and Protection of Private Life

379. The right to privacy and right to private life is the right to keep one's personal life secret. Everything that is part of personal and family life and that an individual does not want to be disclosed must remain secret. This right protects the personal life and the inviolability of the individual's personal sphere.[185] The right enjoys constitutional protection in the Slovenian legal system. The Constitution of the Republic of Slovenia guarantees in Article 35 the inviolability of the physical and mental integrity of every person, his or her privacy and rights of personality.

380. One of the possible violations of the right to privacy, with special importance in the area of healthcare, is unauthorized disclosure of a professional secret. If a doctor unlawfully discloses a secret which he or she has become party to by way of performing his or her tasks, he or she could have committed a crime. But there is no penalty imposed on persons who disclose a secret for the general good or for some other person's benefit when the good or benefit therein is greater than that of withholding the secret. The disclosure of a secret is not unauthorized if the aggrieved party agrees to the disclosure, if the disclosure is permitted or a state body by statutory power decrees that the disclosure should be made. The disclosure is also justified if it is done as a means of a last resort. According to the Contentious Civil Procedure Act[186] (Article 231) and the General Administrative Procedure Act[187] (Article 183), a witness can withhold testimony on facts to which he or she was privy to as a doctor if the obligation applies that the witness must keep as secret what he or she learnt during the performance of his or her profession.

381. The Patients' Rights Act lays down the right to privacy protection in Article 43. The article binds the providers of healthcare services to respect the patient's privacy and especially his or her moral, cultural, religious, philosophical and other personal beliefs during medical care, while taking into consideration medical doctrines.

382. The Act also lays down the obligation to enable the patient to have only the following people present during a medical procedure as a special manner of protecting the patient's privacy:

(1) medical professionals and other collaborators who are involved in the procedure;
(2) people for whom the patient wants to be present if the request is reasonable from the viewpoint of the nature of the procedure;

185. Refer to A. Finžgar, *Osebnostne pravice* (*Personality Rights*) 119 (SAZU 1985).
186. OG RS, Nos 73/2007 (UPB3), 101/2007, 102/2007, 45/2008, 62/2008, 111/2008, 116/2008, 121/2008, 47/2009, 48/2009, 57/2009, 12/2010, 49/2010, 50/2010, 107/2010, 43/2011, 58/2011, 75/2012, 40/2013, 92/2013, 10/2014, 48/2015, 6/2017, 10/2017, 10/2019, 70/2019.
187. OG RS, Nos 24/2006 (UPB2), 105/2006, 126/2007, 65/2008, 47/2009, 48/2009, 8/2010, 82/2013, 175/2020.

(3) people who in an individual case have the right to approve of the medical procedure if the patient does not have disposing capacity and if their presence is possible due to the nature of the procedure; and
(4) other persons, if the law so requires.

383. Persons whose presence is required for the needs of medical education can only be present if allowed so beforehand by the patient (or the person who was authorized for consenting to the procedure if the patient is unable to decide for himself or herself).

384. The Act also lays down a general clause of protecting the patient's right to privacy, stating in paragraph 5 of Article 43 that the patient has the right to demand the implementation of all other suitable and reasonable measures to protect his or her privacy during healthcare.

a. Processing of Data Concerning Health

385. In order to provide uniform, effective and safe administration and management of personal data in the health sector, health institutions and private medical workers are included in a common information system. The processing of health-related data is governed by the Health Care Databases Act. This Act determines the collection of data from healthcare as well as the collection, processing and forwarding of data that is administered, used and exchanged during tasks determined by law by different entities that perform healthcare activities. The gathering, processing and forwarding of data from this database is governed by the Personal Data Protection Act. This Act lays down the rights, obligations, principles and measures that are used to prevent unconstitutional, illegal and unjustified encroachments into an individual's privacy and dignity during the processing of data. The Personal Data Protection Act expressly includes data on the medical condition of an individual (item 19 of Article 6) among sensitive personal data for which it provides greater legal protection. Such data can only be processed if it is done so by medical professionals and other collaborators in line with the Act (item six of Article 13) for the purposes of healthcare protection of the individuals and management or performance of healthcare service. Such data must be specially marked during processing and secured in a way to prevent unauthorized personnel to access it (paragraph 1 of Article 14).

12. Right to Complain

a. General

386. The Patients' Rights Act introduces a special right of the patient regarding a violation of his or her rights. The Act gives the patient, who believes his or her rights laid down in this Act have been violated, the right to be dealt with in the following procedures:

(1) procedure of the so-called first hearing of the violation of patient's rights at the responsible person of the provider of healthcare services, based on the patient's oral request or request in writing (Articles 56–63); and
(2) procedure of the so-called second hearing of the violation of patient's rights at the Commission of the Republic of Slovenia for the Protection of Patient's Rights, also based on the patient's oral request or request in writing (Articles 64–79). This procedure also includes a procedure of mediation.

387. The Act points out that its provisions that govern the procedures to protect the rights of patients in no way encroach in regulations that guarantee supervision over professionalism of health services as well as do not infringe on regulations that deal with health insurance violations.

388. Article 48 of the Act lays down the general procedural principles, which are summarized in nine basic items:

(1) Informing and supporting the patient.
(2) Simple, transparent, quick and efficient solving of the issue.
(3) Free advice and aid of the patient's rights representative.
(4) Impartial and fair treatment.
(5) Adequate and ongoing recording of procedural activities by the participants.
(6) Solving and closing the procedure where the cause for it arose.
(7) Oral procedure, in general.
(8) Exclusion of the public.
(9) Options for peaceful problem solving.

389. Regarding the question of the capacity to sue and be sued in procedures dealing with patient rights, the patients who do not have disposing capacity use *mutatis mutandis* those provisions of this Act that determine a special manner to enforce the rights of such patients. When children's parents are deciding on launching a procedure, consensus is not needed.

The demand for launching procedures can also be launched by the immediate family or people close to the patient, if the patient agrees. Immediate family can also demand the procedures to be launched after the patient's death. Patients who do not have disposing capacity have the right that their cooperation is ensured to the largest extent possible and their opinion, if they are able to express it and if they understand its meaning and consequences, considered in procedures on violation of their rights. Another important general principle is also the assurance that exercising the rights regarding violation of the patient's rights under this Act is not a precondition for demanding a potential judicial protection.

b. The Patient's Rights Representative

390. The Act introduces a new function, the function of the patient's rights representative. The representative's core function is to provide basic information to the patient, provide expert aid and give substantiated guidelines in exercising the rights of patients in healthcare, health insurance and provision of healthcare services. The representative can address proposals, opinions, criticisms or recommendations to the providers of healthcare services, who are obliged to discuss and reply to them. The provider of healthcare services must also give the representative access to all data that he or she required for his or her activities. The patient's medical records and other data are made available to the ombudsman pursuant to the patient's written consent. The representative's activities are not paid for by the patient and are confidential.

391. The representative is not paid for his or her work by the patent. Every province as a rule names one representative, appointed by the province's representation body after a public call for bids. The representative is located in the province's capital. The province provides the necessary conditions for the representative's activities. The representative is entitled to a reward and reimbursement of costs. He or she is appointed for a five-year term and can be reappointed. The candidate must, apart from the general requirements, have a university diploma and at least ten years of experience in the field of law, healthcare, consumer protection or patient's rights. The representative requires written authorization by the patient for his or her activities. Should he or she assess that the patient's claim is manifestly unfounded, he or she is not required to accept the authorization for representation.

c. Human Rights Ombudsman

392. The Act also gives certain powers regarding the protection of patient's rights to the human rights ombudsman. The human rights ombudsman should, in the scale of his or her legal tasks, also monitor the situation in the field of enforcement of patient's rights and, on the basis of such monitoring, request that the responsible national bodies, local community bodies and holders of public powers provide for the conditions for effective enforcement of this Act. The ombudsman appoints one of his or her substitute to deal with the field.

d. Court Protection

393. The patient can also require his or her rights to be protected in a court. Regular courts guarantee the protection of general rights to patients, while the protection of rights stemming from health insurance can be requested with the specialized Labour and Social Court. Regular courts give the patient the possibility to enforce his or her damage claims in line with the general rules of the law of obligations. The criminal court allows the patient to enforce the protection of his or her key rights and values, protected by the Criminal Code of the Republic of Slovenia.

Chapter 2. The Physician-Patient Relationship in Specific Terms

§1. Minor Patients

I. Minor in Slovenian Civil Law

394. According to Slovenian Civil Law, an individual comes of age at the age of 18 years, whereupon he or she is awarded full disposing capacity. A minor can, exceptionally, receive full disposing capacity before turning 18 if he or she enters into marriage. The marriage, however, requires the permission of a court, issued in a non-litigious proceeding, which is only issued if the court believes that a minor is mature enough to perform the rights and duties stemming from such a relationship. Disposing capacity can also be granted to a minor by a court decision if the said minor became a parent, if it believes that he or she is mature enough to provide for himself or herself and the child.[188]

395. Before turning 15, a minor has no disposing capacity. Legal transactions that he or she would conclude are completely invalid, i.e., null. A minor aged between 15 and 18 years has limited or partial disposing capacity. Such a minor can only conclude, without legal representative approval, the legal transactions that are set by law. Pursuant to Family Code,[189] a minor can independently conclude only the legal transactions that are not vital enough to greatly influence his or her life or are not of a nature that they could influence his or her life after becoming of age. More important legal transactions still require consent of the legal representative. But a minor can independently enter into employment and is free to dispose of his or her income.

396. Legal transactions, concluded by a minor without the required consent by the legal representative, are relatively invalid – i.e., can be challenged. Challengeable legal transactions however remain in force until they are annulled.

The rightful claimant of the right to challenge is the minor, while his or her legal representative can challenge the legal transaction in his or her name until the minor reaches 18 years of age. The legal representative must file a suit within one year from getting to know about the reason for challenging and at the latest in three years since the transaction has been concluded. From the child's maturity onwards (or from his or her gaining disposing capacity), the function of the legal representative stops and a different time limit is set in motion for the person of age. Such a person can challenge legal transactions, concluded without the legal representative's consent while being a minor, within three months after becoming of age.

397. The contracting party of the minor can demand repayment of damages from the minor due to the transaction's annulment only if the minor convinced him or her that he or she has disposing capacity.

188. *See* Arts 71–79 of the Non-Contentious Civil Procedure Act, OG RS, No. 16/2019.
189. OG RS, Nos 15/2017, 21/2018, 22/2019, 67/2019.

398. Legal transactions, concluded by a minor without the required consent by his or her legal representative, remain in force if they are later confirmed by the legal representative. The minor's contracting party can require that the legal representative give approval to the transaction. If the latter rejects the transaction or does not provide his or her opinion within thirty days, the legal transaction is considered annulled. The minor's contracting party also has the option to resign from the contract. This option is available if he or she did not know about the minor's lack of disposing capacity or if he or she knew, but was fooled by the minor into thinking that he or she has the legal representative's consent. The contracting party can use this option within thirty days since learning about the lack of minor's disposing capacity or non-existence of consent by the minor's legal representative. This option is not applicable if the minor's legal representative approves of the legal transaction before the contracting party uses the right to resign from the contract.

II. Minor and Medical Law

A. *Informed Consent*

399. The Patients' Rights Act is dealing with the question of informed consent for minors in Article 35, stating that a child younger than 15 years of age is generally not able to give informed consent, unless the doctor assesses otherwise on the basis of the child's maturity. In making a decision on a child's ability to decide on treatment on his or her own, the doctor should as a rule consult with the child's parents or legal guardians.

But the law also states that a child older than 15 years of age is able to give informed consent, unless his or her doctor rules otherwise on the basis of the child's maturity. As is the case for granting the right to informed consent to children younger than 15 years, a doctor should as a rule consult with the child's parents or legal guardians in making a decision not to grant a child older than 15 years the right to decide on treatment on his or her own.

400. When a child is not capable to consent to his or her treatment, the responsibility falls on the parents or legal guardians. In general, the parents decide on treatment jointly. For operations or other procedures entailing great risk or strain for a minor patient, or for treatment involving major consequences for the child, the consent of both parents is required, save in cases where:

(1) one of the parents is unknown or his or her place of residence is unknown;
(2) one of the parents has been stripped of his or her parental rights;
(3) one of the parents cannot state his or her opinion in a timely fashion due to temporary absence; and
(4) one of the parents does not meet the conditions for making decision for his or her own sake.

401. Consent issued on behalf of minors must be registered on a special form (Article 27). If the parents cannot reach a joint decision on consenting to major treatment for their child, they can propose that they be assisted in this by social services. They may even leave the decision up to social services. For all other forms of treatment, consent from the parent present at the time of treatment suffices. If both parents are present and both do not consent to treatment, the doctor seeks the opinion of the consultation body of doctors in view of the interests of the child. If this is not possible, he or she seeks the opinion of another doctor, under the condition that that doctor has not been involved and will not be involved in the treatment of the child. Consent for such treatment of a child is confirmed in writing by at least one of the consenting parents, or the consultation body of doctors, or the consenting independent doctor.

402. The child has the right to have his or her opinion considered to the greatest possible extent in cases where the decision on his or her medical treatment is taken by another person. This is, of course, if he or she is capable of expressing his or her wishes and understanding the consequences of such wishes.

403. Another important new feature of the Patients' Rights Act is the limitation of the right to decide in the name of the minor children that are not able to express their informed consent. Parents or legal guardians cannot reject emergency medical treatment for them (Article 36).

B. Minor and Medical Secrecy and Confidentiality

404. The Patients' Rights Act in the chapter on medical secrecy and confidentiality defines specially for the patient that completes 15 years of age, the right to determine, either by filling out a special form or instructing verbally in the presence of two witnesses of age, to whom, when and which information a doctor or another person authorized by the doctor can, must or must not forward on the patient's health condition. The same rule applies for forwarding information on the health situation that refers to a medical procedure into which the patient under 15 years of age could enter freely. The statement can be issued for an individual procedure or for all future medical procedures or future healthcare with an individual provider of healthcare services.

405. If the patient does not apply this right or cannot do so due to his or her health condition, information on his or her health condition can be communicated to his or her immediate family, close ones and people who are authorized to give a consent to an individual medical procedure or healthcare when the patient does not have disposing capacity.

§2. Incapacitated Adults

406. The Patients' Rights Act deals with the issue of informed consent for incapacitated adults in Article 37. When patients are unable to decide on treatment due to mental health issues or other reasons, the treatment can be carried out only if it is approved by the patient's legal representative. If the patient does not have a legal representative, the institution treating him or her must establish contact with the proper authorities in a bid to name a legal representative. If the doctor concludes that the legal representative is not acting in the best interests of the patient, he or she informs the body that appointed the legal representative and asks it to ensure proper representation of the patient.

407. Until a legal representative is named, the following persons are entitled to exercise, in the specified order, the right to consent or refusal, provided that they are of legal age and have full disposing capacity:

(1) the patient's spouse or partner in cases of civil unions;
(2) the patient's children or adopted children;
(3) the patient's parents or foster parents;
(4) the patient's brothers or sisters;
(5) the patient's grandparents; and
(6) the patient's grandchildren.

If one or more of the above-listed persons deny consent, the doctor shall decide on the course of action on the basis of all of the opinions given and in the patient's best interest.

The patient's legal representative and other persons listed above to decide on behalf of an incapacitated adult patient cannot refuse emergency (life-saving) medical treatment.

408. The same (presented) rules apply to patients who are incapacitated temporarily. Treatment can be administered only if it is approved by the legal representative of the patient. Until a legal representative is named, decisions on consent or refusal are exercised by the same persons as listed above (in the same order). It likewise applies that for such cases a doctor decides on the course of action on the basis of expressed opinions and in the patient's best interest if treatment is refused by at least one of the persons listed. The legal representative and other persons listed above cannot refuse emergency (life-saving) treatment for patients who are temporarily incapacitated.

§3. The Mental Patient and Involuntary Placement

I. General

409. The area of mental disorders and involuntary placement of mental patients is regulated by the Mental Health Act.[190] The Act defines mental disorder as a temporary or permanent disorder in brain functioning, which is shown as altered thinking, emotions, perception, knowledge and perceiving oneself and the environment.

190. OG RS, Nos 77/2008, 46/2015, 44/2019.

Maladjustment to moral, social, political or other society values is not by itself considered a mental disorder. Slovenia uses the classification of mental disorders according to the International Classification of Diseases, Revision 10, published under the aegis of the WHO.[191] In general, patients who are mentally ill also fall under the Patients' Rights Act.

II. Constitution of the Republic of Slovenia

410. The Constitution of the Republic of Slovenia states in Article 51 paragraph 3 that nobody can be forced into involuntary treatment, except in cases defined by legislation. This is because an individual (patient) is treated as a subject and not an object of treatment, so he or she has to be guaranteed active participation regarding treatment and must provide his or her approval. A patient can thus also reject treatment.

411. The right to voluntary treatment is based on the principle of respecting an individual's free will. The latter, however, cannot be invoked in some cases of psychological disorders, due to their nature. Rejecting treatment can also be the result of a mental illness and not a conscious or rational decision by the patient.

412. Also relevant for this area is Article 15 of the Constitution, which states that human rights and fundamental freedoms can only be limited by the rights of others and in cases provided by the Constitution. Exercising constitutional rights must not violate the constitutional rights of others. A mental patient can pose a risk to the lives of others or cause them grievous harm, which can serve as reasonable basis for involuntary commitment. But the latter is only allowed when such restriction forms the only effective way to guarantee the protection of the rights of others.

413. Also relevant for involuntarily hospitalized individuals is a provision in Article 18 of the Constitution, which states that nobody can be subjected to torture, inhumane or degrading punishment or treatment. Conducting medical or other scientific experiments on any individual without his or her free consent is also prohibited.

414. Two other provisions of the Constitution are also important – the one on personal freedom (Article 19 paragraph 3) and freedom of movement (Article 32); both can be affected in case of involuntary commitment, and violations of these rights must in all cases be based on legislation.

---

191. *See* U. Dižovnik, *Pravna ureditev neprostovoljne hospitalizacije v psihiatrični bolnišnici* (*Legal Regulations on Involuntary Hospitalization in a Psychiatric Institution*) 3 (Pravna fakulteta, Univerza v Ljubljani 2011).

415. In June 2015 Slovenian Constitutional Court decided[192] that the third sentence of second paragraph and third sentence of third paragraph of Article 74 of Mental Health Act are unconstitutional. Because of that the mentioned provisions have been repealed (in a period of one year after the decision was published in OG RS).[193] The Constitutional Court namely held that an arrangement which, in cases where a person admitted to a protected ward of a social welfare institution is without disposing capacity, allows his or her legal representative to decide in patient's name without the possibility of a judicial review of the decision to be accepted in this kind of institution, is unconstitutional. The Act regarded this kind of admissions as equal to the admissions upon patient's free and informed consent, which was inaccurate.

416. In July 2019 Constitutional Court decided[194] that the (whole) Mental Health Act is unconstitutional. It ordered the National Assembly of the Republic of Slovenia to eliminate the established unconstitutionality within nine months of the publication of this decision in the Official Gazette.[195] The deadline expired in April 2020, but the new law has not yet been adopted, so the established unconstitutionality has not yet been eliminated.[196] Until then the Mental Health Act, as presented below, remains in force in Slovenia.

417. As part of the review of the constitutionality of the Mental Health Act, the Constitutional Court first had to answer the question whether the existing statutory regulation of admission of persons with mental disorders to the protected ward of a social welfare institution is in accordance with the guarantees from the second paragraph of Article 19 of the Constitution. It ensures that no one shall be deprived of his or her liberty save in the cases and according to the procedure prescribed by law.

418. The Constitutional Court emphasized that in the case of legal regulation of a measure which constitutes an interference with a person's right to personal liberty due to his or her mental disorder, it is not sufficient for the legislator to concretize the execution of the measure only by referring to the aim of the protection. The legislator should also strive to achieve the therapeutic goal of the measure. Already at the legislative level, the conditions for the execution of a measure must be determined in such a way that a factual connection is established between the basis or reason for allowing the deprivation of liberty and the place (institution) and conditions of detention. Determining the conditions for the execution of a measure that has the aim of achieving both, a protective and a therapeutic objective, ensures that the duration of the measure is limited to the time necessary to improve the condition of the detainee to the extent that he or she is able to live independently again,

192. *See* the decision of the Constitutional Court of Slovenia, No. U-I-294/12-20, https://www.uradni-list.si, 2 Dec. 2020.
193. It was published on 26 Jun. 2015.
194. *See* the decision of the Constitutional Court of Slovenia, No. U-I-477/18-19, https://www.uradni-list.si, 2 Dec. 2020.
195. It was published on 5 Jul. 2015.
196. The proposition of a new Act on Mental Health is currently in governmental procedure. *See* https://e-uprava.gov.si, 2 Jan. 2021.

or to prevent the deterioration of her health. Legislative regulation which does not meet the stated requirements regarding the determination of the basis and conditions for the execution of a measure is inconsistent with the second paragraph of Article 19 of the Constitution.

419. The Constitutional Court assessed also the conformity of the statutory regulation from the point of view of the first paragraph of Article 19 of the Constitution. It states that every person has a right to personal liberty. Constitutional judges derived their decision from the constitutional requirement that the court is the only one with the right to order more than just an immediate deprivation of liberty. Pursuant to this requirement, the legislator left the decision on the constitutional admissibility of the measure of admitting a person to a protected ward of a social welfare institution without consent to the court. The law also obliges the courts to determine the specific social welfare institution that will implement the measure. However, as the Constitutional Court pointed out, the constitutional requirement that a court must decide on the admissibility of a measure loses its meaning if the law excludes the court from ruling on the admissibility of ordering a measure in each individual case by deriving from the requirements of the principle of proportionality. The assessed legal regulation namely enables the court to consider only the necessity of the measure regarding the part of the aim of protection which can be achieved by excluding the person from his or her environment outside. However, it excludes the possibility for the court to assess the suitability of the chosen institution from the point of view of ensuring safety and achieving the therapeutic goal of the measure. In the opinion of the Constitutional Court, the regulation that does not enable the court's assessment on mentioned questions is not appropriate and as such does not lead to achievement of a constitutionally permissible goal of this kind of special measures. Therefore it was pronounced as inconsistent with the right from the first paragraph of Article 19 of the Constitution.

420. Finally, the Constitutional Court assessed the conformity of the legal regulation from the perspective of the right of detained persons to the protection of personal dignity during deprivation of liberty (the first paragraph of Article 21 of the Constitution). It found that the legislation, which disregards the requirement for a clear and definite definition of such conditions of detention and excludes the possibility of a court's assessment of the suitability of the specific institution in which the measure is to be carried out, is also contrary to the Constitution.

III. Legislation

A. *Patients' Rights Act*

421. The Patients' Rights Act determines the rights (as well as obligations) of all patients, including mental patients, in its more general way. But it refers to a more special law, the Mental Health Act provisions.

422. The Patients' Rights Act specifically deals with patients with mental health problems in Article 37, where it states that if a patient, due to mental health or other issues affecting the ability to reason, is not able to agree to a medical procedure, the procedure can only be performed if a legal representative permits it. If such a patient does not have a legal representative, the performer of healthcare services must notify the competent body to start the procedure for appointing a legal representative. Should a doctor ascertain that the legal representative does not act in the benefit of the patient, the doctor must notify the body which appointed the legal representative. The latter must immediately make sure that appropriate representation is provided.

423. The Act also provides for a solution for the time when such patient does not yet have a legal representative. In such cases, individuals capable of self-determination who have reached 18 years of age can express consent for undertaking a medical procedure for such a patient. The exclusive order of approval is:

- patient's spouse, partner or same-sex partner;
- patient's children or adopted children;
- patient's parents or adoptive parents;
- patient's brothers or sisters;
- patient's grandparents; and
- patient's grandchildren.

In case that the above-stated individuals do not reach agreement on carrying out the medical procedure, the decision is taken by the treating doctor. In the decision, the doctor considers the stated opinions and the patient's maximum health benefits. It is also important that the appointed legal representative of a patient with a mental disease as well as any of the above-stated next of kin cannot reject emergency medical treatment that the patient might need.

B. Mental Health Act

1. The Procedure of Involuntary Detention of the Patient in Psychiatric Hospital

424. Involuntary hospitalization is a procedure which is decided by the competent court in non-litigious proceedings. This is a procedure for acceptance to the treatment in the psychiatric hospital into its department under special surveillance without consent of a patient – based on a court decision or the special procedure of involuntary acceptance, but only in emergency cases. Involuntary treatment is permitted in mentioned two cases only if the following conditions are met (Article 39 of the Mental Health Act):

- The patient poses a risk to his or her own health and the health of others or causes major damage to his or her assets or assets of others.

- The above-stated risks are caused by a mental disorder, due to which an individual has severely disrupted notions of reality and the ability to control his or her actions.
- The above-stated reasons or risks cannot be averted through other forms of help – for example, treatment outside of a department with special surveillance, outpatient or supervised treatment.

425. All procedures before the court require patient representation by a representative who is an attorney. For a minor or a person of age who was relieved of disposing capacity, his or her legal representative must authorize the attorney. But another procedure applies when a procedure was instituted on his or her proposal. In such a case, a representative is appointed by court.

426. Under court procedure, all participants have the ability to state their views regarding the statements of other participants or to take part in the procedure. A person without disposing capacity but capable of understanding the importance and legal consequence of actions is empowered by the court to manage the proceedings. The court also undertakes a personal hearing except in cases when it decides, after seeing the patient, that this is impossible due to the patient's mental health condition.

Such court procedures are urgent (fast) in nature and the public is excluded. All persons, who take part in the procedure in any way, are bound to keep all information revealed in the procedure secret.

a. Acceptance to Treatment Without Consent of a Patient, Based on a Court Decision

427. The procedure is initiated upon the proposal of the performer of psychiatric treatment, a Centre for Social Work, a supervised treatment coordinator, the patient's next of kin or the state prosecutor as well as a legal representative (for a minor or a person of age who has lost disposing capacity). The proposal is filed with the competent court (in the area where the patient has a permanent or temporary residence or where he or she de facto resides) and must contain the reasons that establish the conditions for involuntary treatment (as described above). The proposal must also include the opinion of a personal doctor or psychiatrist, which must not be older than seven days. If an examination is impossible, a statement about that is provided.

428. The court sends the proposal to the patient within one day of receiving it and instructs him or her that he or she can respond to it within two days of receiving it. The court also instructs the patient that he or she has the right to choose an attorney, otherwise one shall be provided by court.

429. After receiving the proposal described above, the court also orders the patient to be examined. The examination is carried out by a court expert psychiatrist. The psychiatrist must submit expert opinion on the patient's health condition within three days, which must also include an assessment whether it would be possible to use supervised treatment or treatment in a secure ward.

430. The patient can be examined by the doctor against his or her will. The court can, based on expert opinion, decide that the patient be kept in a psychiatric institution for a maximum of two days if such treatment is required due to the nature of the mental disorder or because the patient does not want to submit to an examination. An additional condition is that the psychiatric expert cannot provide an opinion regarding involuntary treatment in a department under special surveillance without the patient being sent for a two-day stay in a psychiatric institution. The patient must be told about the reasons for being committed and his or her rights in an understandable manner. An appeal to such a decision is allowed (within one day of receiving it), and a Court of Second Instance must decide on it within three days. If it is ascertained during retainment that conditions for involuntary treatment in emergency cases are fulfilled, the patient is admitted for treatment.

431. After receiving the expert opinion, the court orders a hearing, at which it takes the decision after meeting the individual in person. The hearing is also used to hear the expert and all others who could provide relevant information for the decision. After the evidence hearing procedure, if the legally required conditions are met, the court decides on sending the individual to involuntary treatment to the department under special surveillance. In its decision the court also determines the period of detention, which must not exceed six months and the name of the institution. If the court ascertains that conditions exist for acceptance of the individual to a secure ward of a social care institution, it issues a decision that the individual be retained there and determines the time of stay, which must not exceed one year. Should the court ascertain that conditions exist for so-called supervised treatment, it also defines the duration of the treatment, which must not exceed six months. If the court ascertains that conditions for any of the above-stated measures are not met, it issues a decision rejecting the proposal. The decision in which the court orders the individual to be detained must be issued within three days after the end of the hearing.

432. An appeal to court decision is allowed, but it does not hold back its execution. The appeal is decided by a Court of Second Instance. This court's decision can be contested also by extraordinary legal means, i.e., a revision.

433. Based on the decision on admission, a psychiatric institution calls the patient to arrive there. The outcome of the mentioned call is explained to the court and patient's attorney. If the patient does not arrive at the institution and does not provide a valid excuse for not doing so, the psychiatric institution's director notifies the court, patient's personal doctor and attorney and orders that the patient be taken there in an ambulance. The director can ask for police assistance in organizing such transport. If the court decision cannot be carried out in such a manner, the psychiatric hospital's director again notifies the court. The court can order forced bringing if it ascertains that the call to the patient for admittance to the department under special surveillance was delivered correctly.

b. Acceptance to Involuntary Treatment in Emergency Cases

434. These are the cases when the nature of an individual's mental disorder requires that his or her freedom of movement is restricted or that his or her interaction with the surroundings is prevented prior to carrying out the above-described procedure. Even in such cases, the conditions from the above-stated Article 39 of the Mental Health Act must be fulfilled in order for such an involuntary treatment to be carried out.

435. The individual is admitted to treatment on the basis of a referral by a personal doctor, psychiatrist or other doctor who examined the individual and discovered that grounds do exist. The referral (must not be older than three days) has to be accompanied by a report on the health condition of the individual which must clearly state that retention is necessary. The patient can also be committed without a referral if police officers, upon detaining an individual in a public place, private place or upon discovering a foreign national who is sought after or has had an arrest warrant issued, presume that conditions for admission to involuntary treatment are met. The police must immediately notify the emergency medical aid services of that.

436. The physician examines such an individual upon admission. If he or she believes that legislative conditions are met, he or she orders the individual to be taken to the nearest psychiatric hospital in an ambulance. If required, the doctor can also restrain the individual until the ambulance arrives. The doctor or another healthcare professional appointed by the doctor must be present in the ambulance. The doctor can also request police assistance during the transport. The police are required to cooperate and offer assistance until the risks, posed by the individual, can be mitigated through adequate health measures.

437. Upon arrival at the psychiatric hospital, the individual is examined by the receiving psychiatrist, who ascertains whether conditions for retaining him or her exist. The doctor must primarily ascertain whether the given case expressly requires that the individual's freedom of movement is restrained or that his or her interactions with the surroundings are prevented before the above-described court procedure is carried out. If the doctor ascertains that such conditions do not exist, he or she refuses to accept the individual. If such conditions do exist, the individual is admitted for treatment and informed of the reasons for being retained and on his or her right to an attorney. Within four hours from receiving the individual, the doctor must notify the individual's next of kin or his or her representative of the fact. The doctor must also notify the institution's director within the same time period, whereupon the director must immediately notify the competent court.

438. The decision on acceptance to involuntary treatment in emergency cases is under the jurisdiction of the court which is located in the same area as the institution. In such a case, the court procedure begins ex officio and immediately after receiving the notice by the institution's director or if learning about such an action in any other way. The court institutes the proceedings, determines an expert and the patient's attorney and at the same time informs the patient that he or she can change the appointed attorney.

439. The judge within one day from issuing a decision on instituting proceedings personally visits the patient and interrogates him or her in the presence of attorney, expert and representative, except if the latter is not possible due to the patient's health condition. The judge explains the reasons for instituting the proceedings and calls upon the patient to state his or her position on the restraining. If the patient agrees with the restraining and confirms it in writing, the court stops the procedure with a decision. The expert examines the patient and issues an opinion on his or her health condition and on whether a milder form of treatment is possible (supervised treatment or treatment in a secure ward). The judge must also interrogate other persons who could provide insightful statements on circumstances important for the decision.

440. The court can pass a special measure, a temporary decision, in which it states that the patient remains under observation at the ward for two days at the most from the issuance of such a decision if this is necessary to determine whether conditions exist for admitting the patient to the department with special surveillance.

441. Within three days after the judge's visit, the court must issue a decision in which it determines whether the individual shall continue to be committed at the department with special surveillance, be released, be transferred to a secure ward of a social security centre or sent to supervised treatment. This decision can also be appealed against at the Court of the Second Instance. This court's decision can also be contested by a revision (an extraordinary legal measure).

2. Extending the Detention, Release and Transfer from the Department with Special Surveillance

442. If the psychiatric institution's director discovers that follow-up treatment is absolutely necessary to avert risks, he or she proposes to the judge to extend the admission. The extension can last for six months at the most per extension. In case the health condition of the committed individual improves and the grounds for retainment disappear, the institution releases the patient and notifies the court about that. The release procedure can also be instituted by the court ex officio. The patient, his or her next of kin, legal representative or lawyer can propose the patient to be released prior to the termination of the due time as set by the court. If the court rejects such a proposal it can set a due date before which another release proposal can be filed. The court can only decide in such a way when the patient's health condition is such that no improvement is expected before the end of the retainment. This due date cannot exceed one month.

3. Rights of Patient in the Department under Special Surveillance

443. The Mental Health Act guarantees the following to all patients admitted to the department under special surveillance:

- the right to mail and e-mail;
- the right to send and receive packages;
- the right to receive visitors;
- the right to use a phone;
- the right to movement; and
- the right to a representative.

The above-stated rights, apart from the right to a representative, can be restricted if necessary – i.e., when the individual poses a threat to himself or herself or others.

444. The patient's representative informs him or her about his or her rights, the manner of their execution, provides tangible guidance and counselling, strives to protect patient rights and checks whether correct records are kept for the patient. The representative can be anyone with at least a high education, passed exam for a representative, five years of work experience in mental health and has not been finally sentenced to an unconditional prison sentence. The patient selects the representative by himself or herself from the list of the representatives. In case of minors or persons of age without disposing capacity, the representative is selected by the legal representative.

4. Special Safety Measures

445. The Mental Health Act uses two special safety measures: restriction of body movement with belts and confinement to one space. These are emergency measures which are used when it is necessary to control a patient's behaviour which poses a threat to his or her life or health or life and health of others or in cases of causing major damage to assets. An important precondition for implementing these safety measures is that such behaviour cannot be prevented with a milder measure. The measures can only be used in exceptional cases and can only last for the amount of time that is necessary. Body restriction with the belt must not last for more than four hours while confinement in a single space cannot exceed twelve hours.

A special security measure is ordered by a doctor who must inform of that to the psychiatric institution's director, the patient's next of kin, his or her attorney and representative in writing, in twelve hours at the latest.

446. The amendment to the Patients' Rights Act in 2017[197] brought also a general regulation on this issue, as it has been noted for a long time that the occasional use of belts is necessary (and practised) also in other healthcare institutions.[198] Since the Mental Health Act regulates these measures only for the field of treatment of mentally ill persons (persons with mental disorders) in psychiatric institutions, the use of these measures outside mentioned limits was illegal.[199]

197. *See* OG RS, No. 55/2017.
198. *See* https://www.zbornica-zveza.si, 6 Jan. 2021.
199. For details, *see* the Art. 31a of Patients' Rights Act.

5. Other Ways to Treat Psychiatric Patients

447. The Mental Health Act introduced some new ways for treating psychiatric patients, especially the so-called supervised treatment and treatment in the community. In the first case, individuals with a severe and recurring mental disorder are treated on the basis of a court decision and under the supervision of a psychiatric institution in the patient's locality. Treatment in the community meanwhile provides help to an individual who no longer requires treatment in a psychiatric institution or supervised treatment, but still requires help in psychosocial rehabilitation, everyday tasks, maintaining living conditions and inclusion into society.

§4. The Dying Patient

I. Euthanasia

A. *General*

448. Euthanasia or 'eu thanatos' (Greek for a good and easy death) is today mainly defined as induced and accelerated death of a terminally ill patient. It is also called 'mercy killing'.

449. Euthanasia is prohibited in Slovenia by the Slovenian Constitution, legislation and by the Slovenian Code of Medical Ethic. The Code explicitly states that a physician should reject euthanasia or physician-assisted suicide. Another negative opinion towards euthanasia was published by the National Medical Ethics Committee in 2018.[200] The above-stated clearly shows that euthanasia in Slovenia is (legally) inadmissible and not admired in practice.[201] However, numerous authors believe that this topic should be debated in a wider social context in the country and not only point out the negative but also list possible positive consequences of euthanasia.[202]

B. *Constitution of the Republic of Slovenia*

450. The Constitution of the Republic of Slovenia indirectly prohibits euthanasia as it states in Article 17 that human life is inviolable. An individual is not given a constitutionally guaranteed right to death. Based on the individual's right to autonomy and capability for self-determination, he or she only has the following

200. The Position of the National Medical Ethics Committee Regarding Treatment of the Dying and Euthanasia, 11 Dec. 2018, http://www.kme-nmec.si, 2 Jan. 2021.
201. *See also* Š. Šifrer, *Evtanazija* (*Euthanasia*) 55–59 (Pravna fakulteta, Univerza v Ljubljani 2011).
202. *See* V. Žnidaršič Skubic, *Civilno medicinsko pravo s poudarkom na vprašanjih, ki zadevajo zaključek življenja* (*Civil Medical Law with an Emphasis on End-of-Life Issue*), in *Razmišljanja o vprašanjih ob izteku življenja* (*Reflections on Issues at the End of Life*) Zbornik referatov in razprav, No. 1/2018, Državni svet RS 29–42 (2018).

rights: the right to reject medical treatment, the right to turn off life support machines and the right to alleviate pain (palliative care). The latter can also be carried out with means that accelerate the individual's death. But the individual has no right to request from another person to intentionally advance his or her death. The direct purpose of the person who takes part in accelerating another's death therefore must never be to kill that person. Such a case would be regarded as murder.

C. Criminal Code

451. The Criminal Code does not use the term 'euthanasia' as the Slovenian Criminal Law system does not recognize a specific privileged form of murder following a request by the deceased. The punishability of euthanasia is thus derived by logical analysis of the structure of the abstract legal norm, itself based on an ethical norm. Because human life is, in accordance with the Constitutional provision, inviolable, we can speak about an inference of a disposition which encompasses the fundamental moral values of the modern society. Anyone, not only a doctor, can commit the criminal act of murder. All forms of participation as well as attempted and futile attempts are punishable. Theoreticians, however, criticize the lack of existence of a milder form of murder, which has existed before (in the former Criminal Code)[203] – mercy killing, killing upon the request of the victim and the like, which also included euthanasia.[204]

452. Soliciting and assisting a suicide is also a criminal act in Slovenia. Whoever intentionally appeals to another person to kill himself or herself or assists him or her in doing so, with the end result being that that person commits suicide, shall be sentenced to between six months and five years in prison. But should whoever under particularly mitigating circumstances assist another person in committing suicide and if that person indeed commits suicide, he or she can be sentenced to not more than three years in prison. If the suicide has only been attempted through the above-stated actions, the court may reduce the punishment of the perpetrator. Because doctors are mainly guided by the 'desire to show mercy' in assisting suicides, such attempts by them will usually be classified as milder forms of assistance in killing, meaning a lower sentence.

453. Voluntary euthanasia is based on the patient's consent to it. However, in Slovenia, the consent of the patient does not legitimize the doctor's actions. It would still fall under the criminal act of manslaughter, in accordance with the first paragraph of Article 115 of the Criminal Code. The situation is different in cases when it comes to the question of respecting the patient's refusal of medical help with a potential or actual fatal outcome. The Patients' Rights Act regulates the right to refuse medical care in Articles 30 and 31. With such a regulation (as presented

203. OG RS, Nos 95/2004 – UPB1, 37/2005, 17/2006, 55/2008, 66/2008, 5/2009.
204. Š. Šifrer, *Evtanazija* (*Euthanasia*) 58 (Pravna fakulteta, Univerza v Ljubljani 2011).

above, under the title of 'Patient Rights') we tried to decline a very solid paternalism also on a field of Criminal Law.[205] However, it soon became apparent that this has not happened as the doctors were still in danger of criminal prosecution while obeying patients' will not to receive treatment if it resulted in their death. That is mainly why in 2012, by change of Criminal Code,[206] the new provision of paragraph 2 of Article 178 of Criminal Code was accepted. The new provision stipulates that if a doctor discontinues treatment at the express written request of a patient (or other person capable of deciding for himself or herself) where he or she refuses assistance even after being instructed on the urgency of the assistance and the possible consequences of refusal, and in the case where the doctor tried again to persuade a patient to change his or her mind, the doctor has not proceeded illegally. However, this regulation does not change the pre-existing principle, that is, that in cases where the doctor had helped the patient nonetheless, he or she would not have performed the crime of coercion.[207]

D. Patients' Rights Act

454. The Patients' Rights Act does not specifically and explicitly mention or deal with euthanasia. However, it does include several provisions that touch on an individual's decisions on ending his or her life. Apart from the right to be informed, cooperate in as well as make independent decisions regarding treatment, the right to comply with previously expressed wishes, the right to refuse treatment and the right to alleviate and prevent suffering must also be stressed. The first four rights were presented in more detail in the general overview of patient's rights, which is why I shall only focus here on the last of the four.

1. Right to Alleviate and Prevent Suffering

455. This right is written down in Article 39 of the Patients' Rights Act. The patient has the right that everything necessary to eliminate or maximally alleviate the pain and other suffering, connected to his or her disease, is done without hesitation. It is also necessary to ensure that treatment of the patient uses professional standards in order to prevent unnecessary pain and other suffering, connected to the medical procedure. Every patient also has the right to suitable palliative care in the final stages of his or her disease or in case of an untreatable disease that causes severe suffering.

---

205. *See* D. Korošec, *Razmišljanje o koncu življenja – kazenskopravni vidik* (*Thinking about the End of Life – The Criminal Law Aspect*), Zbornik referatov in razprav, No. 1/2018, Državni svet RS 13–28 (2018).
206. *See* KZ-1B, OG RS, No. 91/2011.
207. *See* Art. 132 of Criminal Code.

The doctor is therefore obliged to prevent and alleviate physical and psychological pain of a patient that is caused by his or her disease. In cases when curative treatment is no longer efficient or worthwhile, the doctor is required to employ palliative care to achieve the highest possible quality of life for the patient.

Chapter 3. Specific Activities

§1. Reproductive Medicine: General

456. In Slovenia, the freedom of decision on childbirth is guaranteed by the Constitution (Article 55). With this important fundamental freedom, the Constitution enables people (women of childbearing age and men) to exercise their will concerning the questions of whether, when and how many children they will have. Although it is a fundamental human freedom (and not a right), there are, according to the interpretation of the Constitutional Commission, some rights that derive from it – such as:

- the right to diagnose and treat subfertility or infertility;
- the right to prevent pregnancy (birth control and sterilization); and
- for women, the right to terminate pregnancy (the right to abortion).[208]

Access to medical and other means of exercising these rights is guaranteed by the state.[209]

§2. Right to Prevent Pregnancy (Right to Birth Control and Sterilization)

457. The subject of the legislation is not just artificial pregnancy termination but all methods and means to manage fertility known to modern medicine. The Health Measures in Exercising Freedom of Choice in Childbearing Act states regarding birth control that each individual, male or female, has the right to advise on how to prevent pregnancy. Every individual thus has the right to be prescribed the most suitable means of birth control by his or her physician. The type of birth control, when and in what way should it be prescribed is a professional-medical question. Two options exist regarding birth control: temporary (employing various contemporary means) and permanent (sterilization).

I. Minor Female and Temporary Birth Control

458. The right to temporary birth control is a right given to a minor female of sound mind. She can exercise it independently. This means that she does not need parental or guardian representation, approval or cooperation in exercising this right. However, this is only valid if a physician adequately ascertains that the minor

208. *See* K. Zupančič & V. Žnidaršič, *Dva vidika svobode odločanja o rojstvih otrok* (*Two Aspects of Freedom Regarding Childbirth*), in: *Pravo in medicina* 195–249 (A. Polajnar-Pavčnik&, D. Wedam-Lukičeds. Cankarjeva založba 1998).
209. *See* the draft of the Constitution of the Republic of Slovenia (appendix), the interpretation of Art. 55 of the Constitution, by the Constitutional Commission, Poročevalec Skupščine RS, 1/91, 17 Jan. 1992, 23.

patient is of sound mind, meaning she possesses the required ratio and will to make her choice. In such a way, the physician can ascertain whether the temporary birth control means or procedure is the minor female's free choice.

459. In such a case, the minor is regarded as capable of consenting to the procedure and also that she is aware of the consequences of her decision. The latter is not only connected to her ability to understand the consequences and express her own will, but also with the physician's obligation to explain. The physician must, the same as for persons of legal age of sound mind, explain the health condition to minor female and the probable consequences for her health condition upon receiving a medication or undergoing a medical procedure. The physician has to tell her about the manner of execution, the probability of success and outcomes of taking specific birth control means, as well as about potential risks and side effects, negative and/or unpleasant consequences of the planned medical procedure or usage of birth control means. This obligation to explain binds the physician pursuant to Article 20 of the Patients' Rights Act. While explaining the above-stated circumstances, the physician must be delicate, provide the explanation while in direct contact with the patient, in full and on time. When dealing with minor individuals, the physician must also be extra cautious to provide the explanation in an understandable manner and in accordance with the patient's ability to process information. Extra diligence when dealing with children is also enshrined in the Constitution, which guarantees special protection and care for children and their benefits (Article 56). Children, as a specific group of patients, who are provided special protection and care, are also mentioned in the Patients' Rights Act (Article 3, paragraph 3(3) and Article 8).

II. Sterilization

460. Sterilization is carried out on the request of the individual on whom it is to be performed. An individual must be at least 35 years old and of sound mind. However, sterilization can be carried out even if the last two criteria are not met due to health reasons.

461. For a person who is not of a sound mind, sterilization is requested by the parents or a guardian with an obligatory consent by the Centre for Social Work. A minor person who is of sound mind can request to be sterilized by himself or herself; however, the commission that decides on the question must acquire the opinion of the parents or the guardian. The latter is not necessary if the minor already acquired disposing capacity.

462. The sterilization request is filed with the First Level Commission for Artificial Pregnancy Termination. The Commission decides on the request after acquainting the person requesting it with the consequences of such a procedure. If the First Level Commission rejects the request, the individual can request the Second Level Commission to make a decision.

463. Sterilization can only be carried out after a certain period of time has passed since it was approved. The six-month period is mainly meant to give the individual the time to thoroughly think through and consider his or her decision to go ahead with this form of birth control. The six-month period is not used in cases when sterilization is required for health reasons.

§3. ABORTION

I. General

464. Decision on abortion in Slovenia is a constitutional right of a pregnant woman who does not wish to give birth (Article 55 of the Constitution – Freedom of Choice in Childbearing). Legislation gives her the right to abortion, even though such a procedure is (medically and socially) an undesired measure of birth control. Artificial pregnancy termination is always the last resort, as stressed by all documents dealing with family planning. The right to abortion can also be problematic from the standpoint of a woman and her true freedom in making decisions. This is because a pregnant woman is deciding between two unpleasant outcomes: violent pregnancy termination and birth of an unwanted child. Despite that, abortion must be included among the means for regulating childbirth, as it is the only way to prevent giving birth after conceiving. Prevention should be prioritized at all times, especially through the use of modern and reliable birth control means. Research has shown that the number of performed abortions is inversely related to the use of modern birth control means.

II. Legislation

A. General

465. Abortion or artificial pregnancy termination is regulated in the Republic of Slovenia by the Health Measures in Exercising Freedom of Choice in Childbearing Act. The Act invoked a so-called combined solution. In accordance with this solution, artificial pregnancy termination is a medical procedure, carried out on the request of the pregnant woman if the pregnancy has lasted for fewer than ten weeks. Slovenian law sets no other criteria in such a case. Should the pregnancy last more than ten weeks, abortion can only be carried out at the request of the pregnant woman if the dangers from the procedure for her health and future pregnancies are outweighed by the dangers to the pregnant woman and the child in case of continuing pregnancy and birth. Psychological traumas, potentially suffered by the future mother, are also considered here. This, the so-called late abortion, is decided upon by the First and Second Level Commission for Artificial Pregnancy Termination. The decision-making procedure must, understandably, be quick. The First Level Commission for Artificial Pregnancy Termination is composed of a social worker and two physicians (one of the two who also serves as the chairman must be a specialized gynaecologist – obstetrician). The Second Level Commission for Artificial

Pregnancy Termination (the Complaints Commission) meanwhile consists of a social worker and three physicians. The legislation states that all Commission members must have appointed deputies, so that all cases can be solved in a fast and timely manner in practice. After twenty weeks, medical professionals reject pregnancy termination, unless such a procedure is required to protect the life and health of the pregnant woman.[210]

466. The legislation presented above was passed, because the lawmaker was of the opinion that a system of so-called indications for abortion ran contrary to the constitutional principle that abortion is a right of the woman, which can only be restricted due to health reasons.

B. Minor Pregnant or Pregnant Woman Without Sound Mind

467. The procedure for artificial pregnancy termination begins upon request by the pregnant woman. The right to terminate pregnancy can only be exercised by her if she is of sound mind. This means that for the mentioned decision, she must have the needed intellect and will.

468. Artificial pregnancy termination for a pregnant woman who is not of a sound mind is requested by her parents or guardian. But this does not give them the right to replace her will. The decision for abortion is a strictly personal one, meaning that no representation is possible. Despite that the legislation allows the parents (the guardian) to request pregnancy termination for their daughter or protégée who is not of sound mind. In such a way, they do not replace her will, but merely execute their duty to take care of the health and life of their daughter or protégée.

469. In case a minor pregnant female requests artificial pregnancy termination, the healthcare organization, which carries out such procedures, usually notifies the parents or guardian of that request, unless the girl acquired full disposing capacity before becoming of age. This happens when a minor female entered into marriage (after waiving the minor reservation) or has acquired full disposing capacity because she became a mother. Both questions are decided by a court in a non-litigious procedure (Articles 71 and 76 of the Non-Contentious Civil Procedure Act).

470. Pursuant to a direct legislative provision, the request for artificial pregnancy termination also includes approval for the procedure in accordance with healthcare regulations. This applies both in cases when a minor pregnant female of sound mind requests artificial pregnancy termination or if such termination is requested by an adult, of age pregnant woman who was taken away the disposing capacity but is of sound mind.

210. *See* K. Zupančič, *Pravna ureditev prekinitve nosečnosti* (*Legal Regulations Regarding Pregnancy Termination*), in *Pravo in medicina* 202 (A. Polajnar-Pavčnik & D. Wedam Lukić eds., Cankarjeva založba 1998).

471. The main implementing regulation act in the area, passed with the aim to facilitate the execution of the Health Measures in Exercising Freedom of Choice in Childbearing Act, in practice is the Instructions to Execute the Health Measures in Exercising Freedom of Choice in Childbearing Act.[211] Article 7, paragraph 3, of these instructions states that a minor pregnant female is treated with special care with consideration of her family and social circumstances. Such treatment considers and respects her personal decision, both regarding pregnancy termination and notifying the parents.

472. Apart from the Health Measures in Exercising Freedom of Choice in Childbearing Act, which is the fundamental legal resource in this area, the Patients' Rights Act is also used as a legal source in case of minor pregnant females or (adult) pregnant women who are not of a sound mind. The provisions that will mainly be used are the more general ones which deal with the status of children as patients or recipients of healthcare services. I would mainly like to stress Article 3, paragraph 1(1) of the Patients' Rights Act, which states that the principle of maximum health benefits for the patients, especially children, must be considered while exercising the patient rights pursuant to this Act. Article 8, paragraph 1, of this Act also explicitly states that children (and other groups at risk) are provided special rights in healthcare, apart from the rights pursuant to this Act. These rights are under active supervision of the state and are set in other regulations. Another important provision can be found in Article 8, paragraph 3, of the Patients' Rights Act, which states that child healthcare must be suitable to their age and their health condition.

473. Article 35 of the Patients' Rights Act specifically determines the status of children as patients. Pursuant to this article, children are defined as individuals who have not yet turned 18 years of age, except if they have already achieved full disposing capacity. This is due to the fact that it has been determined through proper procedures that such persons have reached physical and psychological maturity and are capable of independent life. This voids the special protection guaranteed for children as such a person is not considered a child anymore.[212]

474. The general legislation (in accordance with the Patients' Rights Act) surmises that a child is not capable of consenting to a medical procedure until the age of 15 years. This assumption can be challenged: a physician can, based on the child's maturity, state on a case-by-case basis that the child is capable of such consent. A child who has reached 15 years is in principle able to give consent, but this assumption can also be challenged, as a physician can assess that this is not the case after examining the child's level of maturity. We have to stress, however, that these rules do not apply to the freedom regarding child bearing. This constitutional freedom, which is the origin of the right to prevent pregnancy and artificial pregnancy termination, is regulated by a specific law, i.e., the Health Measures in Exercising Freedom of Choice in Childbearing Act. This is the decisive piece of legislation in the area and holds precedence over the more general (and more recent) Patients'

211. OG SRS, Nos 15/1977 and 1/1980.
212. *See* K. Zupančič, *Družinsko pravo* (*Family Law*) 157 (Uradni list RS 1999).

Rights Act. This Act is therefore *lex specialis*, which is why we have to act in compliance with its provisions and the provisions of its final implementing regulations in dealing with artificial pregnancy termination and the right to birth control.

475. According to Slovenian legislation, a minor female of sound mind can independently and without parental/guardian/anybody else's cooperation or assent request an abortion for herself. She can also do that if she has been relieved of disposing capacity, if the latter was not done because she has impaired judgment. In accordance with Slovenian law, parents cannot request that abortion be carried on their minor daughter of sound mind. They also cannot prevent pregnancy termination if she wishes to carry it out.

476. The right to terminate pregnancy can thus be exercised by a pregnant woman if she is of sound mind. This means that she must have the judgment and will to follow through. This is ascertained by a physician on a case-by-case basis after a discussion with the patient while carrying out his or her duty to explain. Such regulations were accepted into Slovenian law mainly because artificial termination of pregnancy is one of the most personal decisions an individual can make. This decision, which results in a major medical intervention into the girl's most personal good, her body, should therefore be taken by the girl herself. Freedom of choice in childbearing, as a constitutional right, as a principle belongs to an individual when he or she can begin to exercise it or has already begun to exercise it (in case of a minor pregnant female who wants an abortion or birth control). Parents cannot represent the child at the legal transactions or expressions of will where the child's own decision is required, and this decision definitely belongs to that category. A child must be free in making such decisions. The freedom of decision-making would be negated if the child's will would be replaced by the will of the parents as her legal representatives. Representation and freedom in decision-making are diametrically opposite. Slovenian legislation therefore does not require full disposing capacity to state explicitly personal decisions. And if a child has full disposing capacity regardless of being underage, parental representation is not required anyways.

§4. Assisted Reproduction

477. The right to infertility treatment is prescribed in the Infertility Treatment and Procedures of Biomedically-assisted Procreation Act of 2000.

I. Medical Treatment and Procedures of BMAP

478. The Act deals, as can be seen from its title, with two basic problems: medical treatment of sub and infertility and the special medical procedures which help a person to conceive a child – the procedures of BMAP.

Medical treatment is defined, but not widely regulated, because it is not a legal problem. It is a question to be solved by medical science and the medical profession. In brief, treatment includes establishing the causes for sub and infertility and the removal of those causes through professional counselling, medical and surgical intervention. In the law, there is also a special sub-definition of medical treatment. That is the possibility of depositing one's gametes for possible personal use in the future if there is a serious risk that the concerned person will soon become infertile.

479. The law includes regulation on various techniques of BMAP, but it also stresses two basic principles: (1) the procedures of BMAP are all procedures of fertilizing women with help of biomedical science in a way that is different to natural conception (conception through sexual intercourse); (2) the enumeration of the techniques of BMAP[213] is not exhaustive – in this way the law leaves the door wide open for the use of new techniques that the future development of biomedicine may bring and evaluate as appropriate.

II. Artificial Procreation Should Imitate Nature

480. The writers of the Act were guided by two basic principles. The first was formulated by John Robertson, for American law, with the sentence: 'Freedom to have sex without reproduction does not guarantee freedom to have reproduction without sex.'[214] A similar opinion can be found in the commentaries to Article 8 of the European Convention on Human Rights, which among others guarantees the right to family life that the right to artificial multiplication need not necessarily derive from the right to natural human multiplication (reproduction, procreation).[215] The second principle that was taken into consideration was expressed by Prof. Finžgar with the phrase: '*Procreatio artificiale imitatur naturam*'.[216] It is necessary to imitate nature, to make possible (only) that which nature has deprived us of; unusual and unnatural methods are not acceptable.

481. Taking into consideration these two principles, the law gives the right to BMAP only to couples, married and unmarried, who cannot have children for reasons of infertility. This right is denied to single women and women living in a homosexual relationship with another woman, because we cannot know whether a woman without a (permanent) relationship with a man is infertile or not. Because it is unnatural, this right is also denied to men living with other men. As conception by a dead person is not possible in a natural way, (conscious) post-mortal use of gametes is not allowed. The doctor should not implant into a woman's body donated

213. The methods of BMAP are specifically: (1) intra-corporal fertilization: it consists of placing of the sperm into the reproductive organs of a woman or placing of the ova together with the sperm into her reproductive organs; (2) extra-corporal fertilization: fusion of egg-cells and semen-cells outside the woman's body and the transfer of fertilized ova or early embryos into her reproductive organs.

214. J.A. Robertson, *Procreative Liberty and the Control of Conception, Pregnancy and Childbirth*, 69 Va. L. Rev. 406 (1983).

215. *See* L. Wildhaber, *Commentary to Article 8 ECHR*, in *Internationaler Kommentar zur Europaischen Menschenrechtskonvention* item 192, 75 (H. Golsong et al., 1995).

216. A. Finžgar, *Svobodno odločanje o rojstvih otrok in umetno omogočanje rojstev* (*Freedom of Choice in Childbirth and Artificial Pregnancy Assistance*), Pravnik 354 (1992).

sperm or ova if he or she knows that the donor is deceased.[217] Biomedical participation in surrogate motherhood is also prohibited: BMAP to a woman, who expresses her intention to leave the child she would bear to a third party (surrogate mother) should not be performed. It is especially stipulated that BMAP procedures may only be performed in order to cause pregnancy, and not for other purposes, and that special care should be taken to protect the health of the future child, his rights and well-being (responsible parenthood).

III. Who Is Entitled to BMAP (and When)?

482. As stated above, only couples of opposite sex are entitled to BMAP: a man and a woman living together, either married or not (cohabitation). For BMAP, the partners, married or not, must fulfil certain conditions: they must be of legal age, capable of discernment and otherwise healthy (the exception is an illness that prevents natural conception). The woman must be of childbearing age. Their age and health condition must be in such state that we can expect their ability to fulfil all their parental obligations in the best interest of the child (concern for the child's well-being). BMAP should only be performed in case other previous procedures of curing infertility were either unsuccessful or hopeless. An exception to this demand exists when BMAP could prevent the transmission of a serious hereditary disease to a child.

483. Another special condition for BMAP is formal, free and informed consent: consent of the married or unmarried couples, that should be given in writing, after they have been acquainted with the procedure of BMAP, the chances, possible consequences, and after they have been counselled by a doctor. This consent is valid for a certain period of time and can be renewed or revoked.

IV. Homologous and Heterologous Methods of Fertilization

484. As a rule, couples may be assisted only by homologous methods of fertilization: only their genetic material (ova and sperm) may be used. When there is no hope to achieve conception with their own genetic material or if the use of that could lead to a serious hereditary disease, the law allows exceptional heterologous procedures. In these two cases, the use of donated sperm and ova is allowed. Being a donor is not restricted to men only, as it is in some of the European laws, mostly for the reason that this is the only way of helping an infertile woman to have a child. However, it is prohibited to use (by the same procedure of BMAP) both donated sperm and donated ova. It is prohibited to use a donated embryo, which means the prohibition of transfer of an embryo which is created with donated genetic material

217. The same meaning can be found in the regulation that demands the existence of the marriage or cohabitation of a man and a woman who are assisted with BMAP at the time of the placement of the sperm, fertilized ova or early embryo into the woman's body. Because at the moment of death, the marriage or cohabitation ceases to exist, post-mortem BMAP is not acceptable.

(seen from the point of view of the woman in whose body the embryo is implanted). It is also forbidden to use a sperm or ovum mixture of two or more men and women.[218]

485. Since BMAP with donated genetic material is an exceptional procedure, the conditions for its implementation set by the law are rigorous. This is also true for formal conditions concerning permission for implementation of procedures and selection of performers of these procedures and also for conditions which are, besides general conditions, prescribed for the couple in treatment and specially for the donors of the sperm and ova.

486. Before BMAP is performed, the couple must participate in psychological counselling and should be informed about all the legal consequences of their consent to BMAP with donated material, and the legal consequences of the birth of a child conceived in that way. Male and female donors must be of legal age, capable of discernment and healthy. If a woman is to be fertilized with donated genetic material, for eugenic reasons this sperm may not be used if the donor is related to her in such a way that they could not form a valid marriage. For the same reason, donated ova may not be fertilized with sperm of a man who could not form a valid marriage with the woman donor because they are related.

487. Male and female donors and their donated material must be examined. Donated sperm and ova may be used only if it is determined that they are suitable for fertilization and their use cannot cause any danger the health of the woman or child. This also means that, considering the development of medicine, only the use of previously frozen genetic material is allowed. The genetic material of one donor may be used for BMAP only until two pregnancies are reached (with one or two different women). The reason for this is: the more pregnancies, the more brothers and sisters which could (due to the donor's anonymity) have children in mutual relationships. For reasons of easier supervision over the use of donated material, it is prescribed that donors must always give their gametes to one and the same medical institution. For the performance of BMAP with donated genetic material, the written consent of the donor is needed, after he or she is acquainted with the procedure and the legal consequences of the birth of a child conceived by such a procedure. The donor can always revoke his or her consent. After that, the genetic material must be destroyed.

488. One medical institution in the country keeps a unified register of data about all donors, and it enters data which is important especially for the health and identification of future children into this register.[219]

---

218. Reasons: this method does not imitate nature; the child's (genetic) father and mother are actually unknown; there is no information important for the child's health.
219. Management of medical documentation in Slovenia – *see*: V. Flis, *Medicinska dokumentacija in pravice bolnikov* (*Medical Records and Patient Rights*), Pravna praksa, No. 410/98, 27.

V. Medical Data: Professional Secrets

489. Employees in medical institutions which perform BMAP must keep as secret all information about donors, women fertilized with donated material, their husbands or cohabitation partners and children conceived in this process. In this way, in principle, the anonymity of the participants in the procedure is guaranteed.

VI. Anonymity of the Donor Versus the Right of a Child to Know His or Her Origin

490. When writing the act, the special question arose of whether to keep the donor's anonymity also in relation to the child conceived with donated genetic material.[220] The idea that prevailed was that if we, *de lege ferenda*, abolished anonymity, and if the legislation enabled a child conceived with BMAP to know his or her genetic parents' identity (donor of sperm and ova), and not only information about them important for his or her health, this could bring about many unpleasant consequences for his or her genetic parents, who at the time of donation did not have the intention to form a parental relationship with him or her. They now live their own personal and family lives in which there is no place for this child. However, there are the social parents, who were able to get the child by means of donation (implementation of freedom of choice in childbearing). They could, on the basis of the right to privacy and to family life, demand this child to be only theirs. Revealing the donor's identity could also weaken the relationship between a child and his or her social parents, which certainly is not in his or her best interest. The possible benefit of the child's personal identification, which is said to be necessary for his or her development and formation of personality, does not compensate for such bad side effects. In theory, there are opposing opinions about the child's right to know his or her genetic parents' identity.

491. According to the solution in our law, the child may, for health reasons (which should be interpreted extensively: we can include, for instance, psychological problems caused by uncertainty of origin among them), demand from the medical institution to be shown data on the donor, important for his or her health. Those are basically the information needed to diagnose a child's disease for treatment. A child should be capable of discernment and minimum 15 years old. The child's legal guardian can get to know these data only with permission of the court in a special civil procedure for non-litigious matters (because his or her interests can be opposite to those of the child), if exceptional, health-related reasons are given.

---

220. *See*: M. Končina, *Osebnostne pravice otroka in njihovo pravno varstvo, Pravni vidiki otrokovih pravic* (*Personal Rights of a Child and Their Legal Protection, Legal Aspects of Child Rights*), ČZ Uradni list RS 104–106 (1992), K. Zupančič & V. Žnidaršič, *Dva vidika svobode odločanja o rojstvih otrok* (*Two Aspects of Freedom Regarding Childbirth*), in Pravo in medicina, Cankarjeva založba 242 (Pravna fakulteta, Univerza v Ljubljani 1998) and V. Žnidaršič & T. Pipan, *Določanje očetovstva in materinstva za otroka spočetega z zdravstveno pomočjo* (*Determining Fatherhood and Motherhood for a Child, Conceived Using Bio-Medically Assisted Procedures*) 45–47 (1995).

VII. Special Rules for Treatment of Genetic Material

492. One of the basic principles should be mentioned at the beginning: it is prohibited to give or receive payment for donated germ cells. For ethical reasons and for reasons of protection of the well-being of the future child, the law pays special attention to the treatment of gametes and embryos. We have legal regulation of use, examination, preservation and research of genetic material.

493. Gametes and embryos may only be used for BMAP. They should only be handled and examined in accordance with the purpose of BMAP: making pregnancy possible. Certain treatments may only be permitted for the prevention of serious hereditary diseases: fertilization with a semen-cell selected for its gender chromosome or genetic research (prenatal diagnostics). Interventions into hereditary structure are permitted only if they are specially laid out by statute. Prohibited activities are: cloning (creation of an embryo with the same genetic cell-structure as another embryo, living or dead person), creation of hybrids and chimeras (e.g., fertilization of a human egg-cell with the semen-cell of an animal or fertilization of an animal egg-cell with the semen-cell of a human, changing of an embryo through the fusion of embryos and parts of other human or animal embryos) and the placing of such embryos into a human body or an animal, the placing of human germ cells or embryos into an animal or the placing of animal germ cells or embryos into a human body. It is also prohibited to develop an embryo outside the human body for longer than fourteen days, as well as to use the tissue of an embryo created with BMAP. The creation of human embryos (only) for research purposes is prohibited. The same is true for enabling the development of human embryos out of germ cells whose genetic structure has been changed. They must not be placed into a human body or an animal. Changing of the genetic structures of cells which are part of an embryo is also prohibited. The word 'mostly', situated at the beginning of the enumeration of these prohibited actions, expresses the fact that this enumeration is not exhaustive.

494. All the ova obtained in one cycle may be fertilized outside the woman's body. It is not permitted to implant all of them into a woman's body. Because of the possibility (danger) of multiple pregnancy (and as a result, the destruction of all of them), only three embryos may be implanted. Any remaining embryos are preserved and can be later placed only into the body of the woman of the couple who started the BMAP procedure and gave their consent to it. The couple must fulfil the conditions prescribed by the legislation for persons who want to be entitled to the right to BMAP, at the time when these embryos are to be placed into the woman. Placing can be performed only if it is based on their mutual written request. Thus, the donation of an embryo is prevented.

495. The preservation of sperm and ova is, for medical reasons, necessary in heterologous methods with donated genetic material, whereas in homologous methods this question arises mostly when a person wants to store his or her genetic material for the use in the future. Embryos would be preserved if they are superfluous and may not be placed into a woman's body. A man, woman or child who will, because of his or her illness, (most probably) become infertile in the future, is entitled to preservation of his or her gametes, for he or she could use them later. At that time, he or she will have to comply with all the conditions prescribed by this law.[221]

VIII. The Preservation of Gametes and Embryos

496. Gametes and embryos may only be stored in a specially authorized medical institution, and for five years at most. If it is allowed by the State Commission for BMAP, for exceptional, medical reasons, the time of preservation of gametes can be prolonged for an additional five years. The prolongation is based on the request of the person whose gametes are in question. This person can be minor, if he or she is capable of discernment. When this is not true, his (her) parents or his (her) guardian has the right to ask for the prolongation of preservation. After the expiration of these terms, the gametes should be destroyed, and the embryos are left to die. Exceptionally, under certain conditions mentioned below, research on these embryos is allowed. During the time of their preservation, no one is entitled to dispose of gametes and embryos, neither the person they derive from nor any other person. The institution that preserves them must not give them up to anybody.

IX. Research

497. Research work on gametes (at all stages of their development) and embryos may be performed only if its aim is to protect and to improve human health. For such research on embryos, the written consent of the couple who are being assisted with BMAP is needed. There must also be a permission from a special institution: the State Commission for BMAP, which should be approved also by the National Medical Ethics Committee. In addition, research work may only be permitted on embryos which are not, regarding the development of medicine and experience, suitable for implantation into a woman's body or for preservation. It can also be done on preserved embryos which are intended for destruction (the expiry of the time of preservation).

X. Medical Institutions Licensed for BMAP

498. Since some people cannot exercise their constitutional freedom of choice in childbearing without biomedical assistance which enables conception, and since it is a very complex and delicate activity, which could threaten especially the human right to personal dignity, it is necessary for the law to regulate particularly those questions concerning the subjects who practice this activity.

221. *See* Art. 3 of the Infertility Treatment and Procedures of Biomedically-assisted Procreation Act.

499. In the first place, the law determines that BMAP procedures can only be carried out in medical institutions that are licensed for these activities by the Minister of Health. This institution is in the act called a centre for BMAP (hereinafter 'centre'). A licence can be granted only to a medical institution that has suitable specialists and equipment for performing BMAP, according to the demands of contemporary biomedical science and experience, and that could also, in certain cases, provide psychological and legal counselling. The Minister can revoke the licence, especially, for example, if the centre severely violates the regulations of the statute. BMAP with donated material can only be performed in a centre (or centres), which was (were) especially appointed by the Minister.

500. Within the centre, individual BMAP procedures are performed by a group of biomedical specialists. The leading role belongs to a doctor (specialist gynaecologist and obstetrician) who also decides on the biotechnological procedures. For every BMAP procedure, the professional counselling body (medical council, expanded to include other experts, for instance lawyer, social worker) must give its consent to and in that way executes the function of internal supervision within the centre. For BMAP with donated genetic material, the consent of this body is insufficient. The State Commission for BMAP must give its permission as well.

501. The law acknowledges the right of conscientious objection: specialists (doctors and other biomedical experts and medical workers) are not obliged to perform BMAP or to participate in it.[222]

502. The centres have to keep the records on BMAP which must contain all the data important for the performance of procedure and the data about significant circumstances with regard to the child. They also have to report to the State Commission for BMAP on the procedures performed. The data of the records are a professional secret.

503. From the above brief review of the legal regulations on the performers of BMAP, it follows that it could be performed in public as well as private medical institutions if they fulfil the conditions for obtaining a licence. As it is nevertheless the work of a team of specialists from different areas (at least two: medicine and biology), it is evident that a licence cannot be given to a single doctor, unless it is given to him or her as the owner of the medical institution. The performance of BMAP is therefore restricted to medical institutions, i.e., hospitals.

XI. The State Commission for BMAP

504. According to the law, the State Commission for BMAP, which besides medical professionals includes experts of other profiles, is formed by the Ministry

222. The situation is similar to conscientious objection at the abortion cases. *See* K. Zupančič & V. Žnidaršič, *Dva vidika svobode odločanja o rojstvih otrok* (*Two Aspects of Freedom Regarding Childbirth*), Pravo in medicina, Cankarjeva založba 212–214 (1998).

of Health, in order to discuss and solve all important questions with regard to the execution of the statute. Some of the tasks of this Commission are explicitly stated:

- the Commission shall give its opinion with regard to the question of whether a certain health institution fulfils the conditions for performing BMAP to the Minister of Health;
- the Commission shall give its opinion with regard to the question of whether a certain centre may practise BMAP with donated genetic material;
- give its permission for the implementation of a certain BMAP procedure with donated material;
- give permission for research work; and
- discuss the reports from centres and acquaint the minister with the findings of these reports.

505. Other tasks of the State Commission derive mainly from its function of supervision over the work of centres and its advisory function (also to the Minister, for example, about regulations on the execution of this law). The State Commission will most likely have a crucial influence on the creation of health policy with regard to BMAP. The English Human Fertilization and Embryology Authority served as an example in the creation of this Commission and its working domain, but we did not accept their solution regarding committees within the Authority. Our Commission can, in order to assist its work, form permanent or periodic working bodies and demand the opinions of different experts.

XII. Maternity and Paternity for Children Conceived with Biomedical Assistance

506. The Infertility Treatment and Procedures of Biomedically-assisted Procreation Act used to deal also with questions of determination of origin and parenthood (maternity and paternity) for children conceived with biomedical assistance. Because these are problems of Family Law, the new regulation on this field, that is, the Family Code), arranged those questions by itself and derogated the solutions in a mentioned healthcare act. Nevertheless, the basic solutions stayed the same: the father of a child conceived with donated sperm is his or her mother's husband or the man who (with full knowledge of his deed – informed consent) agreed to this kind of BMAP. The mother of a child, conceived with donated ova, is woman who gives birth to the child and has given informed consent to this kind of BMAP procedure.[223]

223. *See*: V. Žnidaršič & T. Pipan, *Določanje očetovstva in materinstva pri otrocih, spočetih z zdravstveno pomočjo* (*Determining Fatherhood and Motherhood for a Child, Conceived Using Bio-Medically Assisted Procedures*), Pravnik, No. 9–10, 1997, 555–580.

§5. ORGAN TRANSPLANTS

I. General

507. Transplants are procedures for removing a body organ or tissue from one person and implanting it into another person. Transplants also include preparation, keeping and storage of organs and tissues. Nowadays transplants have more or less become routine in solving certain health-related issues; however, it is necessary to point out that they still deeply encroach on the essence of being human, an individual's life and its quality. While this could be claimed for all medical procedures, the risks involved in transplants are surely much higher.

508. A specific characteristic of transplants is that they by their nature include third persons, i.e., organ donors: dead or living individuals. This characteristic poses additional problems to procedures connected to transplants. Transplants represent a deviation from the classical disease treatment relationship, i.e., a relationship between two subjects: the patient and the doctor.

509. The beginnings of transplants in Slovenia go back to 1970, when a kidney donated by a living donor was successfully transplanted for the first time.[224] The first act in this area, the Removal and Transplantation of Human Body Parts for Medical Purposes Act,[225] was adopted in Slovenia in 1985. It was in its entirety superseded by the Removal and Transplantation of Human Body Parts for the Purposes of Medical Treatment Act[226] in 2000. In 2015 it was replaced by a new act: Act Regulating the Obtaining and Transplantation of Human Body Parts for the Purposes of Medical Treatment (Transplant Act).[227]

II. Organ Donors

510. Pursuant to Slovenian law, organ donors can be alive or dead.

A. *Dead Donors*

511. The fundamental criterion for removing body parts from a deceased person is that such a person has been certified dead. This procedure follows the so-called dead-donor rule principle, which states that an organ donor must not die in order to perform the donation nor die because his or her body parts have been removed. Slovenia accepted the so-called brain death legal standard, which states that death occurs after all brain functions have irreversibly stopped, including the functioning

224. *See* https://www.slovenija-transplant.si, 5 Jan. 2021.
225. OG SRS, No. 42/1985.
226. OG RS, Nos 12/2000 and 61/2007.
227. OG RS, No. 56/2015.

of the brainstem.[228] The Transplant Act defines two types of death: the mentioned brain death and the death after a final stop of a heart. In both cases the death should be established with certainty, in accordance with medical criteria and on a prescribed manner. Brain death is certified by a committee, composed of at least two doctors, which has to produce a record and sign it. Their decision should be independent and unanimous. Members of the committee must not be involved in transplantation procedure or in any way connected to it. In case of an ordinary cardiopulmonary death, the latter is ascertained by a doctor, according to a standardized procedure and at the place of death. A doctor who determines death is also not allowed to cooperate at transplantation procedures.

1. Consent for Removal

512. The Transplant Act states that during a lifetime every person, who is capable of deciding on his or her own medical treatment independently, has a right to decide upon a question of donation of his or her body parts after death. He or she can declare or refuse to give his or her agreement to donation in writing. This kind of declaration (i.e., option) is made on a special form, in front of an authorized individual or organization, which is authorized to carry out activities in the area of searching for organ transplant donors. A declaration could also be made in electronic form or orally. The latter applies for a person who is (due to different reasons) not capable to make a written declaration. In that case the presence of a selected personal physician and two adult witnesses is required.

513. On the basis of written consent for organ donation it can be removed from donor upon his or her death after his or her close ones have been noticed (if they are reachable). It does not mean that the Transplant Act gives them the right to consent to or oppose organ removal, which is why it is called a solid system of expressing consent.[229]

514. Slovenian regulations regarding organ and tissue transplants from dead people also use the so-called presumed consent for donation. This means that organ or tissue removal is allowed also in cases when the deceased person has not declared his or her decision on a matter during a lifetime. The Transplant Act thus states that this kind of removal of body parts can only be made to a deceased person who is a citizen and resident of the Republic of Slovenia and whose close ones do not oppose to the removal. Namely, if they are reachable, at least one of them should be informed of the intended removal and also on their right to reject it. They should be also given the appropriate time for making this kind of decision. If persons who

228. *See* Rules on medical criteria, methodology and procedures for certification of the brain death and on the composition of the Commission for the certification of the brain death, OG RS, Nos 70/2001 and 56/2015. The Rules state that brain death occurs after all the brain areas cease to function (the brainstem and both hemispheres) for a person, who is kept alive on life support.

229. S. Tevž, *Nekateri pravni problemi presaditve človeških organov* (*Some Legal Issues Regarding Human Organ Transplants*) 13 (Pravna fakulteta, Univerza v Ljubljani 2004).

were close to the deceased are not reachable, the removal of a body part is not allowed. If the deceased is not a Slovenian citizen or resident, his or her body parts can be removed for transplantation purposes only in case of explicit consent, given by his or her close ones. They should also declare in writing that they are not aware of the deceased's opposition to donation of body parts.

515. The Transplant Act separately defines the removal of body parts and their use for transplantation in a case of the aborted embryos. It is allowed only if a woman who carried the embryo has been exhaustively informed of the purpose of the intended donation and has also given her written consent to it. A physician who executed the abortion should not be cooperating at the procedure of transplantation and should not be interested in it in any possible way. It is also specifically stressed that because of a decision for donation of body parts of the embryo it is not allowed to change the decisions regarding the procedures, time and other circumstances connected with the abortion.

516. Slovenian transplantation law deals also with the question of removal of body parts in cases when deceased are minors or adults without capacity of discernment. In these cases the removal is allowed only with the consent of their legal representatives. Their consent is not required if minors (or adults without capacity of discernment) agreed in removal during their life and they were capable to understand the meaning of their statements.

517. A special issue presents the removal of body parts with the approval of an investigating judge. Namely, if it is obvious that there will be, due to circumstances that cause death of a certain person, a forensic autopsy, the removal of body parts (if all of the criteria of transplantation law are met) could only be allowed if approved by the investigating judge.

B. Living Donors

1. General

518. The second group of people who can donate organs or tissues are living donors. Their legal position is, understandably, quite different from that of the dead donors.

519. The Constitution states in Article 35 that all people are guaranteed inviolability of their physical integrity, and that an individual can dispose of such right in a certain sense when he or she allows for interventions to his or her body, especially in cases of treatment. As removing an organ or tissue represents a huge intervention of body integrity and can potentially threaten the health and life of the donor, donations from a living person hold special importance. Because a donor donates a healthy part of his or her body, the procedure results in loss and damage for the donor. Ethically speaking, we could say this also breaches the principle of charity and harmlessness. Despite that, the generally accepted position nowadays is that a violation of body integrity of a healthy individual is acceptable if the person is guided by humanitarian reasons and if the risk is within acceptable boundaries.

520. The prevailing position is that the legal nature of disposal with organs and tissue of a living person can be understood as a gift, but as a gift in a form of a real contract. This means that consent on the removal of an organ or tissue means no obligations to the donor, because it can be revoked up until the start of the medical procedure. Liability or binding legal transactions, with which a person binds himself or herself to removal of his or her own body organs or tissues, would be null and void as they would be opposed to morals. The relationship that is created with organ and tissue relocation does not fall under the law of obligations.

2. Tissues and Organs That Can Be Donated

521. The Transplant Act prescribes that removal of body parts from a living donor is allowed if the risks to his or her health are within acceptable limits as set by medical criteria. An additional demand is that the risk must not be out of proportion in regards to the expected benefits for the recipient. In accordance with the risk criteria, the practice as well as legislation created the distinction between renewable tissues (regenerative tissues) and non-renewable (non-regenerative) tissues.

522. The removal of non-renewable tissues entitles much larger risks, which is why Slovenian legislation in principle only allows the removal of renewable tissues. Exceptionally, a kidney, part of liver and part of lungs can be removed in order to be transplanted to a person with whom a donor is connected genetically, through family relations or emotionally. It is allowed only in the case when an organ from a deceased donor cannot be received in a reasonable amount of time or whether the use of an organ by a living donor ensures a much better possibility of getting well than other forms of treatment for terminally malfunctioning kidneys, liver or lungs. Removal in such cases is only allowed after preliminary approval by the Ethics Commission for Transplants. With explicit consent of a woman who delivered a child the hematopoietic stem cells, tissue from the detached umbilical cord of a live-born child and tissues or cells that would otherwise be destroyed after the birth of a child can be collected and stored. Cells collected in this way can be used for related or unrelated transplantation.

3. Donor Consent

523. In accordance with the principle of physical integrity protection, an individual's body can only be intervened upon his or her expressed consent. Removal without consent is a criminal offence. In order to maintain the validity of consent, it is necessary that the donor is free from all inappropriate influences and pressures and must be sufficiently informed to consider the risks, benefits and consequences of this Act. The normal requirements regarding the informing of the donor about the procedure are not applicable, because this is a non-therapeutical procedure in nature. This is why obligations regarding information disclosure for the donor are stricter than towards the recipient. The use of the so-called therapeutic privilege is prohibited.

524. The Transplant Act states that donor consent only relates to the planned procedure. It must be in writing and an expression of free will. It must be formed on the basis of an adequate explanation on the nature, purpose and course of the procedure, the probability of its success and usual risks. It is also stressed that the explanation must not be suggestive. The doctor must also notify the donor that he or she has the right to individual consultation regarding the risks to his or her health with a doctor who will not take part in the transplant procedure and is not his or her personal doctor.

525. The only valid consent is the one given by a person of legal age, who is capable of reasoning. It could be attached to a condition that a transplantation is performed to a particular person. A consent can be withdrawn in writing at any time before the beginning of removal. For particularly justified reasons the regenerative parts of the body can be removed from a person younger than 18 years or to a person who is not capable of reasoning, if transplantation is aimed to benefit someone with whom he or she is genetically, emotionally or family related. For this kind of transplantation procedures the preliminary written approval by the Ethics Commission for Transplants is needed.

526. If the donor is not of age or is not capable of reasoning, the consent is given by his or her legal representative. In cases when an individual refuses the donation, even if there is the consent of his or her legal representative, the removal of body parts is not allowed.

C. Prohibition of Trafficking with Body Parts

527. The transplant activity uses the principles of altruism, voluntariness and gratuitousness. The latter mainly means that parts of the human body, which are *res extra commercium*, can only be donated and in no case sold or traded for a different benefit (material or non-material gain). However, the principle of gratuity does not cover all payments. Pursuant to Slovenian legislation, the prohibition does not apply for payments of medical or technical services in connection with the removal and transplanting. It is also allowed for a donor to be reimbursed for loss of income and compensated for travel costs, connected to organ or tissue donation. The donor is also entitled to free treatment after the procedure as well as suitable compensation if he or she suffers an unexpected aggravated consequence to his or her health as a direct consequence of the removal. The fact that is the most important is that the stated payments do not mean payments for an organ or an incentive for donation, but mainly to reinstate the financial state of the donor, as it was before the removal.

This relates to the covering for his or her actual loss. Advertising the need for body parts and their availability, if the aim of it is offering or seeking profit or similar benefits, is prohibited.

D. Organ and Tissue Recipients

528. Organ or tissue transplant is a way of medical treatment for an organ or tissue recipient, which is why this procedure also requires express agreement by the recipient. The Transplant Act (similar as with donor consent) requires a full consent in writing, which has to express an individual's free will, formed on the basis of a suitable explanation on the nature, purpose and course of the procedure, the probability of its success and usual risks. In case of a recipient who is not of age or not capable of reasoning the transplantation is not allowed, in cases where a legal representative has given his or her consent, but the recipient opposes to the procedure and is capable of understanding the meaning of his or her decision.

E. Allocating Organs and Tissues

529. In transplanting human organs and tissues, one of the open and very relevant issues is the allocation of organs and tissues. The problem mainly lies in the lack of human tissues and organs, as well as monetary means to cover the costs for all transplant requirements. Allocation is made on macro and micro levels. The amount of the financial means that should be allocated for transplants (political issue) and the criteria based on which patients are put on waiting lists (medical issue) are decided on the macro level. On the micro level, it is decided which of the several individual patients on the waiting list will receive the available organ or tissue.

530. Transplants in Slovenia (pursuant to the Heath Care and Health Insurance Act) are paid by compulsory health insurance. The Transplant Act states that organs and tissues taken from a deceased person have to be used in accordance with the rules of the medical profession and the principle of just access to this manner of treatment in accordance with regulation on recipients' waiting list. Allocation criteria differ depending on the organ type. Slovenia is a member of Eurotransplant, within which all recipients, who are compatible with the tissue, are allocated to a priority list:

- regarding the number and type of tissue compatibility;
- points are additionally added for the waiting period; and
- distance from the removal and transplant centre.

F. Organizational Aspect of Transplanting Organs and Tissues

531. Slovenia in 1992 started forming the national transplants network, even though the then valid act did not contain organizational provisions. The network was established in 1998. The current Transplant Act prescribes the activities of removal and transplantation of body parts to be carried out in donor and transplantation centres licensed by the Ministry of Health. The role of donor centres is gathering the body parts, and the role of transplantation centres is to transplant them. Both kind of institutions are functioning under the conditions prescribed by law and specially issued permissions. In accordance with the law, donor centres have their own hospital transplantation coordinators who organize activities within the hospital and maintain the link to Slovenia Transplant. Transplantation centres appoint clinical transplantation coordinators who take care for organization of preparation of recipients, for entries on the waiting list of recipients and regular medical checks of recipients and possible recipients. Apart from the mentioned hospital coordinators, there are also central transplantation coordinators who have to coordinate activities among the donor centres and transplantation centres. They also have to arrange procedures connected to organ exchange and destruction.

532. The institutions listed above are connected through the Organ and Tissue Transplant Institution of the Republic of Slovenia (Slovenia Transplant), set up by the Government of the Republic of Slovenia. This functions as a public health institution and is financed from the state budget. Slovenia became a full Eurotransplant member in 2000. This means that organ exchange for Slovenia is being carried out within its network, which also includes the waiting lists for Slovenian patients. This mainly means that the most suitable donors are being sought for kidneys throughout the Eurotransplant area. Regarding allocation of other organs, where the requirements of tissue compatibility are a bit lower, regional allocation takes precedence, and only if no recipient exists in the donor's country, the organ is allocated to other Eurotransplant areas. An exception is when a Eurotransplant area patient urgently needs the organ for survival. Also being considered is the principle that the number of sent and received organs should be about the same at the end of the current year.

§6. Research (Experiments) on Humans

I. General

533. We have recently been witnessing rapid scientific developments and discoveries in numerous fields of human work and activities. A day hardly passes by without us learning about a new invention that will facilitate or prolong our life. The scientific fields or areas that stand out in several ways in this regard definitely include biomedicine. Biomedicine achieved enormous progress lately, which was completely unimaginable even a few decades ago. We can but guess how far new discoveries in this field will lead us.

II. Research on Humans

A. *Introduction*

534. Two important values, which are at the same time legally protected rights, meet in the field of biomedical research: the freedom of scientific research on the one and the wish and need for the respect of human life and dignity on the other hand. Research on humans is a morally and ethically very sensitive issue where it is paramount to abide by the ethic guideline that even the most important end cannot and must not justify the means. A similar principle could be expressed in another way through the application of the well-known Oviedo Convention Guideline – that the interest of an individual must always take precedence over the interests of the society or science. While it is true that we all highly praise and in principle support the progress that could be made, especially in medicine, by well-conducted, sincere and not too restricted scientific research, it is also true that numerous hazards and scruples are appearing in this field. One of the major scruples is that there exists a great danger of dehumanization and treating of a person as the means to reach an end and not as the end itself. Law can be one of the instruments (but not the only one) that can help in mitigating such risks, manipulations and abuse.

535. The principle of human dignity guarantees the basic human right to life as well as the right to self-determination, which is why an individual must in principle agree to all procedures that are carried out on him or her by third persons. This means that the implementation of the right to self-determination, when speaking of patients or other individuals who take part in (biomedical) research, is always subjected to the patient's wilful approval after being explained the procedure (the rule of informed consent). This consent, which is only valid if the individual received and understood exhaustive information on the planned intervention into his or her bodily or mental integrity before its launch, is the fundamental precondition for any medical intervention and, of course, for any therapeutic and other biomedical research on humans.

B. *Regulation*

1. General

536. The Republic of Slovenia does not have a separate (national) act that would regulate the field of biomedical research as such. The basic document binding the Republic of Slovenia in this field is the Convention on Human Rights and Biomedicine and its Additional Protocol Regarding Bio-medical Research. On the field of clinical trials of medicinal products on humans, Slovenia implemented EU directives in the field.

2. The Oviedo Convention

537. It stresses in its preamble that a human being must be respected as an individual and as a member of the human species as well as includes a special chapter on the issue of scientific research in the field of biology and medicine and in principle declares such research as free. It also binds such research by its provisions and by the provisions of the legislation in individual countries that are parties to the document. It also specifically defines the conditions that have to be met in order to allow a research on a human being to be carried out: there is no alternative of comparable effectiveness to research on humans; the risks which may be incurred by that individual are not disproportionate to the potential benefits of the research; the research project has been approved by a competent body after independent examination of its scientific merit, including assessment of the importance of the aim of the research, and multidisciplinary review of its ethical acceptability; the individuals undergoing research have been informed of their rights and the safeguards prescribed by law for their protection; the necessary consent has been given expressly and in writing and may be freely withdrawn at any time.

538. The Convention specifically defines the protection of individuals who are not capable of consenting to the research in a valid manner. Such individuals are given special protection through measures to prevent abuse that prevent inadmissible encroachments into their health as well as bodily or mental integrity. Exceptionally, it is also permissible to carry out research on such individuals if all the following conditions are met: there is no alternative of comparable effectiveness to research on humans; the risks which may be incurred by that person are not disproportionate to the potential benefits of the research; the research project has been approved by a competent body after independent examination of its scientific merit, including assessment of the importance of the aim of the research, and multidisciplinary review of its ethical acceptability; the persons undergoing research have been informed of their rights and the safeguards prescribed by law for their protection; the results of the research have the potential to produce real and direct benefit to his or her health; research of comparable effectiveness cannot be carried out on individuals capable of giving consent; the legal guardian of the individual who is unable to consent to the research in a valid manner has given his or her consent (such consent has to be given specifically for such purpose and in writing); the individual is not adverse to the research.

539. The Convention furthermore states that, apart from the existence of special safeguarding provisions of national legislation (these have so far not yet been passed by Slovenia), it is permissible to carry out the research which is not expected to result in direct benefits for the health of the individual concerned if the following conditions are also met: there is no alternative of comparable effectiveness to research on humans; the risks which may be incurred by that person are not disproportionate to the potential benefits of the research; the research project has been approved by a competent body; the individual who will be included in the research must be acquainted with his or her rights; the issues that the research is purported to address cannot be carried out on individuals who are capable of providing their consent; the legal guardian of the individual who is unable to consent to the research in a valid manner has given his or her consent specifically for the research and in writing; the research has the aim of contributing, through significant improvement in the scientific understanding of the individual's condition, disease or disorder, to the ultimate attainment of results capable of conferring benefit to the person concerned or to other persons in the same age category or afflicted with the same disease or disorder or having the same condition; the research entails only minimal risk and minimal burden for the individual concerned.

3. Council of Europe Additional Protocol Regarding Biomedical Research

540. Slovenia signed the Additional Protocol to the Convention on Human Rights and Biomedicine regarding biomedical research. It entered into force on 1 September 2007 and applies to all research activities in the field of health protection that include health-related treatment on individuals. The Protocol substantiates the fundamental provisions of the Convention regarding biomedical research on individuals but does not deal with, for example, the issues of research on in vitro embryos, leaving this field to national legislation.

541. One of the basic principles in the field of carrying out biomedical research on individuals is that the consent of the patient or the individual on whom the research will be carried out has to be acquired for any procedure (treatment, examination, test). It should therefore be mentioned here that a provision of the Patients' Rights Act will be used alongside the provisions of the Convention, which are directly applicable in the Republic of Slovenia. The Act defines the right to consent for treatment as part of the wider right to self-determination regarding treatment and introduces the principle of the patient's right to decide by himself or herself on treatment under conditions that are set by the Act. The Act forbids any health treatment or care to be administered to a patient, who is capable on deciding about himself or herself without his or her prior free and wilful consent, which has to be made on the basis of received explanations, except under cases determined by law. The patient has the right to actively participate in selecting the method of treatment after being given the necessary explanations on the treatment or procedure. The principle of free and wilful consent is not only established for health treatment or therapeutic procedures but also for several special procedures that the Act expressly defines and in which the patient participates. The examples of such special procedures include: taking part in the learning process, especially in the presence of other people, during the administering of healthcare; the use of health data for purposes that do not represent treatment; acquainting third parties with medical files; communicating information on the medical condition to third parties; carrying out research on biological material that was obtained from the patient; the use of the body or parts thereof after the patient's death for medical training and scientific research; donations of organs, tissues or cells during life or after death, and participating in medical research.

4. Clinical Trials of Medicinal Products on Humans

542. Slovenian legal regulation of clinical trials of medicinal products is harmonized with EU legal acts on the field;[230] in 2014 also the Regulation EU No. 536/2014 – the so-called Clinical Trial Regulation – was approved.[231]

543. Clinical trials of medicinal products are in Slovenia also regulated by Medicinal Products Act and Rules on clinical trials of medicinal products.[232] Execution of the mentioned act is a competence of a special Agency for Medicinal Products and Medical Devices of the Republic of Slovenia (AMPMD). Besides legal rules, the European Commission's principles and guidelines for good clinical practice on clinical trials and principles of ethics in medicine should be respected. It is also important that the protection of personal data is provided.

544. Medicinal Products Act determines clinical trials on medicinal products in Articles 30–42. Clinical trials of medicinal products for use in human medicine are defined as researches on healthy individuals or patients that have the aim to discover or verify clinical or pharmacological effects of the medicine on test, to reveal its adverse side effects or to examine its absorption, distribution, metabolism and secretion. All of the explained is done in order to prove safety and efficacy of a tested medicine. Medicines are clinically tested by the providers of healthcare services that have the staff, authorized to prescribe drugs, in accordance with legal rules and principles of good clinical practice.

Clinical trial of a certain medicine can start only after the results on analytical and non-clinical pharmacological and toxicological testing of medicinal products have been submitted and the medicine should not affect genetic germ line of the participants. Non-routine medicinal product, ready for advanced therapy, may not be clinically tested.

Before starting a clinical trial of medicinal product the process has to be notified to AMPMD. In case it involves a medicinal product intended for gene therapy, therapy with somatic cells, including xenogeneic cells, and the medicine that contains genetically modified organisms, a permission of AMPMD must be obtained. An application for a clinical trial of medicine for human use must be accompanied by opinion of the National Medical Ethics Committee. In a decision-making process AMPMD can take into account the assessment on the given clinical trial already made by other Member States of EU. It is prescribed by law that the proposer of clinical trial must, before its beginning, insure his or her responsibility for possible damage that could arise out of the procedure. For the reasons of protection of public health and health of participants in clinical trials AMPMD can decide on temporary or permanent discontinuation of clinical trial.

Medicinal Products Act arranges also the so-called non-interventional clinical trials of medicinal products where selection of patients, method of treatment, selection of medicines and their prescription, medical examinations and monitoring of

230. *See* https://ec.europa.eu, 2 Jan. 2021.
231. *Ibid.*
232. OG RS, No. 54/2006.

patients do not deviate from the established method of treatment and are in accordance with approved or prescribed dosage, method of use on indication area. This kind of clinical trials should be notified to AMPMD and they should also obtain the opinion of the National Medical Ethics Committee. It is important that with their execution the prescription or use of involved medicinal product is not encouraged. A patient should be informed on his or her inclusion into non-interventional clinical trial. The fact that he or she is participating in it must not be the reason for changing of existing appropriate therapy. The cooperating doctor must receive the prior consent of his or her employer if the latter is financed from public funds. The doctors are not allowed to receive payment for their cooperation in trials that are carried out during their working hours; they can only receive compensation for their work in free time.

545. In the scope of clinical trials the Medicinal Products Act regulates also the compassionate use of medicines. The latter is defined as process of giving a medicine with new substance that represents important therapeutic, scientific and technical innovation and is already in the process of issuing of marketing authorization or in the process of clinical trial. It can be used for the group of patients with chronic or serious exhausting disease that cannot be satisfactorily cured with medicines that already have marketing authorization. AMPMD is issuing permissions for implementation of compassionate use of medicine in practice. According to Article 83 of the Regulation No. 726/2004 of the EP and of the Council of 31 March 2004,[233] it obtains the opinion on that of the Committee for Medicinal Products for Human Use, established at European Medicines Agency.[234]

546. Clinical trials of medicinal devices in Slovenia are dealt with in Medical Devices Act and Rules on Medical Devices.[235] They are both harmonized with the EU legal documents on the field. They are generally dealing with the ways of finding out the safety and the capacity of medicinal device according to the purpose of using that was foreseen by the producer.

III. Research on Human Embryos

A. General

547. For obvious reasons, the moral and ethical discourse about researches on humans gets especially intense when performing biomedical research on embryos. This is especially true for research projects carried out on in vitro pre-embryos that were only recently created and do not purport to achieve therapeutic aims but could

233. Regulation No. 726/2004 of the EP and of the Council of 31 Mar. 2004 (consolidated text 30 Mar. 2019) – laying down Community procedures for the authorization and supervision of medicinal products for human and veterinary use and establishing a European Medicines Agency. *See* https://eur-lex.europa.eu, 2 Jan. 2021.
234. *See also* https://www.ema.europa.eu, 2 Jan. 2021.
235. OG RS Nos 37/2010 and 66/2012.

result in their destruction. The positions on these issues, by various countries, international organizations and other subjects, religious groups, biomedical researchers, jurists, philosophers, biomedical ethics experts and all other individuals are very different and diverse.

548. In the Republic of Slovenia, an embryo that is implanted into a mother's body does not have a special legal status as it is not treated as a person under Civil Law. The embryo is considered as a part of the mother's body, and its rights are as such only indirectly protected through the protection of the rights of the mother. These safeguards are written down in the Constitution of the Republic of Slovenia as well as the Health Measures in Exercising Freedom of Choice in Childbearing Act (HMEFCC). In line with the Slovenian Constitution, the embryo has no guaranteed right to life.

549. However, the status of the embryo outside of the mother's body that was conceived with the aid of in vitro fertilization is somewhat different. The latter presents a separate entity in a way and also has a certain legal position. Because it cannot be given the protection by its mother, its special situation is provided by in the safeguarding provisions of the Infertility Treatment and Procedures of Biomedically-assisted Procreation Act.

B. Regulation

1. Oviedo Convention

550. Regarding research on in vitro embryos, the provisions of the Oviedo Convention have to be followed in Slovenia. Namely, the document explicitly deals with research on embryos that are conceived with the use of in vitro fertilization. In line with the provision of the Convention, the countries can by themselves decide whether to allow the carrying out of research on pre-embryos or not. The Convention also tasks the countries that decide to allow pre-embryo research to provide for a suitable legal protection of such embryos. However, the Convention also brings an important and, we could also say, an explicit prohibition: it prohibits the creation of human embryos (solely) for the purpose of scientific research.

2. National Legislation

a. Conditions That Have to Be Met

551. Infertility Treatment and Procedures of Biomedically-assisted Procreation Act allows research on germ cells and pre-embryos, created with the aim to carry out the BMAP procedures, solely for the purposes of protecting and improving humankind's health. All research in the field must have a specific health purpose and cannot be carried out for commercial or other purposes. Research on embryos that are created through in vitro fertilization procedures falls under the more stringent provisions of the Act. If we take into account the greater ethical issues regarding such procedures, such a decision is undoubtedly well founded and understandable. The first condition that has to be met in order to allow research on pre-embryos is that such research cannot be carried out with comparable efficiency on animal embryos or in other ways. The Act also says that research can only be carried out on pre-embryos that are confirmed by biomedical science to be unfit to be implanted into a body of a woman or stored and on those stored embryos that would otherwise be left to die after the time limit for their keeping, as defined by the Act (five years) has passed. The Act also demands the written consent for research on pre-embryos of either spouses or cohabiting partners who are undergoing BMAP procedures. Such research must moreover be allowed by the National Commission for BMAP and approved by the National Medical Ethics Committee. The Act moreover states that modern achievements in medicine and experience as well as proved global practices and the general rules of medical ethics have to be considered in carrying out research on pre-embryos. The Act explicitly says that the approval and supervision by both the Commissions (the National Commission for BMAP and the National Medical Ethics Committee) is also required during the implementation and the use of any new methods of in vitro fertilization, so long as they are believed to be in an experimental phase.

b. Prohibited Actions

552. A separate provision of the Act explicitly prohibits the following actions in carrying out BMAP procedures: allowing the growth of an embryo more than fourteen days old outside of the body (after the primitive streak has developed); allowing embryos to be created solely for scientific purposes; allowing the creation of human embryos from germ cells whose genetic identity has been altered and the implantation of such embryos into humans or animals; using parts of the embryo, created by the BMAP procedures, except in cases specifically allowed by the Act; allowing the creation of embryos with the same genetic identity or embryos whose genetic identity is identical to another living or dead person (cloning); fertilization of a human egg-cell with animal sperm or an animal egg-cell with human sperm or changing the embryo by transplanting parts of other human or animal embryos, that is, allowing the creation of hybrids and chimeras; implanting an embryo that was created by the above-mentioned controversial procedures into a human or an animal; implanting a human germ cell or human embryo into an animal; implanting an animal gamete or an animal embryo into a human; deliberately changing the genetic identity of the cells that form a part of the embryo.

c. Preservation of Embryos

553. Spare embryos that are not used for reproductive purposes or for (allowed) research projects are kept for a specific period of time. The Act limits that period to five years. After that period expires, the embryos are explicitly required by the Act to be left to die.[236]

236. The wording can be somewhat contentious from the viewpoint of the legal status of the embryo as it implies that the embryo was 'living'.

d. Penal Provisions

554. The Infertility Treatment and Procedures of Biomedically-assisted Procreation Act also includes penal provisions. A legal entity which, contrary to the provisions of the Act, allows a procedure that alters the genetic identity of an embryo, genetic research on the embryo or allows the gender of the embryo to be selected, is fined with a penalty of between EUR 2,000 and 15,000. The same fine also applies to a legal personality that fails to store the embryos in line with the provisions of the Act or, for example, trades in them. Such violations are also subject to a fine between approximately EUR 200 and up to EUR 10,000 for the person in charge of the legal entity.

IV. Human Stem Cell Research

A. General

555. Stem cells are cells of a special type and are given special treatment by the medical profession. They are especially praised for their ability to develop into numerous different types of cells or tissues under specific conditions. This means that stem cells could in the future be used to successfully treat numerous currently untreatable diseases or allow the transplants of one's own tissue or organs without fears of rejection by the body. However, new and revolutionary discoveries in this field of medicine and biomedicine will not come without extensive research.

556. From the ethical and the legal point of view, the decisive piece of data regarding stem cell research is whether these cells were acquired from human embryos (embryonic stem cells) or from the tissue of adults. Stem cells are not found in embryos only but also in adults and can therefore be acquired from the tissues of the already born humans, for example from their bone marrow or the blood in the umbilical cord, skin. Some of the authors in the field claim that embryonic stem cells have so far proved themselves to be the most effective; however, the point of contention here is that acquiring such cells leads to the destruction of the embryo. Other sources reject such findings and state that stem cells acquired from adults seemed to have proved better at treating certain diseases.

557. Researches on stem cells that the scientists acquire from (living) humans (adults or children) are not morally or ethically contentious in any extraordinary manner, meaning that they are acceptable under the same conditions as all other similar biomedical research. Research in this field is governed by the same legal regulations (national and international) that completely protect the individual on whom the research is being carried out, his or her bodily and mental integrity, health and other human rights.

558. In the case of embryonic stem cell research however, the situation is completely different. Here we are dealing with human embryos acquired in vitro from which certain materials are extracted after being a few days old and before they differentiate into specific cells. This material, meaning the embryonic stem cells, can potentially be used to grow specific tissues in a human body, but also leads to the inevitable death of the embryo. This is where the moral and ethical and consequently the legal points of view regarding such research become contested. Despite being one of the most promising techniques in the field of biomedicine that could lead to a huge improvement in treating certain diseases, such research does not only trigger approval and hope but also strong concern and stiff opposition. The root of the problem lies in the confrontation between the freedom of scientific research and the desire and need to respect the human life and dignity. The issue (similarly to the issue of abortion or BMAP) also brings back in all force all of the contentious and as of yet indeterminate issues of the legal, moral and ethical status of an embryo.

B. National Legislation

559. The provisions of the Infertility Treatment and Procedures of Biomedically-assisted Procreation Act that were already presented above under the title Bio-medical Research on Embryos are relevant and applicable in the Republic of Slovenia also for a specific type of research such as the research on embryonic stem cells, so they will not be listed in detail again here.

V. Cloning

560. The Slovenian Infertility Treatment and Procedures of Biomedically-assisted Procreation Act prohibits the cloning of a human being in its entirety. The Act states that it is prohibited to allow the creation of embryos with identical hereditary material or embryos that are hereditary identical to a living or a dead individual. The Republic of Slovenia is obliged to respect the prohibition of cloning also on the basis of the Oviedo Convention, especially the separate Protocol to the Convention entitled the Additional Protocol to the Convention for the Protection of Human Rights and Dignity of the Human Being with regard to the Application of Biology and Medicine, on the Prohibition of Cloning Human Beings.

561. The Protocol brings a complete prohibition of cloning, including therapeutic and reproductive cloning, while some other international documents that only discuss the prohibition of such procedures that can lead to a cloned human being (beings) could lead us to believe that they only prohibit reproductive cloning. Some people believe that even the wording of the Protocol includes a legal void that could lead to an interpretation that reproductive cloning only is prohibited. This is so, because the term 'human being' is not specifically defined in the document, which could lead to various interpretations.[237]

237. *See* T.K. Harvey & J.V. McHale, *Health Law and the European Union* 273 (Cambridge University Press 2004).

VI. Bio-banks

562. There is no special regulative framework on the question of bio-banks in Slovenia; however, we adopted several legislatives measures that consist of constitutional provisions, international conventions, laws, regulations, codes of practice and so forth, which are potentially applicable to bio-banks.[238]

563. The topic is in Slovenia mainly arranged with the act that was accepted on the bases of the EU Tissue and Cells Directives.[239] It is the Act on Quality and Safety of Human Tissues and Cells, for the Purposes for Medical Treatment[240] which regulates all of the issues that are dealt with by the directives and in line with the directives' principles.

564. This Act is also used for stem cells, meaning both blood-forming stem cells from the bone marrow, the peripheral umbilical cord blood, the reproductive cells and stem cells acquired from adults as well as embryos. The Act refers to the fact that donating, acquisition, storage and the use of reproductive cells are governed by the provisions of the Infertility Treatment and Procedures of Biomedically-assisted Procreation Act.

565. The Act established a separate unit for the activities of the tissue and cell institutions which is responsible for carrying out the provisions of the Act as part of the Agency for Medicinal Products and Medical Devices of the Republic of Slovenia. Among other things, the agency also issues permits to institutions for tissues and cells for carrying out any of the activities regarding the acquisition, testing, treatment, preserving, storing, allocating and distributing tissues and cells meant for the treatment of people. The agency's job is also to take care that all the described activities are carried out as a public service in public healthcare institutions that are given the permit by the agency.

566. Regarding the safety of data and confidentiality of the procedure for donating germ cells, the Act refers to the provisions of the core Act, the Infertility Treatment and Procedures of Biomedically-assisted Procreation Act, which includes a separate regulation on the issue that is in line with the guidelines of the tissue directives.

567. In Slovenia, there is one public umbilical cord blood bank, which is organized within the Blood Transfusion Center of Slovenia. From 1 December 2014, the latter no longer accepts samples, as they have assessed that they obtained enough of them. It means that given the number of inhabitants in Slovenia, the needs for the

238. *See* J. Sander & P. Bard, *The Legal Regulation of Biobanks*, National Report: Slovenia, http://web.ceu.hu, 2 Jan. 2021.

239. The parent Directive (2004/23/EC) which provides the framework legislation and two technical directives (2006/17/EC and 2006/86/EC), which provide the detailed requirements of the parent directive.

240. OG RS, Nos 61/2007 and 56/2015.

samples are fully met.[241] However, some sources state that closing of the programme happened mainly due to a lack of funds, as the state did not want to invest in it.[242] However, the first private biobank came to life in Slovenia in 2008.[243]

568. There are some basic differences regarding the question of saving the genetic material in a public or private biobank. Private bank is named as family umbilical cord blood bank, it saves samples for autologous treatment (autologous transplants). It means that a patient receives his or her own (stem) cells, and the cells are basically the property of the child. Parents receive a notification of successful storage, and the storage is payable. The availability of cells is unlimited: they are available at any time and immediately. Public umbilical cord blood bank uses samples for allogeneic treatment. People donate umbilical cord blood and make it available to other patients. They are not informed about the (un)successful storage. As the recipient of sample is unknown, there is always a risk of a rejection reaction. Storage is free of charge, but cell availability is limited: there is a standardized process of finding a suitable donor for patients in need, and success is not guaranteed. They also have very strict criteria for storage: only 30% of umbilical cord blood collected meets the criteria of public banks. The rest of the blood is put into research or discarded.[244]

§7. TRANSSEXUALS

I. Legal Framework

569. Slovenia does not have specific regulations in place to govern the issue of transsexuals or sex change. However, the Civil Register Act[245] contains a provision dealing with data entered into the register (Article 4, paragraph 11), which also lists sex change. In accordance with Article 37 of Rules on the Implementation of the Civil Register Act[246] a change of sex is entered on the basis of a decision of the competent authority. The basis for issuing the decision is a certificate from the competent medical institution or a doctor, which shows that the person has changed gender. Before entering a gender change in the register, the registrar must request the determination of a new Personal Registration Number (PRN). An extract from the birth register is issued with information on the new sex, without a note on the change of sex.

---

241. *See* http://www.ztm.si, 7 Jan. 2021.
242. *See* https://www.sta.si, 7 Jan. 2021.
243. *See* https://www.biobanka.si, 7 Jan. 2021.
244. *See* http://www.ztm.si, 7 Jan. 2021.
245. OG RS, Nos 11/2011-UPB2 and 67/2019.
246. OG RS, Nos 40/2005, 69/2009, 77/2016, 102/2020.

II. Current Situation

570. Sex change has been carried out in Slovenia for almost fifty years; however, the number of cases is low, averaging at less than four a year. Sex change applicants mainly want to change their sex from female to male. Slovenia employs a commission for sex change, composed of a psychiatrist, endocrinologist, urologist, gynaecologist and a plastic surgeon. All the procedures are headed and coordinated by psychiatrists, and a specific protocol is in place for persons who want to have a sex change.

571. The procedure starts with a psychiatric session. In order for the applicants to be accepted into further treatment, they have to visit a psychiatrist for two years. The psychiatrist must assess how pertinent the desire for the sex change is and to what extent the applicant's 'ego' is trapped in a wrong body. The procedure then continues with hormonal therapy. Patients are sometimes satisfied only by attaining gentler or rougher features, grow or lose body hair and the like. However, those who want to go all the way can apply for surgical changes as well. Such procedures involve an urologist, gynaecologist and a plastic surgeon. The transition from one sex into another is a long-term process, which lasts for approximately four years. The entire procedure is listed under treatment of a disease in Slovenia, which means that it is paid for by the health insurance funds.[247]

572. Nowadays in Slovenia the awareness of a problematic position of our current regulation in the field of transsexuality is increasingly coming to the fore. Because of its deficiencies it could namely present a danger for violation of human rights and fundamental freedoms of transsexual people. For this reason, there are different proposals regarding the question how to regulate the issues of legal recognition of gender.[248] Most of the proposers believe that the new legislation should not only contain provisions on the regulation of cases where (medical) change of gender occurs, but also cases when it should come to the recognition of gender on the basis of self-identification of a person. *De lege ferenda* we should also take account of the reform that excluded transsexuality from the International Classification of Diseases – ICD 11.[249] We should consider the fact that it no longer falls under the definition of mental illness. Some authors believe we should (as some other jurisdiction did – for example, Germany on 1 January 2019)[250] also introduce a gender-neutral marker of official gender data that would present the abolition of the existing binary sexual system.[251] When drafting new regulation, we should also

247. *See* S. Zonta, *Spremembe spola v Sloveniji že 40 let* (*Sex Changes in Slovenia for the Past Forty Years*), interview with Franci Planinšek, MD, http://www.rtvslo.si, 2 Jan. 2020.
248. *See* https://transakcija.si, 2 Jan. 2021.
249. *See* https://www.euro.who.int, 2 Jan. 2021.
250. *See* https://www.euronews.com, 2 Jan. 2021.
251. *See* https://transakcija.si, 2 Jan. 2021.

take into account the Recommendation of the Council of Europe[252] that legal recognition of gender should be regulated in a way that is fast, accessible and transparent.

573. The public debate in Slovenia in 2019 showed that the Government is aware of a problem of legally insufficient regulation in the field of transsexuality – at least we could make such a conclusion for some of its departments. Among them are the Ministry of the Interior, Ministry of Labour, Family, Social Affairs and Equal Opportunities,[253] while others showed a little less of awareness. For example, the Ministry of Health insists that, from a medical point of view, there are only two biological sexes: male and female.[254]

§8. Human Genetics

I. General

574. Slovenia does not have legislation in place to systematically (specifically) deal with human genetics. Patients who are under any kind of genetic treatment enjoy the legal protection to the same extent as all other patients, meaning that general regulations of patient rights *mutatis mutandis* apply to the users of genetic services as well. To that extent, Slovenia mainly employs international legal instruments, especially the Convention on Human Rights and Biomedicine, the Additional Protocol to the Convention on Human Rights and Biomedicine Regarding Biomedicine Research and the Additional Protocol to the Oviedo Convention regarding Genetic Testing for Health Purposes.

575. The experts have been saying and warning that the area of medical genetics, also in Slovenia, contains huge ethical dilemmas, and that absence of legislation in such a delicate area is not desirable. Practical genome research is being carried out in Slovenia, as are genetic studies and research on patients. The country has several genetics laboratories in public institutions, and private companies have begun marketing such research to a large extent, which has brought quite a few problems and ethical dilemmas in practice. The initiative to pass a law in this area was adopted by the Ministry of Health, and an expert team was put together to draft a suitable bill. At the time of writing this monograph, the bill is not yet available to the public.

---

252. *See* Resolution 2048 (2015), Discrimination against transgender people in Europe, https://pace.coe.int, 2 Jan. 2021.
253. The latter relied particularly on the Protection Against Discrimination Act, OG RS, No. 33/2016, 21/2018.
254. *See* https://predlagam.vladi.si, 2 Jan. 2021.

II. Biomedically-Assisted Procreation

576. A very narrow scope of genetic research is dealt with by the Infertility Treatment and Procedures of Biomedically-assisted Procreation Act. The Act states in Article 31, paragraph 2 that genetic research of embryos in the early stages of development can only be carried out in cases of severe genetic illness or if required for a successful execution of a BMAP procedure.

III. Prohibition of Discrimination Based on Genetic Heritage

577. Slovenian legislation does not include specific provisions that would prohibit discrimination on the basis of genetic heritage (excluding the above-mentioned Convention and Protocols). Nevertheless, the Slovenian Constitution provides protection from all kinds of discrimination. It states in Article 14 that everyone shall be guaranteed equal human rights and fundamental freedoms irrespective of national origin, race, sex, language, religion, political or other conviction, material standing, birth, education, social status, disability or any other personal circumstance. An individual's genetic heritage could undoubtedly be included under the 'any other personal circumstance' part of the provision.

578. General protection is also afforded by the Protection Against Discrimination Act and by the Patients' Rights Act, which include among the general principles in Article 3, the principle of respect for personality and dignity, in such a way that nobody gets socially ostracized because of his or her health situation and its causes, consequences and circumstances or the health service that the patient received. This is undoubtedly also true for the procedures of genetic testing or for unveiling genetic heritage.

579. The Health Services Act meanwhile states that healthcare professionals and all other collaborators must, when performing their tasks, treat everybody in the same manner and under the same criteria as well as respect their constitutional and legal rights, and that the only criterion for precedence lies in the urgency of medical treatment (Article 45).

Part III. The Physician in Relation to the Healthcare System

Chapter 1. Relations with Other Healthcare Providers

§1. PHARMACISTS

580. The pharmaceutical sector is regulated in Slovenia by a special law, the Pharmacy Practice Act. Pharmacies provide an important activity within the framework of performing healthcare service, as they serve to guarantee the supply of medicinal products for the population and healthcare institutions and also treat patients pharmaceutically. Apart from the basic activity (selling medicinal products), pharmacies can also provide ancillary medicinal substances, prosthetic appliances, body care and other health protection products, sell veterinary medicines manufacture and check the quality of medicinal products and health preparations and provide advice and counsel in prescribing and use of medicinal products.

581. The holder of pharmacy activity is a Master of Pharmacy with a licence. In his or her work, he or she must be impartial and professionally independent and comply with the Code of Pharmacy Deontology. Pharmacy activity is performed at the primary, secondary and tertiary levels of healthcare. The network of pharmacy activities at the primary level is provided by municipalities, and at the secondary and tertiary levels by the state. The pharmacy activity is carried out in pharmacies, pharmacy subsidiaries or in a convenient supply of medicines, which can be organized by a doctor in a place that is at least 10 km away from the nearest pharmacy. The head of the pharmacy is responsible for the organization of work and the professional implementation of the pharmacy activity.

582. The pharmacy must have adequate supplies. All medicines on the market in the Republic of Slovenia must be provided no later than within twenty-four hours of the order or the next working day.

583. Advertising of the pharmacy activity is not allowed with the view to promote selling of medicines. However, it is permitted to inform the public about a pharmacy activity that has an informative, health-educational or scientific purpose.

The pharmacy must not – through a variety of market approaches – encourage excessive and uncritical purchases of medicines and other health-preserving products.[255]

584. The pharmacy activity is financed from public and private funds. Pharmacies can be organized as public institutes or a concession may be granted for the performance of a pharmacy activity – either to a natural person who is a pharmacy operator or to a legal person in which the pharmacy operator, which is also its management body, has more than a 50% share in capital of that legal entity (i.e., the concessionaire).

585. The concession is granted for a fixed period of not less than fifteen years and not more than thirty years. The Ministry of Health issues consent to the concession act on the basis of the opinion of the Chamber of Pharmacy and the Health Insurance Institute of Slovenia.

586. The concession is granted on the basis of a public tender. The criteria for selecting a concessionaire are: professional qualifications, experience and references of the pharmacy operator and the accessibility of the pharmacy location. A concession contract is concluded with the entity to which the concession has been granted.

587. Hospital pharmacy is a special form of pharmaceutical activity, organized by a hospital. It is an independent organizational unit of the hospital that provides a supply of medicines for treating patients within the hospital. The pharmacy activity can also be performed by other providers or entities, for example, a teaching pharmacy, which can be organized by the faculty that carries out the study programme of pharmacy (in order to carry out its educational programme). Pharmacy activity can also be organized in social welfare and other institutions, as well as within the military health service.

588. The pharmacy activity can be started from the day of obtaining the permission from the Ministry of Health. With a special permit, it is also allowed to organize an online pharmacy. Pharmaceutical professionals are master of pharmacy and master of pharmacy specialists and pharmaceutical technicians. The former can work independently after obtaining a licence and the latter after completing an internship and passing a professional exam. After completing the study and the professional exam, the Master of Pharmacy must perform a six-month professional introduction period. Only then the Chamber of Pharmacy grants him or her a licence to perform pharmacy activities.

255. For regulation of competition in the field of pharmacy, *see* A. Fatur, K. Podobnik & A. Vlahek, *Competition Law in Slovenia* 141–172 (Wolters Kluwer 2020).

589. The licence is granted for seven years, with the possibility of renewal. Proof of professional training must be provided to renew the licence. If the individual does not have the latter, he or she must pass a test of professional competence. The licence may be revoked permanently or temporarily due to a major professional deficiency or error at work.

590. Prescription medicines can be dispensed by a licensed Master of Pharmacy, over-the-counter medicines which are available only in pharmacies can be delivered also by a pharmaceutical technician but under the supervision of a Master of Pharmacy. However, medical devices can be dispensed by both, and the same goes for over-the-counter medicines, which are sold also in specialist shops. Only masters of pharmacy with additional specialization in homeopathy are authorized to advise and dispense homeopathic medicines.

591. The Pharmacy Practice Act also contains special provisions on the preparation of magistral and the production of galenic medicines in pharmacies. The field of pharmacovigilance is particularly highlighted: the alleged adverse reactions to magistral and galenic medicinal products are to be reported to national pharmacovigilance centres in accordance with the same rules as arranged for other medicines. The provider of the pharmacy activity where the medicine was prepared or manufactured is responsible for the damage due to the inadequate quality of the produced magistral or galenic medicines.

592. Pharmacy providers must unite in the Slovene Chamber of Pharmacy. Pharmacy professionals, however, can join it on a voluntary basis. The Chamber cares for the reputation, credibility, development of the pharmacy business and represents the interests of its members.[256]

593. Supervision of the pharmacy activity is carried out by pharmaceutical inspectors of the body responsible for medicinal products, the Information Commissioner, labour inspectors and official veterinarians.

§2. Nurses and Midwives

594. The Health Services Act not only regulates the status of physicians and dentists but also other healthcare professionals and co-workers, including nurses and midwives. The latter can perform healthcare services if they have proper professional education, are professionally trained to perform the work independently and fulfil other prescribed criteria. The Minister of Health adopted a special Order on the list of professions in healthcare,[257] which defines their area of work and difficulty levels for work in the area of healthcare services.

256. For more detailed elaboration of its competences, *see* Art. 96 of the Pharmacy Practice Act.
257. OG RS, No. 4/2014.

595. Healthcare professionals and co-workers can independently perform work in healthcare services after completing their traineeships and passing the professional exams. Healthcare professionals have to do the traineeship for six months. Exception to that rule are graduate nurses (male or female) and graduate midwives (male or female), who can perform their activities without the above-mentioned conditions if the following conditions are met: they have completed an appropriate first-cycle study programme lasting at least three years and can be further expressed by equivalent ECTS credits; it comprises at least 4,600 hours of theoretical and clinical education or training, where the duration of theoretical education presents at least one-third and the duration of clinical training at least half of the minimum duration of the training.

596. All performers in individual healthcare areas must be entered into a register and hold a valid licence. Maintaining the register and awarding licences have been entrusted to the Nurses and Midwives Association of Slovenia by the Minister of Heath.[258]

A licence is awarded for a predetermined time, i.e., a period of seven years, and can be extended on the basis of proofs on professional competence to continue work. A licence can be revoked in case of discovered larger professional errors.

597. Healthcare professionals and co-workers with higher, high professional or university education specialize to perform the more demanding tasks at specific (specialist) health professional areas. The manner and course of such specializations and other details are set by the Minister of Health.

598. Healthcare professionals and healthcare associates with higher or high professional education or with a university degree specialize in individual narrower health professional fields in order to perform more demanding tasks of healthcare activities. The types, duration and content of the specialization, the procedure for conducting the specialist examination and the appointment of the examination commission for healthcare workers and healthcare associates are conveyed to the Nurses and Midwives Association of Slovenia.[259]

599. A healthcare professional or healthcare associate who has obtained a professional qualification in another Member State of the European Union, a country of the European Economic Area or the Swiss Confederation shall be entitled to have his or her professional qualification recognized in accordance with the procedure governing the recognition of professional qualifications. After the recognition of the professional qualification, the healthcare worker or healthcare associate is entered into the register on the basis of the application. The application for entry in the register of healthcare professionals shall be accompanied by: (1) a certificate from an authorized educational institution on the successful completion of a test of knowledge of the Slovene language; (2) a certificate from a competent authority or organization from another Member State of the European Union, a country of the

258. *See* https://www.zbornica-zveza.si, 3 Jan. 2020.

259. For more details, *see* https://www.zbornica-zveza.si, 3 Jan. 2020.

European Economic Area or the Swiss Confederation, which, when submitted, may not be more than three months old and showing the registration with the competent authority or organization and that a person has not been dealt with in disciplinary proceedings or criminal or any other proceedings from which a ban on practising a profession arises (or a ban on practising a profession has been imposed); (3) proof of recognition of the professional qualification. The minimum conditions for qualifications and acquired rights laid down in Directive 2005/36/EC for professions subject to the automatic recognition of professional qualifications shall be determined by the Minister for Health. Nurses (male and female) are bound by the Code of Ethics in Nursing and Care[260] and midwives by the Code of Ethics for Midwives.[261]

§3. Paramedical Professionals

I. General

600. Healing activities are regulated in Slovenia by the CAM Act. The Act defines such medicine as an activity performed by healers with the intention of improving the health of the user of their services, including measures and activities, based on CAM systems and methods. Such activities must be performed in a way that does not harm health. CAM activities include traditional Chinese medicine, Ayurveda (traditional Hindu medicine), homeopathy and other forms of healing.

II. CAM Methods

601. The fundamental CAM methods are, with respect to the basic manner of performance, defined as:

(1) 'Methods of interaction between mind and body' – these are the methods that enhance mental capacity to influence body functioning.
(2) 'Biological methods' – in these methods, the treatment and prevention of diseases is based on the use of foodstuffs, medicinal plants and micronutrients.
(3) 'Manipulative and body-based methods' – in these methods, the treatment and prevention of diseases is achieved by moving body parts.
(4) 'Energy methods' – these methods exert their effects through the biofield and by influencing the biofield.

III. Healers

602. Healers are natural persons of age with at least a completed secondary medical education or at least a secondary professional education and who have passed an exam on health areas prescribed by the Minister of Health. They must also

260. OG RS, No. 13/2017.
261. *See* OG RS, No. 71/2014.

obtain a valid licence. Special forms of CAM, such as homeopathy, chiropractic and osteopathy can only be performed by persons, who, apart from fulfilling the previous requirements, also have a diploma from a faculty of medicine.

603. Healers should, by a rule of law, perform CAM practice in conformity with their Code of Professional Ethics, adopted by the CAM Chamber. It is not the case in practice since until today the CAM Chamber has not yet been established, and also their Code of Professional Ethics has not been accepted.[262] The Act foresees two corporate entities, namely companies and private entrepreneurs, as well as individual persons, who carry out CAM practice independently while holding a valid licence.

604. In order to obtain the permission to perform CAM practice for natural persons who are citizens of other EU Member States, EEC area or the Swiss Confederation or in case of legal persons, established in accordance with the law of those countries, the provisions of the Act regulating services on the internal market are used along with the provisions of this law. A company, established in one of the countries mentioned above and performing CAM services in accordance with the regulations of that country and does not have a seat in the Republic of Slovenia, can still perform such practices in accordance with the act regulating services on the internal market and pursuant to the CAM Act. Before starting with its duties, such a company must report its activities to the Ministry of Health.

IV. CAM Services Users

605. A healer must obtain a written consent by a service user to a CAM system or method prior to treatment. The statement must at the least contain information that the user of CAM services is acquainted with the type of the system or method, the mode of the system or method application and the fact that possible refusal of an already performed medical treatment may adversely affect his or her health. When the service user is a minor up to 15 years of age or a person under care, the healer must obtain a written consent from the person's parent or caretaker.

606. If a healer suspects that the service user shows symptoms of a severe disease or that his or her chronic condition has aggravated, he or she must immediately suggest the user to seek medical help and document the proposal in the records. In no case can a healer dissuade the user of services from seeking medical treatment.

607. At the request of the service user, a personal physician may deliver his or her opinion on the suitability of a CAM system and method with respect to the diagnosis or the service user's condition.

262. Other legal duties, imposed by law to their professional chamber, are performed by the Ministry of Health.

608. The service user has the right to quality and safe CAM services, to privacy at every CAM treatment, to inspect the documentation that refers to him or her and to transcribe or copy data from that documentation. The service user also has the right to request that a transcript or copy of the documentation is forwarded to another healer or the service user's physician.

Should the service user be unhappy with the provided CAM service, he or she can lodge a written complaint within fifteen days of the last use of the service. The healer must respond to the complaint in writing within fifteen days of receiving it. The service user may then lodge an appeal against the reply with the Chamber on Complementary and Alternative Medicine (CAM Chamber) within fifteen days of receiving the reply. The same shall apply if the healer/company fails to respond to the service user's complaint within fifteen days of receiving it.

V. Healer's Practice

609. Healers are obliged to carry out CAM practice with due care and diligence and shall not impose or omit any acts that adversely affect the health of service users. Should a healer dissuade a service user from medical treatment or fail to refer him or her to such treatment when necessary, the healer holds liability for the consequences of the user's missed medical treatment. However, should the service user not provide the healer with true information about his or her health state, fails to observe the healer's instructions or fails to cooperate in the protection, promotion and restoration of health, the healer cannot be held liable.

Similar to physicians, healers must also be insured against any damage that the service user could suffer as a result of CAM treatment.

610. Advertising CAM services by healers must not be misleading, i.e., must not contain vagueness or excessive exaggerations relating to the effectiveness of CAM methods, which might exploit the service user's inexperience or lack of knowledge for profit-making purposes.

All equipment and appliances used by the healers in performing CAM practice must be in compliance with the regulations governing product safety.

VI. CAM Chamber

611. The CAM Act establishes the CAM Chamber, which is tasked with recording, recognition and supervision of CAM systems and methods being implemented. The CAM Chamber is also tasked with passing the code of ethics for healers, checking their conduct and taking measures in connection with code violations. The CAM Chamber should moreover award, extend and revoke licences to healers. It should also manage and maintain their register as well as plans; it should supervise and implement professional training of its members and check their competence. Since this part of regulation never came to life in practice (as mentioned above, the CAM Chamber has never been established), the practical solution is that the Ministry of Health is in charge for all of the mentioned assignments.

A. CAM Licence

612. The licence is a public document, which proves the professional qualifications of the healer for independent implementation of individual CAM systems and methods, and is awarded to the healer for a period of seven years. The healer must fulfil the following conditions before obtaining the licence:

(1) hold at least a secondary education in the area of healthcare or at least a secondary vocational education and has passed a test of knowledge in healthcare contents;
(2) have the competence to implement an individual CAM system or method;
(3) possess an active knowledge of Slovene and, in bilingual areas, of the language of the ethnic community; and
(4) hold proof of not having been convicted for a wilful criminal offence with a final imprisonment sentence of more than six months, or that he or she has not been served a security measure prohibiting the pursuit of his or her profession.

613. In order to renew a licence, a healer must, during the period of the licence's validity, refresh and improve his or her knowledge in the area of CAM through training and education. Ministry of Health can revoke the licence temporarily or permanently. The licence may be permanently revoked due to grave professional misconduct; when the healer's actions or absence of action irreversibly or severely affected the service user's health or even resulted in his or her death; if the healer is convicted for an wilful criminal offence prosecuted ex officio in connection with CAM service implementation; if the healer has failed to obtain evidence regarding the fulfilment of criteria for obtaining or renewing the licence in a legitimate manner; has provided false information in order to obtain or renew the licence or has dissuaded his or her patients from seeking medical treatment.

614. The licence may be revoked for a certain period of time if it is discovered that a healer threatens the health or life of the service user through his or her actions; if the healer has been served a security measure prohibiting his or her performance of CAM practice and if the healer was convicted for an wilful criminal offence prosecuted ex officio to imprisonment for six months or more. A temporary revocation of the licence can last for five years at the most. Following the cessation of reasons for the temporary licence revocation or after the expiry of the time determined for that, temporary licence revocation period, the healer may reapply for the licence.

615. After awarding the licence, the CAM Chamber (in practice Ministry of Health) must enter the healer into the register. A healer is deleted from the register if he or she expresses the wish not to be listed in the register; if his or her licence was permanently revoked; in case of permanent incapacity to work and upon death.

VII. Professional Supervision

616. The supervision over the implementation of the provisions of the CAM Act is carried out by the Health Inspectorate of the Republic of Slovenia, the inspection body in charge of personal data protection and inspection bodies in charge of supervising product safety.

§4. Hospitals

617. A hospital is a stationary institution, which provides twenty-four-hour care, diagnostics, treatment and rehabilitation for the ill and injured, usually for various states of illness and surgery statuses. A hospital can also provide its services as an outpatient institution.

Slovenia has two University Clinical Centres (in Maribor and Ljubljana) and several general and specialist hospitals, which are labelled according to their specialty.

618. A general hospital is defined as a hospital which provides various treatments to people from all age groups with different health conditions, various illnesses or impairments and is at the same time not a university hospital. The Health Services Act defines it as a healthcare institution for treatment of several types of illnesses with a specialist outpatient service and accommodation at least for the areas of internal medicine, surgery, paediatrics, gynaecology and obstetrics.

619. A specialist hospital is meanwhile an institution, which primarily accepts patients with a specific illness or impairment of a vital system or is intended to diagnose and treat illnesses and conditions for persons of a specific age group or for diagnosing and treatment of long-term illnesses and conditions. The Heath Services Act defines a healthcare institution for specialist outpatient and hospital treatment of a specific disease or a specific population group as an institution which has to fulfil the same conditions as a hospital, but with accommodation, diagnostic and other capacities adjusted for its purpose. Such institutions in Slovenia include psychiatric hospitals, gynaecology and obstetrics institutions, the Institute for Oncology, and the like.

620. Two independent maternity hospitals operate in Slovenia (in Postojna and Kranj), and the two University Clinical Centres (in Maribor and Ljubljana) also have their own maternity hospitals, while maternity wards can be found at all ten Slovenian general hospitals.

621. Inpatient service is carried out as a healthcare activity on the secondary and tertiary levels and constitutes performing the activities of clinics, clinical institutes or clinical departments as well as other authorized healthcare institutions.

622. Almost all hospitals in Slovenia are public healthcare institutions. Private practice in this area is very limited.

The public healthcare network is determined by the Republic of Slovenia after acquiring preliminary opinions from interested municipalities or cities. A public healthcare service must also be organized in a way that emergency medical assistance is available at all times to the citizens of the Republic of Slovenia, including emergency transport and provision of emergency medicinal products as soon as possible and as near as possible to the source of the issues and also during transport. The conditions and manner of performing emergency healthcare are governed by specific regulations.[263]

623. Tertiary activities include scientific and research as well as educational and schooling activities for faculties of medicine and other high and higher-education institutions. It also includes performing the most demanding in- or outpatient healthcare services which are impossible and unpractical to be performed at lower levels due to their professional, personnel, technological and organizational complexity. Clinics, within the framework of their activities (clinical institutes or clinical wards), perform the most complex specialist in- and outpatient treatment, formulate the doctrine of step-by-step diagnostics and treatment within their own areas and forward such information to other hospitals, physicians and other healthcare professionals. The latter also cooperate with the competent chambers in drafting and providing postgraduate education to physicians, dentists, other healthcare professionals and healthcare professionals with high education. Healthcare services or programmes, performed at the tertiary level, are set by the Ministry of Health.

624. Accreditation and certification procedures are the tools for assessing the quality of the operation of a health institution on the basis of a selected standard. Accreditation is a public recognition of a health organization by a health accreditation body on the achievement of accreditation standards. The accreditation is renewed every three years. Certification is the process of obtaining a certificate for managing systems according to the ISO 9001 standard or another ISO standard and does not cover clinical quality standards. The certificate is renewed for five years. Healthcare providers decide on accreditation and certification at their own discretion. The obtained certificate represents a confirmation of the quality of operation of the health institution, but only if the efforts for quality and safety are constant and all employees in the health institution are actively oriented towards this goal.

625. Clinical guidelines are recommendations for the best care of certain medical conditions, taking into account the available evidence on the most successful approaches. They are systematically formulated attitudes that assist physicians and other healthcare professionals, as well as patients, in making decisions about appropriate healthcare in specific clinical circumstances. Clinical guidelines do not replace the knowledge and experience of the physician, but are a tool for making decisions about the most appropriate measures for an individual patient, as they offer an answer to what and why. Clinical guidelines are the basis for the development of treatment standards and can make an important contribution to the design

263. *See* Rules on Emergency Medical Services (*Pravilnik o službi nujne medicinske pomoči*), OG RS, Nos 81/2015, 93/2015.

of clinical pathways, the education and training of healthcare professionals, and informing patients about the intended course of healthcare.

626. Professional standards and treatment protocols are recommendations adopted by the competent professional body of an individual health profession to achieve the optimal level of regulation in a particular area and provide an answer to what and how. The development of clinical guidelines and professional standards is the domain of the profession. The Ministry of Health has issued a Slovenian Guidance Manual,[264] which takes into account some established models of guidelines, such as the SIGN (Scottish Intercollegiate Guidelines Network), the German Agency for Quality in Medicine (Arztlichen Zentralstelle Qualitatssicherung, AEZQ) and the International Guidelines Network, GIN).

I. Relations Between Physicians and Hospitals

627. In accordance with the Health Services Act, a healthcare institution which carries out secondary level activities, is headed by the institution's council. The council is composed of representatives of the founder, the institute's workers, representatives of insurers or other users and representatives of the municipality or the city where the institute performs its activities. The composition and the proportionality of the representatives in the council are set by the founder with the act on establishment.

628. The director of the healthcare institution is appointed by and relieved by the council in agreement with the founder. The director must have high professional education and at least five years of work experience. If the management functions and the professional leadership functions are not separated, the director must have obtained a high education of a professional degree from the relevant health area. In case these two functions are separate, professional activities in a healthcare institution is carried out by an expert head who obtained a high education professional degree from the relevant health area and has at least five years of professional experience. The professional collegiate body of the healthcare institution is the expert council, whose tasks, composition and manner of formation are set in more detail by the institution's statute.

629. The Minister of Health in agreement with the Minister of Education, Science and Sport, sets the conditions that the healthcare institution must fulfil in order to perform practical classes for pupils and students of the faculty of medicine and other medical educational institutions. The institution which meets the requirements for such activities is awarded the title of Educational Institution by the Ministry of Health.

630. The Health Services Act states that healthcare professionals must not leave their workplace until they are replaced, even though their working hours have

264. *See* https://www.gov.si, 4 Jan. 2021.

ended, if this could pose a threat to the health of people. Healthcare professionals must provide emergency medical aid, care and treatment during strike as well. Overtime work cannot on average exceed eight hours a week. The maximum amount of weekly overtime work is defined as an average limitation within a certain time period that must not be longer than four months. The calculation of the average does not include annual leave and sick leave. In case of a written approval by a healthcare professional, overtime work can exceed the stated limitations, but such approval must show the weekly number of overtime hours which the working individual still agrees to and the time of validity of his consent. The employer must record a specific registry on overtime work and, if necessary, submit it to the competent supervisory bodies and representative trade unions.

631. A healthcare professional is entitled to a continuous daily rest period of at least twelve hours and a continuous weekly rest period of at least twenty-four hours. If necessary to guarantee healthcare within the agreed scope, the minimum daily and weekly rest periods can be guaranteed as an average over two months. In order to guarantee standby hours, the continuous working hours of a healthcare professional can amount to thirty-two hours at the most, with work as part of full working time amounting to ten hours a day at the most and sixteen hours at the most within two consecutive working days. A written approval by the healthcare professional is required for continuous work of more than sixteen hours.

632. Duty is a specific form of work, composed of the hours of presence at the workplace (inactive hours) and the hours of performing services (active hours). All standby hours are counted towards the working hours as regards the right to take a break and the time to rest. Payment for active and inactive hours differs and is set in the collective bargaining agreement. Payment for standby hours is counted towards the basis for contribution towards retirement and disability insurance. A physician who has reached 50 years of age, as a rule, does not have to perform standby duties.

633. Continuous standby means availability outside of the workplace over the phone or through other means with the aim to provide counsel or arrival to the workplace if necessary. The longest acceptable time to arrive to the workplace is set by the employer. Standby payments are set in the collective bargaining agreement. Such hours are not included under working hours.

634. The Fiscal Balance Act brought amendments to the Health Services Act in the sense of performing competitive activities by physicians. It defined as competitive activities healthcare services, which a healthcare professional, employed in a public healthcare institution or at another legal or natural person which performs healthcare activities within the framework of a public healthcare service, performs on the basis of a work contract or other Civil Law contract at another healthcare service provider within the framework of a public healthcare network. Performing such activities is therefore linked to a written approval by the employee. The latter will only be issued if the following conditions are met:

- Such activities will not cause any damages to the public healthcare institution or cause a disturbance in performing the activities of such institution.
- The public healthcare institution does not have a need for any additional or extra work or work that would exceed obligations stemming from the full working hours of a healthcare professional.
- The healthcare professional entirely fulfils his or her work obligations regarding the amount and type of performed healthcare services, as set in the employment contract.
- The healthcare professional does not reject overtime work, readiness and potential other types of work at his or her employer.
- Work for another public healthcare institution does not prevent the healthcare professional from enjoying the daily and weekly rest as well as annual leave.

635. If a physician, contrary to the above-stated, performs activities at a competitive healthcare institution, this fact can serve as grounds for an extraordinary termination of employment. At the same time, this can also mean his or her liability for damages, caused by the performance of the competitive activity.

636. The Health Services Act also determines when a public healthcare institution can enter into a work contract for providing healthcare services with a healthcare professional. These are the cases when such performance of healthcare activities is economically more efficient and if:

- it is impossible to conclude an employment contract regarding the provision of healthcare services which are the subject of the agreement due to their temporary nature or their lesser extent; and
- a once-only increase in the scope of healthcare institution's services for the needs of compulsory healthcare is being implemented.

The public healthcare institution cannot guarantee the contractual obligations towards the Health Insurance Institute of Slovenia with its existing personnel. A work contract can be concluded for a maximum of twelve months. Entering into such a contract in order to perform healthcare services with an employee already working at the institution is not allowed, unless the healthcare services being talked about are being performed as part of the national screening programmes or other special programmes, approved by the Minister of Health, with guaranteed financing.

637. The amount for evaluating physicians' activities as part of the financial plan of the institution is agreed annually between the Ministry of Health, the Medical Chamber and the Health Insurance Institute of Slovenia. The amount is determined on the basis of the workplaces for physicians within the public healthcare service network, the collective bargaining agreement for physicians and the legislation. The amount presents the starting point to set the price and the scope of programmes within the agreement on the performance of services stemming from mandatory health insurance and on the basis of the law regulating healthcare and health insurance. The wages of doctors who work as public servants are set pursuant to the law setting the wage system in the public sector, its implementing regulation acts and collective bargaining agreements. Private practitioners with a concession receive full payment for their work, as agreed in their contract with the institution. The methodology for setting the price of medical services, which are not subjected to compulsory health insurance, is set by the Minister of Health upon proposal by the Medical Chamber.

A. *Private Practitioner*

638. If a private practitioner wants to perform his or her activities, he or she must, among other things, ensure adequate premises, equipment and, should the nature of the work so demand, personnel. A private practitioner can bid for the premises in a public healthcare institution in order to guarantee proper premises. If a public healthcare institution and a private practitioner bid for the same premises, the founder awards them to the applicant with a better bid. One of the conditions for ensuring adequate premises and equipment is fulfilled if a private practitioner concludes a contract on renting or using them with a suitable healthcare institution.

639. A private practitioner must moreover, apart from other medical services, guarantee his or her patients continuously available urgent medical aid, rescue transport, laboratory and other diagnostic and therapeutic procedures in accordance with the nature of his or her activity. In order to provide such services, he or she must establish connections and cooperate with the nearest healthcare institution or other private practitioners. In order to perform more complex or extensive activities, private practitioners can join medical cooperatives.

§5. Health Insurance

640. For more details on health insurance, *see* General Introduction, §2, B, 3, a and C above.

Selected Bibliography

Books and Articles

Albreht, T., et al. 'Slovenia, Health System Review', *Health Systems in Transition*, 18, no. 3. Copenhagen, 2016.

Balažic, J., et al. *Zakon o pacientovih pravicah s komentarjem* (*Patients' Rights Act with Commentary*). Ljubljana: GV Založba, 2009.

Bavcon, L., et al. *Kazensko pravo, splošni del* (*Criminal Law, General Part*). Ljubljana: Uradni list RS, 2009.

Brulc, K. *Odškodninska odgovornost za zdravniško napako* (*Liability to Damages for Medical Errors*), Master's Paper. Ljubljana, 2007.

Bubnov Škoberne, A. & G. Strban. *Pravo socialne varnosti* (*Social Security Law*). Ljubljana: GV Založba, 2010.

Bužinel, M. *Prostovoljno zdravstveno zavarovanje v Sloveniji in izbranih državah EU* (*Voluntary Health Insurance in Slovenia and Selected EU Countries*). Ljubljana: Ekonomska fakulteta, Univera v Ljubljani, 2006.

Cigoj, S. *Teorija obligacij: splošni del obligacijskega prava* (*Theory of Obligation: General Part of Law of Obligation*). Ljubljana: Uradni list RS, 2003.

Čizmić, J. 'Bioetika i medicinsko pravo' ('Bioethics and Medical Law'). *Medicina* 44, no. 2 (2008).

Dižovnik, U. *Pravna ureditev neprostovoljne hospitalizacije v psihiatrični bolnišnici* (*Legal Regulations on Involuntary Hospitalization in a Psychiatric Institution*). Ljubljana: Pravna fakulteta, Univerza v Ljubljani, 2011.

Fatur, A., K. Podobnik & A. Vlahek. *Competition Law in Slovenia.* Alphen aan den Rijn: Wolters Kluwer, 2020.

Finžgar, A. 'Svobodno odločanje o rojstvih otrok in umetno omogočanje rojstev' ('Freedom of Choice in Childbirth and Artificial Pregnancy Assistance'), *Pravnik* 9-10 (1992).

Finžgar, A. *Osebnostne pravice* (*Personality Rights*) Ljubljana: SAZU, 1985.

Flis, V. 'Medicinska dokumentacija in pravice bolnikov' ('Medical Records and Patient Rights'), Pravna praksa, No. 410/98.

Flis, V. & J. Reberšek Gorišek. 'Pojasnilna dolžnost – kako obsežna in v kakšni obliki' ('Obligation to Explain – What Is Its Scope and What Form Should It Take'), *Medicina in pravo* (2004).

Selected Bibliography

Grmek Košnik, I. & T. Albreht. 'Načrtovanje števila zdravnikov in zobozdravnikov v zdravstvu – metode, uporabnost, omejitve in odvisnosti' ('Physician and Dentist Workforce Planning Methods, Applicability, Limitations and Dependence'), *Zdravstveno varstvo journal* 45 (2006).

Hervey, T.K. & V.J. McHale. *Health Law and the European Union.* Cambridge: Cambridge University Press, 2004.

Kersnik, J. *Kakovost v zdravstvu* (*Quality in Health Care*), 2nd edn. Ljubljana, Association of Family Physicians, Zbirka PIP, 2010.

Kersnik, J. 'Kakovost v sistemu zdravstvenega varstva v Republiki Sloveniji, Pregled stanja, Poročilo za WHO' ('Quality of the Health Care System in Slovenia, Overview, Report for the WHO'), available at http://www.drmed.org, 29 Dec. 2020.

Kerstin Petrič, V. & A. Maresso. *Slovenia*, in *Organization and Financing of Public Health Services in Europe: Country Reports*, ed. B. Rechel et al., https://www.ncbi.nlm.nih.gov.

Kogovšek Sajovic, Š. *Pravna ureditev zdravistva* (*Legal Regulation of Complementary and Alternative Medicine*). Ljubljana: Pravna fakulteta, Univerza v Ljubljani, 2020.

Koman Perenič, L. 'Odškodninska odgovornost zdravstvenih delavcev, Kako odloča Vrhovno sodišče RS' ('Liability for Damages of Medical Professionals – History of Supreme Court Decisions'), *Javna uprava*, year 42, no. 2/3 (2006).

Končina, M. *Osebnostne pravice otroka in njihovo pravno varstvo, Pravni vidiki otrokovih pravic* (*Personal Rights of a Child and their Legal Protection, Legal Aspects of Child Rights*). Ljubljana: ČZ Uradni list RS, 1992.

Korošec, D. *Medicinsko kazensko pravo* (*Medical Criminal Law*). Ljubljana: Pravna fakulteta and Cankarjeva založba, 2004.

Korošec, D. 'Razmišljanje o koncu življenja – kazenskopravni vidik' ('Thinking about the End of Life – The Criminal Law Aspect'). *Zbornik referatov in razprav*, No. 1/2018, Državni svet RS, Ljubljana, 2018.

Krušič Mate, Z. *O pravici do zasebnosti v medicini* (*On the Right to Privacy in Medicine*), Master's Paper. Ljubljana, 2007.

Manohin, A., et al. 'Dileme v zvezi z bolnikovim zavračanjem transfuzije krvi' ('Dilemmas Connected to the Patient's Refusal of Blood Transfusion'). *Isis* 20, no. 1 (2011).

Morovič, B. & B. Simčič. *Nacionalna strategija razvoja financiranja zdravstvene dejavnosti (2010–2020)* (*National Strategy to Develop Health Care Financing (2010–2020)*). Ljubljana, 2010, http://www.vlada.si.

Možina, D. & A. Vlahek, *Contract Law in Slovenia.* Alphen aan den Rijn: Wolters Kluwer, 2019.

Musek, J. *Raziskovanje vrednot v Sloveniji in vrednotni univerzum Slovencev* (*Research of Values in Slovenia and the General Values of Slovenians*), http://www.prihodnost-slovenije.si.

Pajntar, M., I. Verdenik & B. Leskovšek. *Kakovost v zdravstvu Slovenije* (*Quality of Health Care in Slovenia*), https://vestnik.szd.si.

Pavliha, M. 'Analiza obveznih individualnih zavarovanj v Sloveniji' ('Analysis of Compulsory Individual Insurance in Slovenia'). *Podjetje in delo*, year XXV, no. 6 (1999).

Pirš, B. 'Imamo v Sloveniji dovolj zdravnikov in zobozdravnikov?' ('Are There Enough Physicians and Dentists in Slovenia?'). *Zdravstveni vestnik*, year 76 (2007).

Pogačnik, A., P. Gabrijelčič & A. Zavodnik. *Mednarodna izhodišča in prostorski razvoj Slovenije* (*Slovenia's International Positions and Spatial Development*). Ljubljana: Fakulteta za gradbeništvo in geodezijo, Univerza v Ljubljani, 2001.

Polajnar Pavčnik, A. *Obligacijski vidiki razmerja med bolnikom in zdravnikom* (*Obligational Aspects of the Relationship between Physician and Patient*). Ljubljana: Pravo in medicina, Cankarjeva založba, 1998.

Polajnar Pavčnik, A. 'Varstvo ustavnih človekovih pravic med zdravljenjem' ('Safeguarding Constitutional Human Rights during Treatment'). *Podjetje in delo*, 24, nos 6-7 (1998).

Robertson, J.A. 'Procreative Liberty and the Control of Conception, Pregnancy and Childbirth'. Virginia Law Review (1983): 69.

Sander, J. & P. Bard. *The Legal Regulation of Biobanks*. National Report: Slovenia, http://web.ceu.hu.

Sivec, S. *Odškodninska odgovornost zdravnika* (*Liability for Damages of a Physician*). Graduation Thesis, Ljubljana, 2008.

Strohsack, B. *Odškodninsko pravo in druge neposlovne obveznosti (obligacijska razmerja II)* (*Tort Law and Other Non-trade Obligations. Obligation Relations II*). Ljubljana: Uradni list RS, 1996.

Šifrer, Š. *Evtanazija* (*Euthanasia*). Ljubljana: Pravna fakulteta, Univerza v Ljubljani, 2011.

Tevž, S. *Nekateri pravni problemi presaditve človeških organov* (*Some Legal Issues Regarding Human Organ Transplants*). Ljubljana: Pravna fakulteta, Univerza v Ljubljani, 2004.

Trontelj, J. 'Pojasnila k stališču Državne komisije za medicinsko etiko o ravnanju z umirajočimi in evtanaziji' ('Clarifications of the Position of the National Medical Ethics Committee Regarding Treatment of the Dying and Euthanasia'). *ISIS*, no. 6 (1997).

Vencelj, N. *Sistem zdravstvenega varstva v Republiki Sloveniji – analiza ukrepov za zmanjševanje izdatkov za zdravila* (*Healthcare System in the Republic of Slovenia – An Analysis of Measures to Reduce Costs for Medicinal Products*). Ljubljana: Fakulteta za družbene vede, Univerza v Ljubljani, 2004.

Vlahek, A. *Kakšne kazni lahko doletijo Slovenijo zaradi kršitve skupostnega prava?* (What Sanctions May Be Imposed on Slovenia for Breaching Community Law?), Podjetje in delo, 30, no. 8 (2007).

Vlahek, A. *Zahtevki naročnika v primeru nepravilne izpolnitve podjemne in gradbene pogodbe* (*Remedies of the Ordering Party in Cases of Improper Performance of Contract for Work and Building Contract*), in: X. dnevi civilnega in gospodarskega prava, Institute for Comparative Law at the Faculty of Law in Ljubljana, 12–13 April 2012, Ljubljana.

Vlahek A. 'Development of Consumer Collective Redress in the EU: A Light at the End of the Tunnel?', *Baltic Yearbook of International Law, Kluwer Law International*, 18 (2020).

Wildhaber, L. 'Commentary to Article 8 ECHR', in Internationaler Kommentar zur Europaischen Menschenrechtskonvention, ed. Golsong H., et al. Köln: Carl Heymanns Verlag, 1995, item 192.

Zadnik, V. & J. Šelb. 'Osnovni vzroki smrti s kazalniki umrljivosti v Sloveniji v letu 2001' ('Main Causes of Death with Mortality Indicators in Year 2001'), Zdravstveni vestnik no. 72. Ljubljana, 2003.

Zonta, S. *Spremembe spola v Sloveniji že 40 let* (*Sex Changes in Slovenia for the Past 40 Years*). Interview with Franci Planinšek, MD, http://www.rtvslo.si.

Zupančič, K. *Pravna ureditev prekinitve nosečnosti* ('Legal Regulations Regarding Pregnancy Termination'), in *Pravo in medicina*, ed. A. Polajnar-Pavčnik & D. Wedam Lukić. Ljubljana: Cankarjeva založba, 1998.

Zupančič, K. *Družinsko pravo* (*Family Law*). Ljubljana: Uradni list RS, 1999.

Zupančič, K. & V. Žnidaršič. 'Dva vidika svobode odločanja o rojstvih otrok' ('Two Aspects of Freedom Regarding Childbirth'), in *Pravo in medicina*, ed. A. Polajnar-Pavčnik & D. Wedam-Lukič. Ljubljana: Cankarjeva založba, 1998.

Žnidaršič, V. & T. Pipan. *Določanje očetovstva in materinstva za otroka spočetega z zdravstveno pomočjo* (*Determining Fatherhood and Motherhood for a Child, Conceived using Bio-medically Assisted Procedures*). Ljubljana: Pravna fakulteta, Univerza v Ljubljani, 1995.

Žnidaršič, V. 'Dedovanje po prejemniku denarne socialne pomoči' ('Inheritance after the Recipient of Financial Social Assistance'). *Delavci in delodajalci*, 12, no. 2/3 (2012), 375-388.

Žnidaršič Skubic, V. *Civilno medicinsko pravo* (*Civil Medical Law*). Ljubljana: Uradni list, 2018.

Žnidaršič Skubic, V. 'Civilno medicinsko pravo s poudarkom na vprašanjih, ki zadevajo zaključek življenja' ('Civil Medical Law with an Emphasis on End-of-Life Issue'), in *Razmišljanja o vprašanjih ob izteku življenja* (*Reflections on Issues at the End of Life*), edited by Marjeta Tratnik Volasko. Zbornik referatov in razprav, no. 1/2018, Ljubljana, Državni svet RS, 2018.

Internet

https://old.delo.si
https://www.arso.gov.si
https://www.tnp.si
https://www.dnevnik.si
http://www.stat.si
https://www.onko-i.si
https://www.nijz.si
http://www.prihodnost-slovenije.si
http://www.zzzs.si
https://www.eurofound.europa.eu
https://www.hspm.org
http://www.drmed.org
https://www.ncbi.nlm.nih.gov
http://www.un.org
https://op.europa.eu
http://www.mf.uni-lj.si

https://www.uni-lj.si
https://www.zdravniskazbornica.si
https://vestnik.szd.si
https://core.ac.uk
http://www.drmed.org
https://zdrzz.si
https://www.nlzoh.si
http://www.szd.si
http://pisrs.si
http://www.sodisce.si
https://www.uradni-list.si
http://www.kme-nmec.si
https://www.slovenija-transplant.si
https://ec.europa.eu
https://eur-lex.europa.eu
https://www.ema.europa.eu
http://web.ceu.hu
http://www.rtvslo.si
https://transakcija.si
https://www.euro.who.int
https://www.euronews.com
https://pace.coe.int
https://predlagam.vladi.si
https://www.zbornica-zveza.si
https://www.gov.si
http://www.ztm.si
https://www.sta.si
https://www.biobanka.si

Selected Bibliography

Index

The numbers here refers to paragraph numbers.

Index

Index

www.ingramcontent.com/pod-product-compliance
Lightning Source LLC
Chambersburg PA
CBHW071444230926
51846CB00001B/335